SPIDER-MAN

FRIENDLY NEIGHBORHOOD

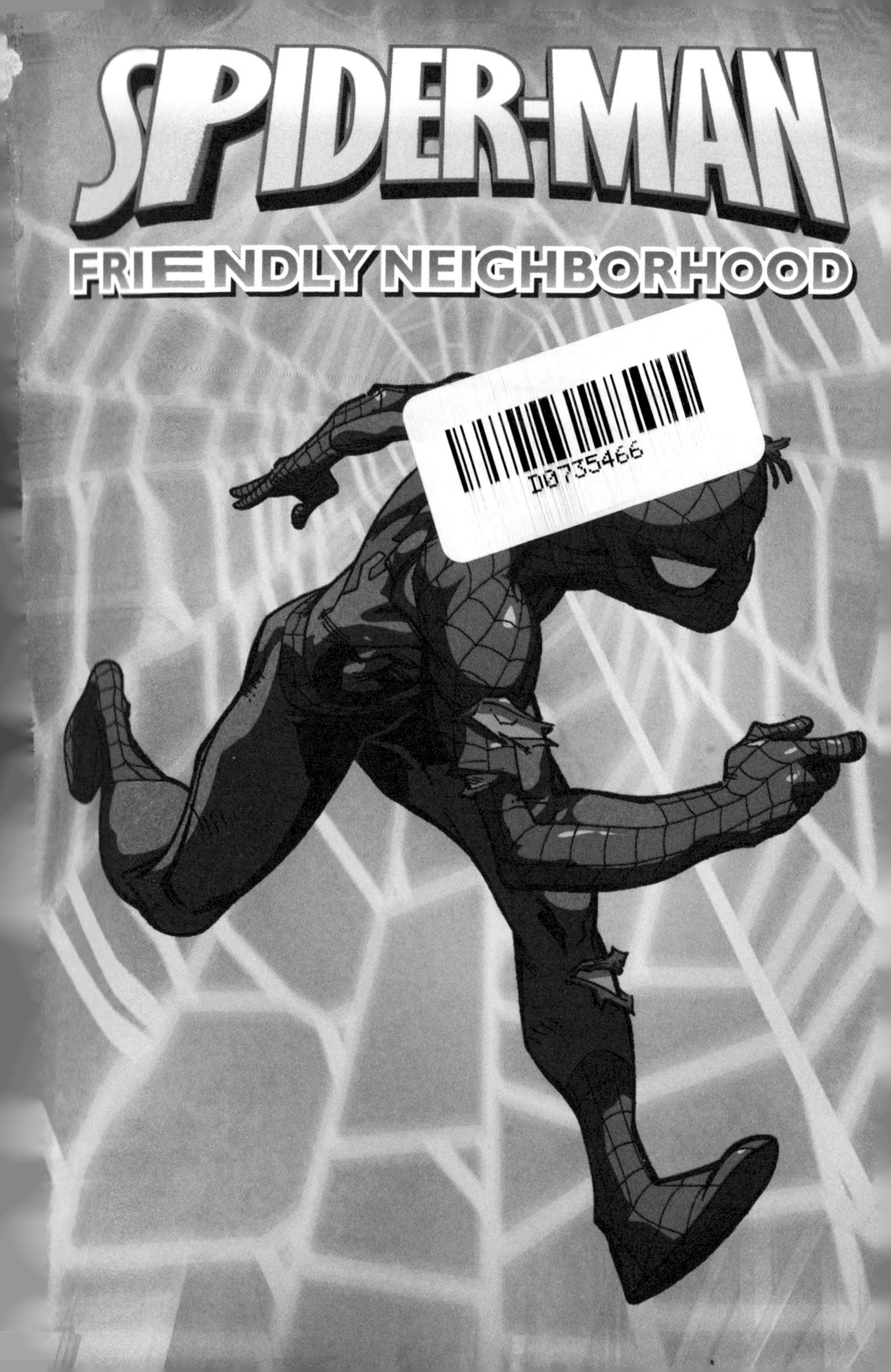

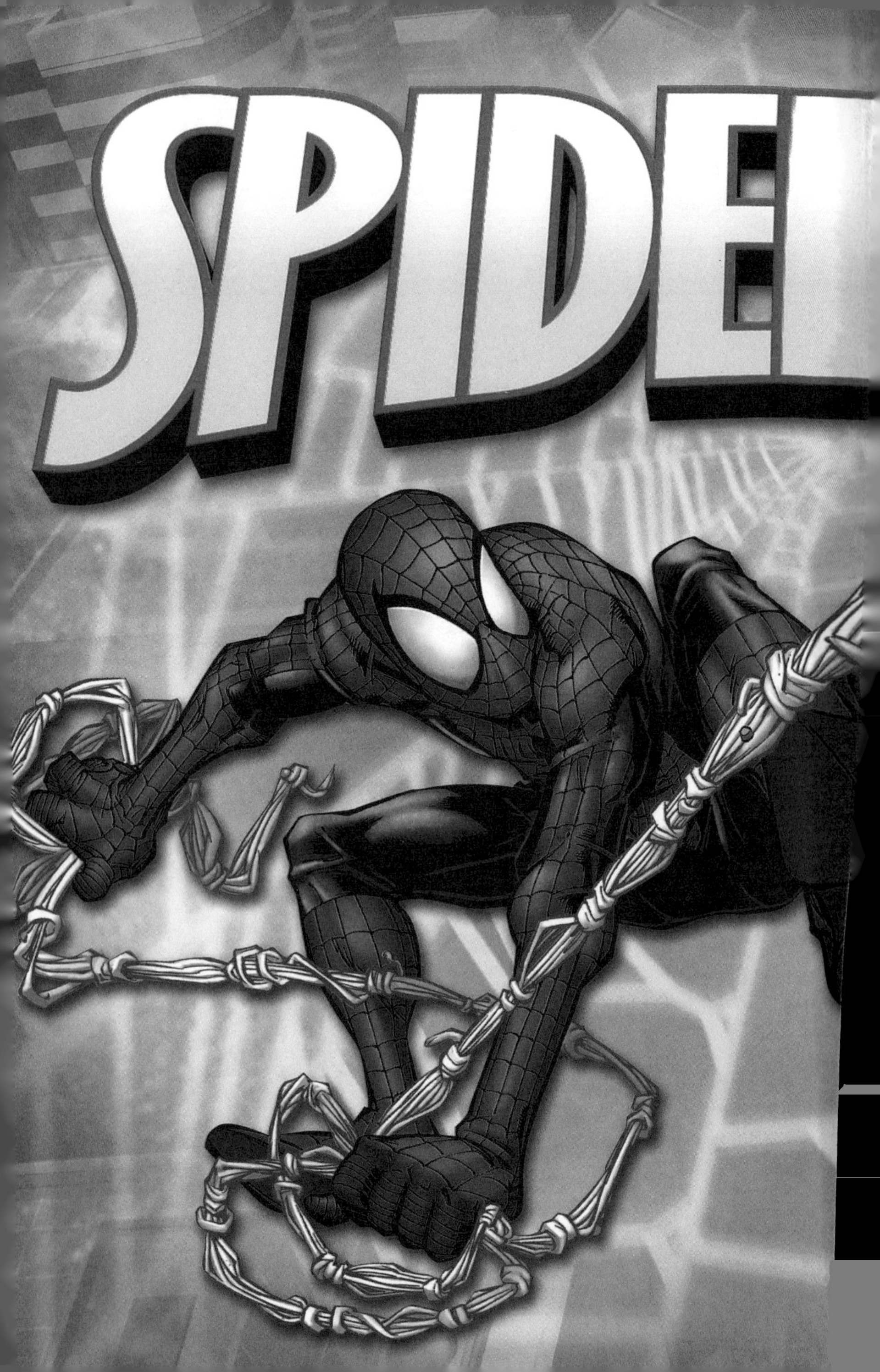
SPIDE

R-MAN

FRIENDLY NEIGHBORHOOD

Writer: **Paul Tobin**
Pencilers: **Rob Di Salvo (Issues #13 & 15)**
& Matteo Lolli (Issues #14 & 16)
Inkers: **Terry Pallot (Issues # 13-14 & 16)**
& Rob Di Salvo (Issue #15)
Colors: **Sotocolor**
Letters: **Dave Sharpe**
Cover Artists: **Barry Kitson with Guru eFx (Issue #13),**
Patrick Scherberger with Edgar Delgado (Issues #14-15)
& Ale Garza with Chris Sotomayor (Issue #16)

Assistant Editor: **Rachel Pinnelas**
Associate Editor: **Tom Brennan**
Senior Editor: **Stephen Wacker**

Collection Editor: **Cory Levine**
Editorial Assistants: **James Emmett & Joe Hochstein**
Assistant Editors: **Matt Masdeu, Alex Starbuck & Nelson Ribeiro**
Editors, Special Projects: **Jennifer Grünwald & Mark D. Beazley**
Senior Editor, Special Projects: **Jeff Youngquist**
Senior Vice President of Sales: **David Gabriel**

Editor in Chief: **Axel Alonso**
Chief Creative Officer: **Joe Quesada**
Publisher: **Dan Buckley**
Executive Producer: **Alan Fine**

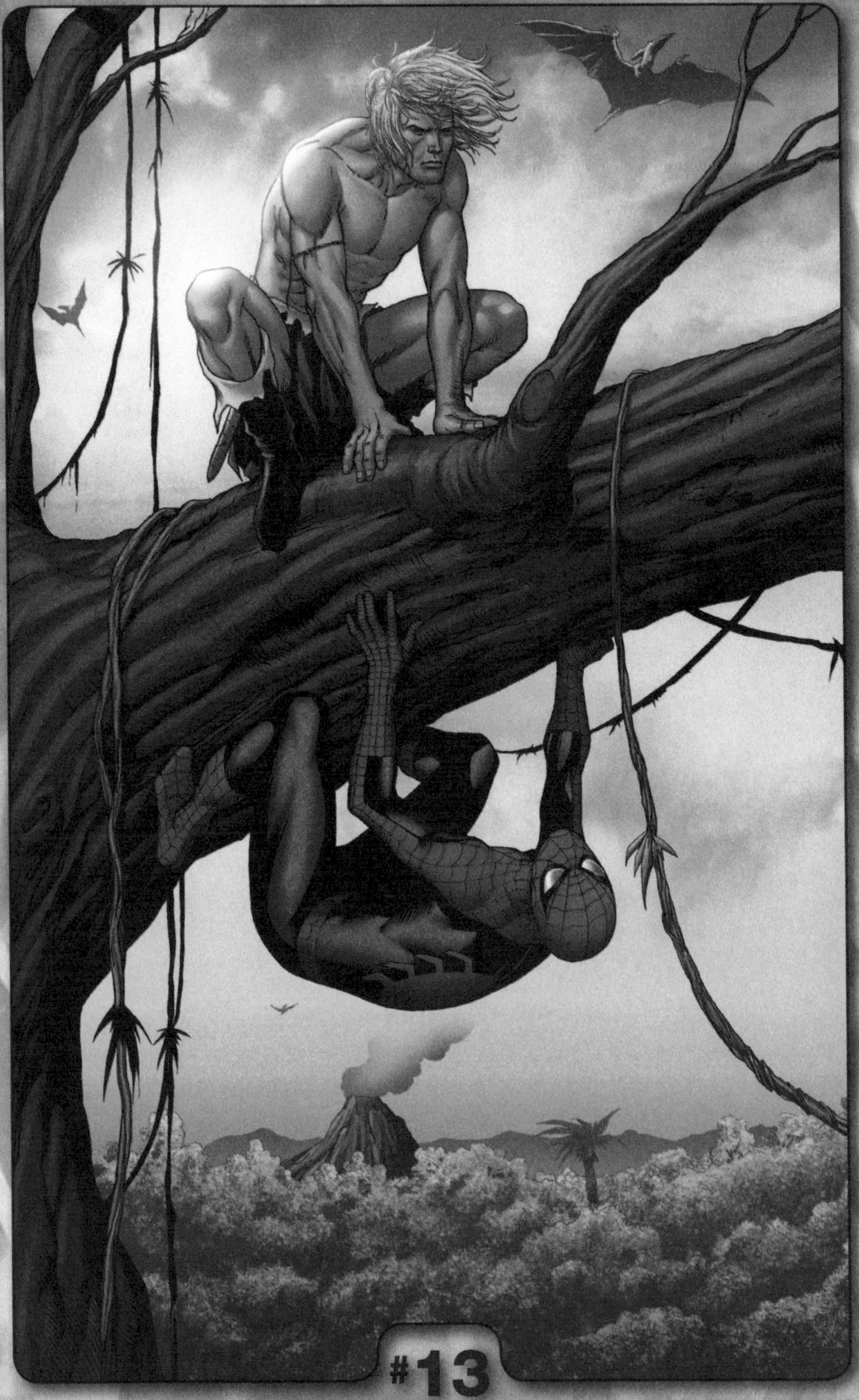
#13

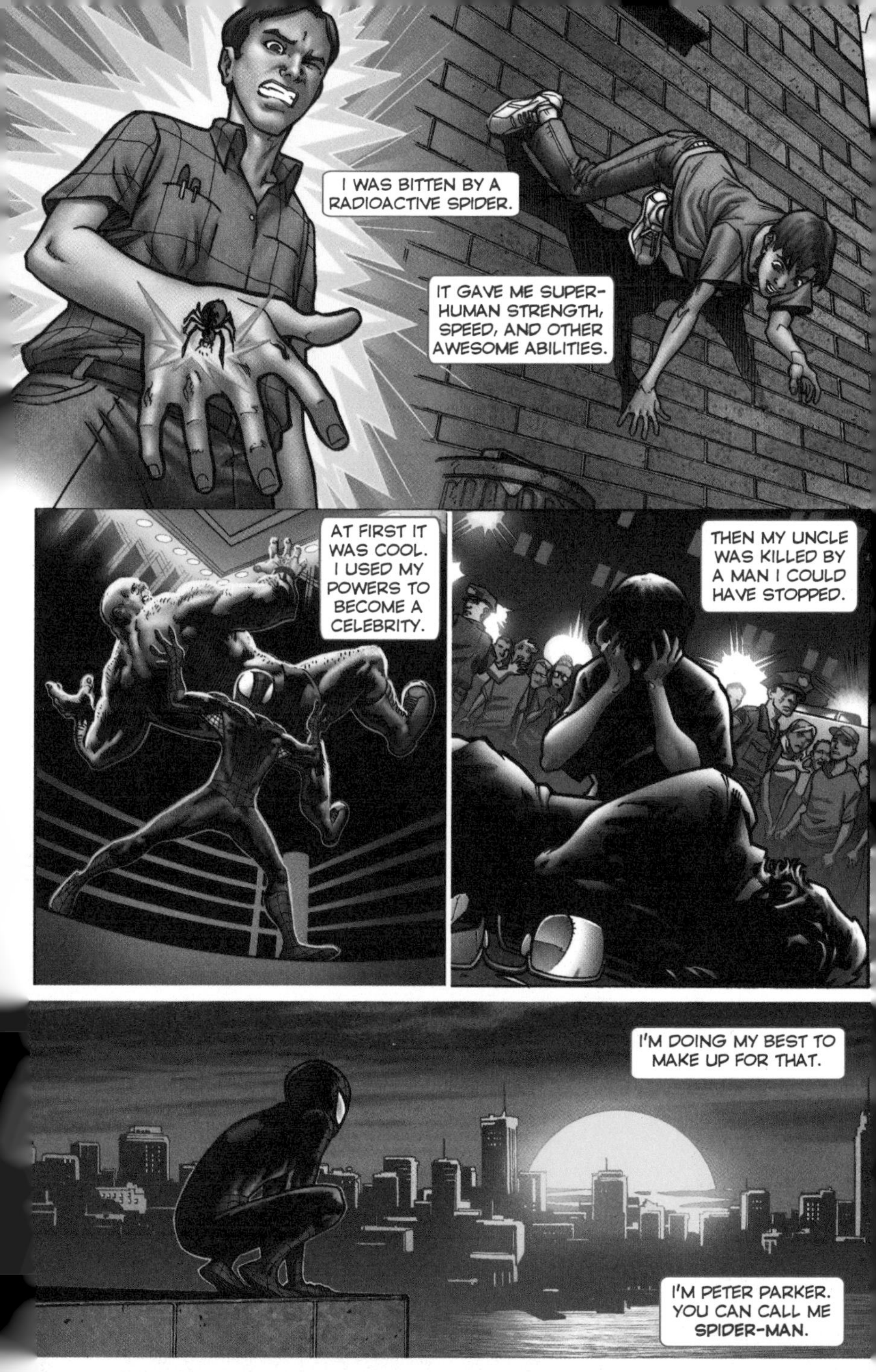
I WAS BITTEN BY A RADIOACTIVE SPIDER.
IT GAVE ME SUPER-HUMAN STRENGTH, SPEED, AND OTHER AWESOME ABILITIES.
AT FIRST IT WAS COOL. I USED MY POWERS TO BECOME A CELEBRITY.
THEN MY UNCLE WAS KILLED BY A MAN I COULD HAVE STOPPED.
I'M DOING MY BEST TO MAKE UP FOR THAT.
I'M PETER PARKER. YOU CAN CALL ME SPIDER-MAN.

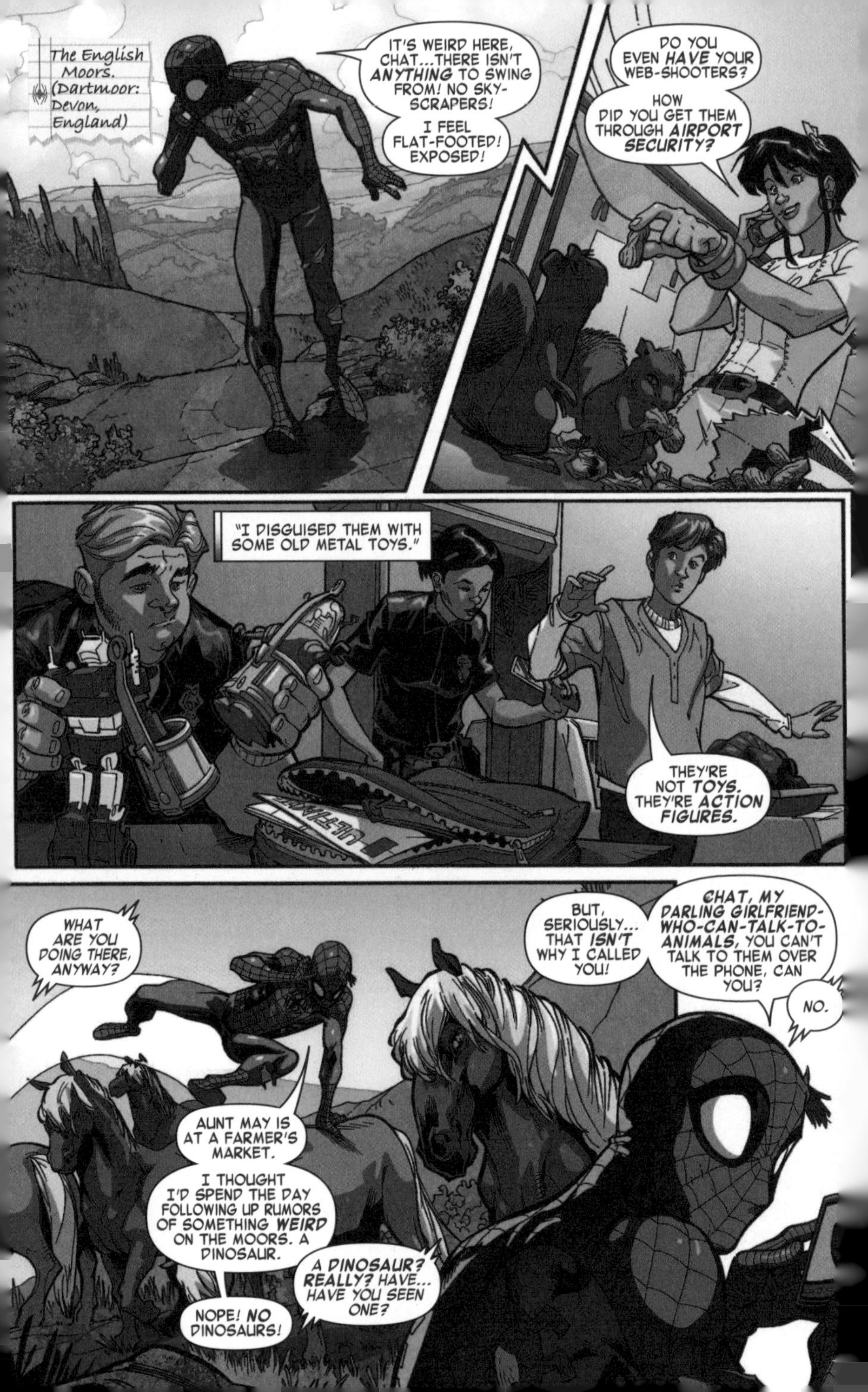
The English Moors. (Dartmoor: Devon, England)
IT'S WEIRD HERE, CHAT... THERE ISN'T ANYTHING TO SWING FROM! NO SKY-SCRAPERS!
I FEEL FLAT-FOOTED! EXPOSED!
DO YOU EVEN HAVE YOUR WEB-SHOOTERS?
HOW DID YOU GET THEM THROUGH AIRPORT SECURITY?
"I DISGUISED THEM WITH SOME OLD METAL TOYS."
THEY'RE NOT TOYS. THEY'RE ACTION FIGURES.
WHAT ARE YOU DOING THERE, ANYWAY?
AUNT MAY IS AT A FARMER'S MARKET.
I THOUGHT I'D SPEND THE DAY FOLLOWING UP RUMORS OF SOMETHING WEIRD ON THE MOORS. A DINOSAUR.
A DINOSAUR? REALLY? HAVE... HAVE YOU SEEN ONE?
NOPE! NO DINOSAURS!
BUT, SERIOUSLY... THAT ISN'T WHY I CALLED YOU!
CHAT, MY DARLING GIRLFRIEND-WHO-CAN-TALK-TO-ANIMALS, YOU CAN'T TALK TO THEM OVER THE PHONE, CAN YOU?
NO.

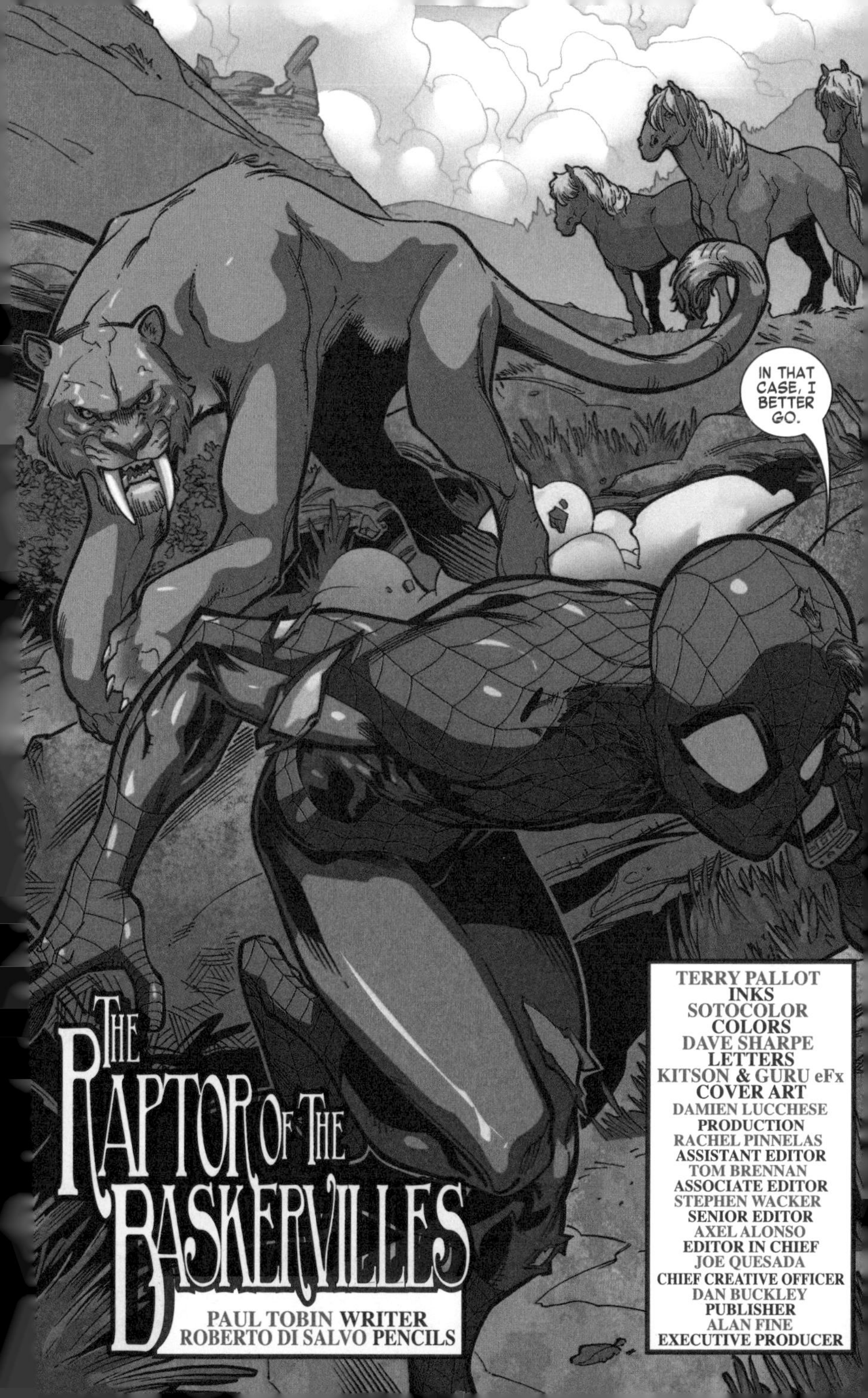
IN THAT CASE, I BETTER GO.
THE RAPTOR OF THE BASKERVILLES
PAUL TOBIN WRITER
ROBERTO DI SALVO PENCILS
TERRY PALLOT
INKS
SOTOCOLOR
COLORS
DAVE SHARPE
LETTERS
KITSON & GURU eFx
COVER ART
DAMIEN LUCCHESE
PRODUCTION
RACHEL PINNELAS
ASSISTANT EDITOR
TOM BRENNAN
ASSOCIATE EDITOR
STEPHEN WACKER
SENIOR EDITOR
AXEL ALONSO
EDITOR IN CHIEF
JOE QUESADA
CHIEF CREATIVE OFFICER
DAN BUCKLEY
PUBLISHER
ALAN FINE
EXECUTIVE PRODUCER

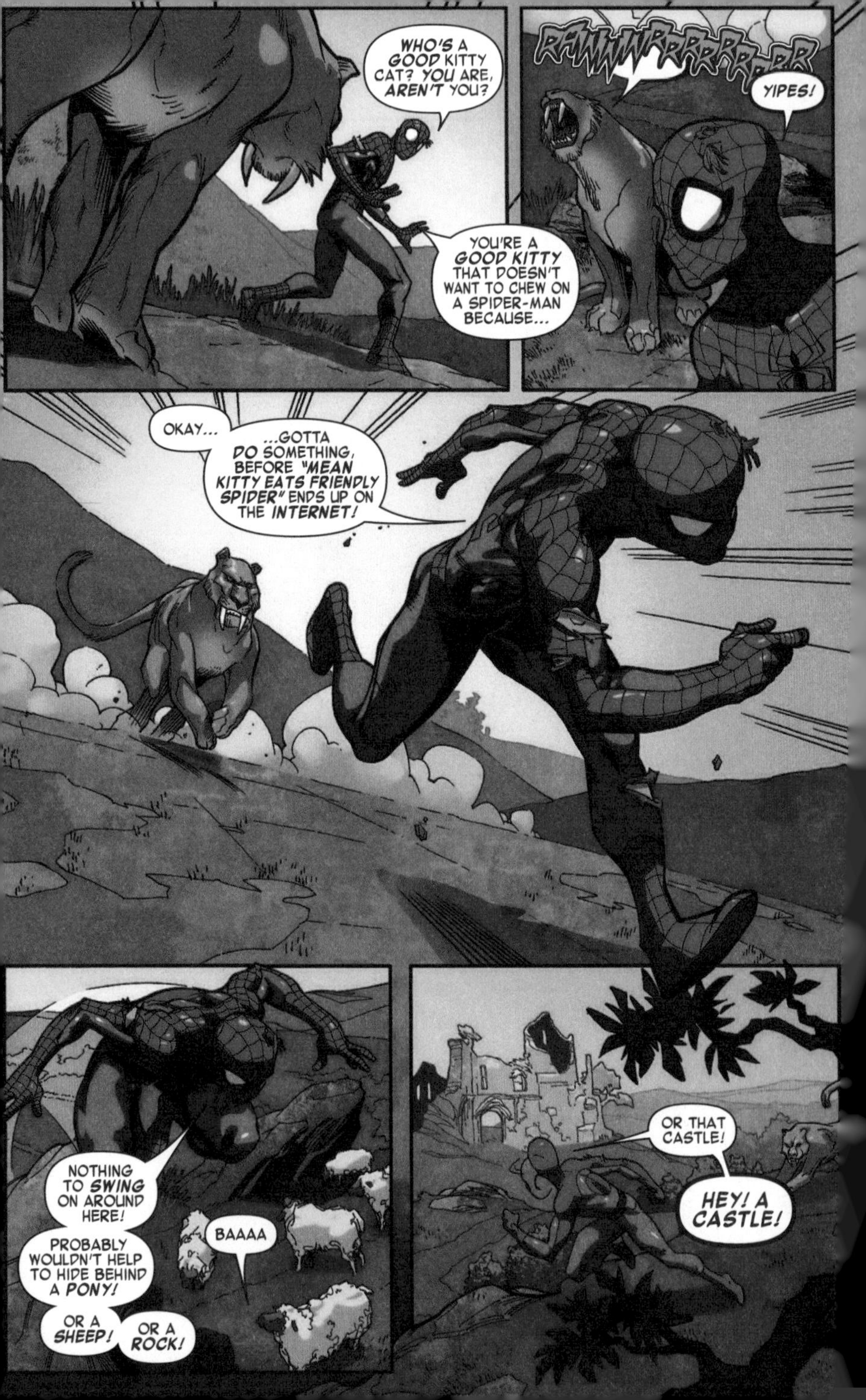
WHO'S A GOOD KITTY CAT? YOU ARE, AREN'T YOU?
YOU'RE A GOOD KITTY THAT DOESN'T WANT TO CHEW ON A SPIDER-MAN BECAUSE...
RAWWWRRRRRRRRRR
YIPES!
OKAY...
...GOTTA DO SOMETHING, BEFORE "MEAN KITTY EATS FRIENDLY SPIDER" ENDS UP ON THE INTERNET!
NOTHING TO SWING ON AROUND HERE!
PROBABLY WOULDN'T HELP TO HIDE BEHIND A PONY!
BAAAA
OR A SHEEP!
OR A ROCK!
OR THAT CASTLE!
HEY! A CASTLE!

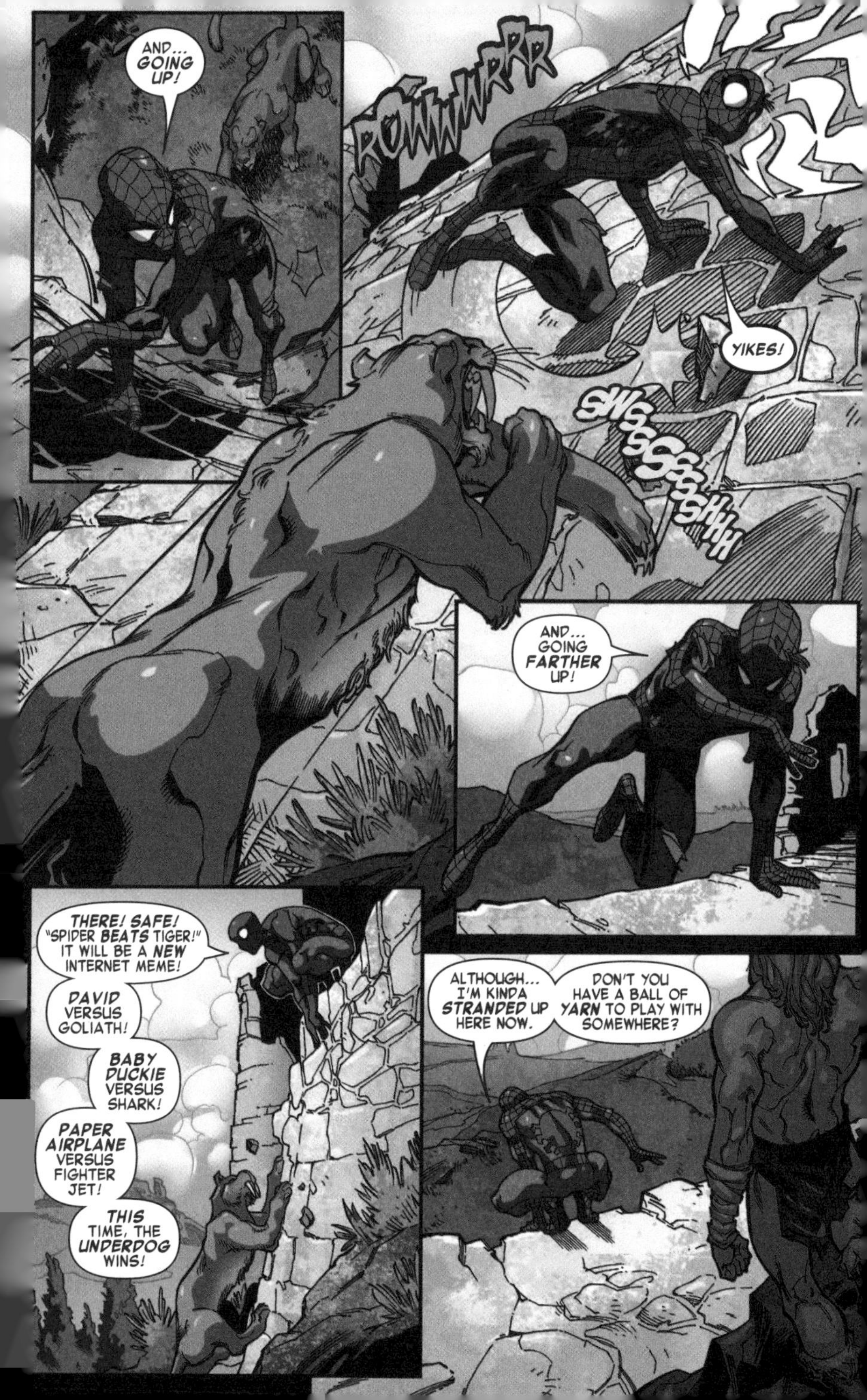
AND... GOING UP!
ROWWWRRR
YIKES!
SWSSSSSSHHH
AND... GOING FARTHER UP!
THERE! SAFE! "SPIDER BEATS TIGER!" IT WILL BE A NEW INTERNET MEME!
DAVID VERSUS GOLIATH!
BABY DUCKIE VERSUS SHARK!
PAPER AIRPLANE VERSUS FIGHTER JET!
THIS TIME, THE UNDERDOG WINS!
ALTHOUGH... I'M KINDA STRANDED UP HERE NOW.
DON'T YOU HAVE A BALL OF YARN TO PLAY WITH SOMEWHERE?

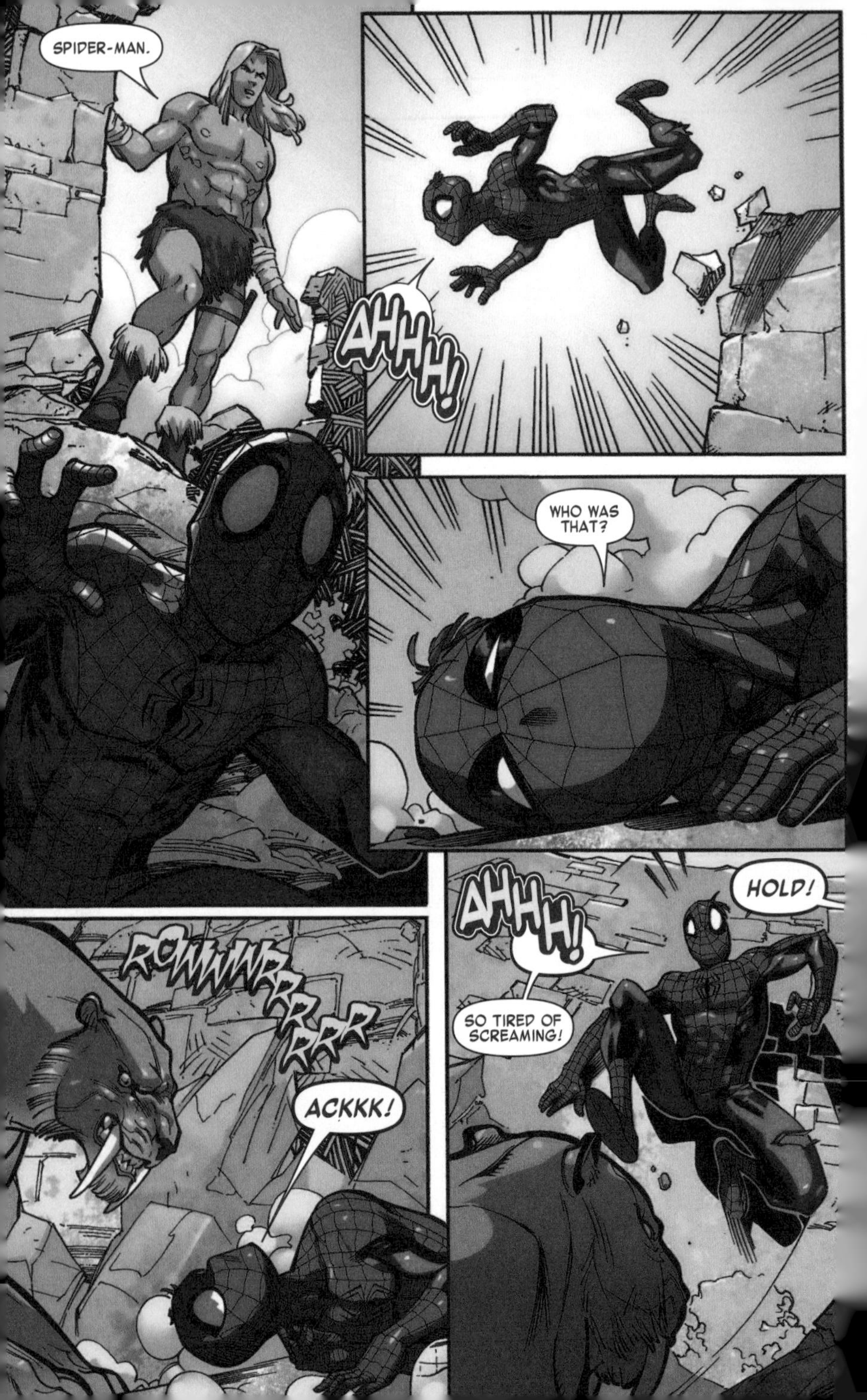
SPIDER-MAN.
AHHHH!
WHO WAS THAT?
ROWWWRRRRRR
ACKKK!
AHHHH!
HOLD!
SO TIRED OF SCREAMING!

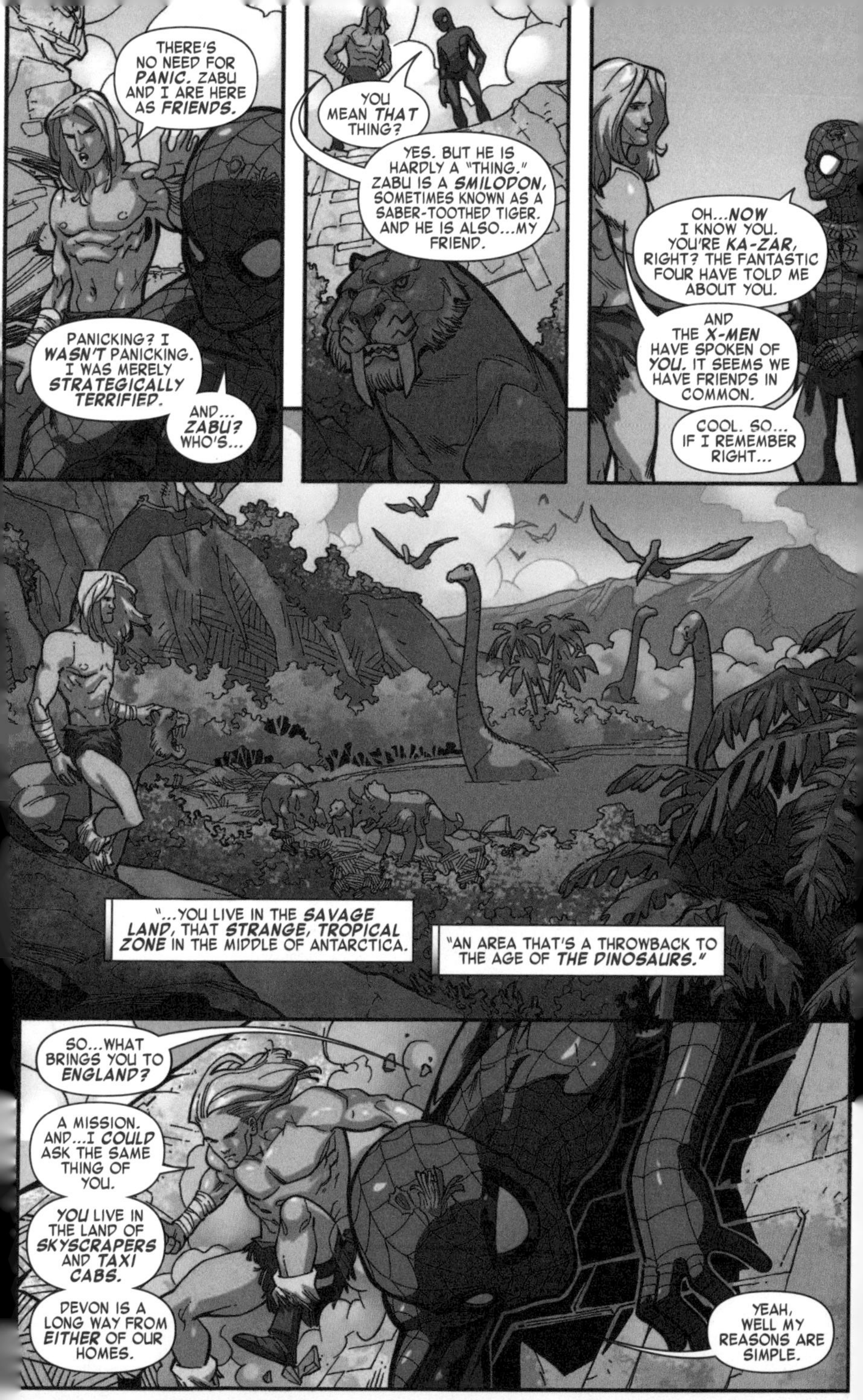
THERE'S NO NEED FOR PANIC. ZABU AND I ARE HERE AS FRIENDS.
PANICKING? I WASN'T PANICKING. I WAS MERELY STRATEGICALLY TERRIFIED.
AND... ZABU? WHO'S...
YOU MEAN THAT THING?
YES. BUT HE IS HARDLY A "THING." ZABU IS A SMILODON, SOMETIMES KNOWN AS A SABER-TOOTHED TIGER. AND HE IS ALSO...MY FRIEND.
OH...NOW I KNOW YOU. YOU'RE KA-ZAR, RIGHT? THE FANTASTIC FOUR HAVE TOLD ME ABOUT YOU.
AND THE X-MEN HAVE SPOKEN OF YOU. IT SEEMS WE HAVE FRIENDS IN COMMON.
COOL. SO... IF I REMEMBER RIGHT...
"...YOU LIVE IN THE SAVAGE LAND, THAT STRANGE, TROPICAL ZONE IN THE MIDDLE OF ANTARCTICA.
"AN AREA THAT'S A THROWBACK TO THE AGE OF THE DINOSAURS."
SO...WHAT BRINGS YOU TO ENGLAND?
A MISSION. AND...I COULD ASK THE SAME THING OF YOU.
YOU LIVE IN THE LAND OF SKYSCRAPERS AND TAXI CABS.
DEVON IS A LONG WAY FROM EITHER OF OUR HOMES.
YEAH, WELL MY REASONS ARE SIMPLE.

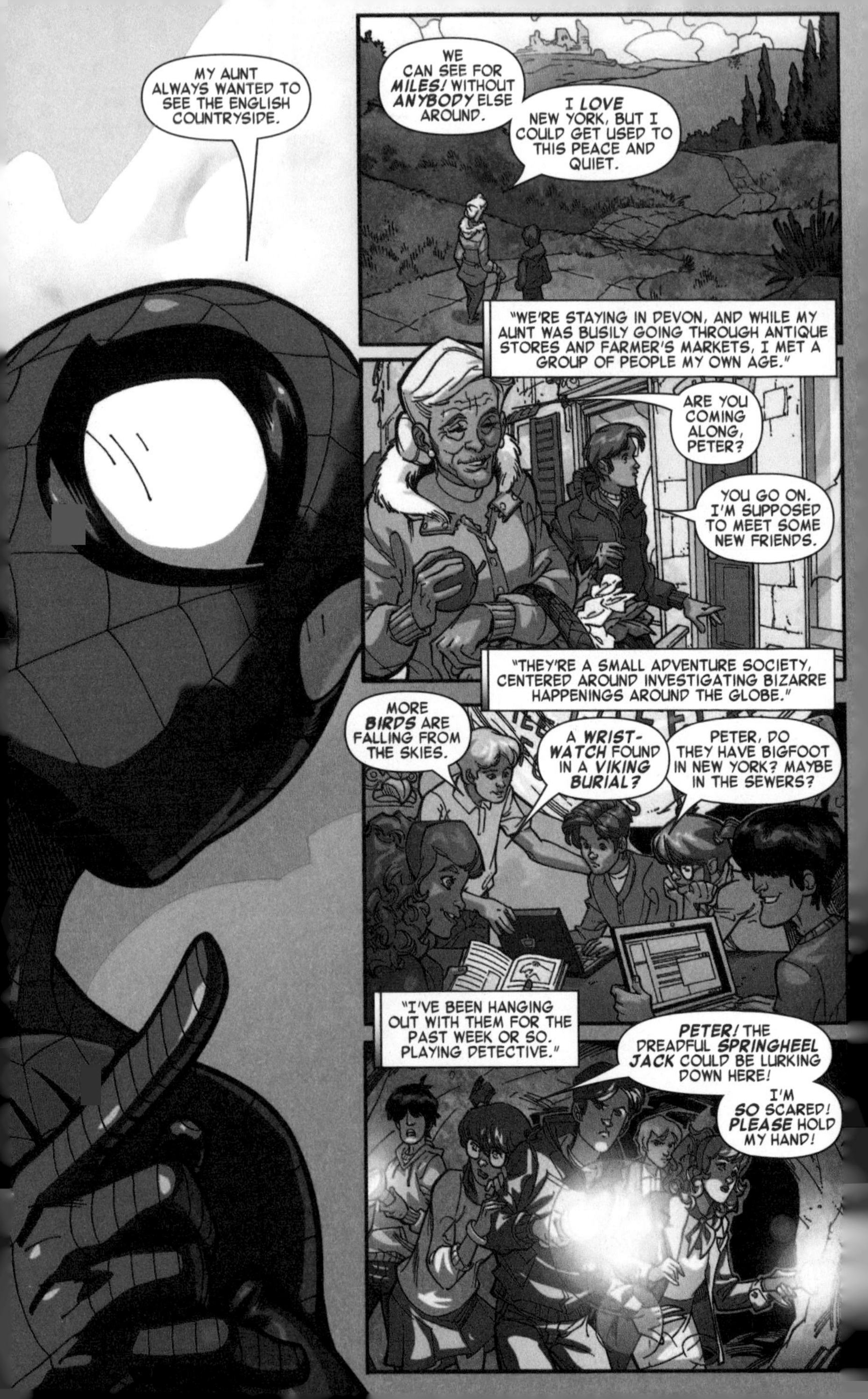
MY AUNT ALWAYS WANTED TO SEE THE ENGLISH COUNTRYSIDE.
WE CAN SEE FOR MILES! WITHOUT ANYBODY ELSE AROUND.
I LOVE NEW YORK, BUT I COULD GET USED TO THIS PEACE AND QUIET.
"WE'RE STAYING IN DEVON, AND WHILE MY AUNT WAS BUSILY GOING THROUGH ANTIQUE STORES AND FARMER'S MARKETS, I MET A GROUP OF PEOPLE MY OWN AGE."
ARE YOU COMING ALONG, PETER?
YOU GO ON. I'M SUPPOSED TO MEET SOME NEW FRIENDS.
"THEY'RE A SMALL ADVENTURE SOCIETY, CENTERED AROUND INVESTIGATING BIZARRE HAPPENINGS AROUND THE GLOBE."
MORE BIRDS ARE FALLING FROM THE SKIES.
A WRIST-WATCH FOUND IN A VIKING BURIAL?
PETER, DO THEY HAVE BIGFOOT IN NEW YORK? MAYBE IN THE SEWERS?
"I'VE BEEN HANGING OUT WITH THEM FOR THE PAST WEEK OR SO. PLAYING DETECTIVE."
PETER! THE DREADFUL SPRINGHEEL JACK COULD BE LURKING DOWN HERE!
I'M SO SCARED! PLEASE HOLD MY HAND!

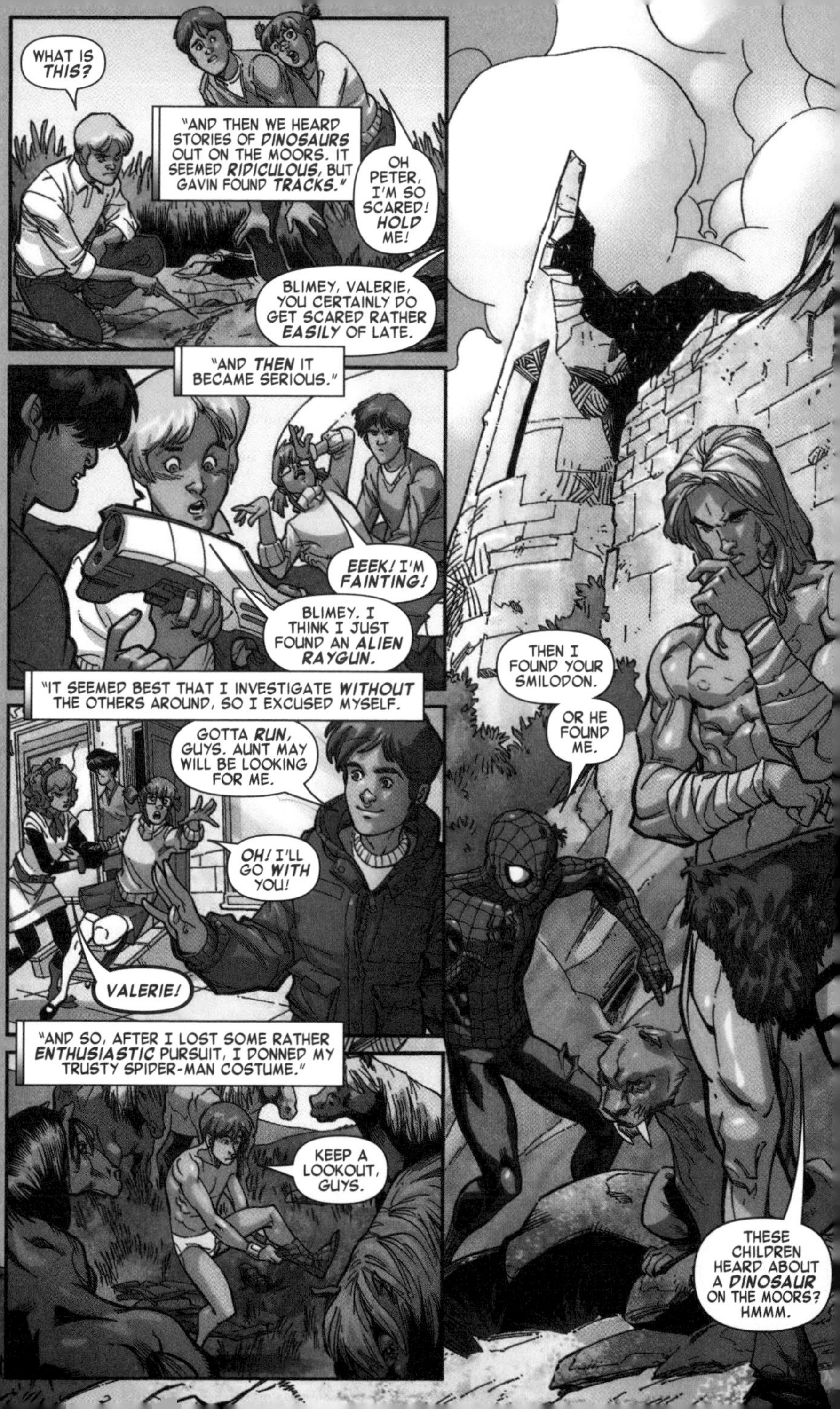
WHAT IS THIS?
"AND THEN WE HEARD STORIES OF DINOSAURS OUT ON THE MOORS. IT SEEMED RIDICULOUS, BUT GAVIN FOUND TRACKS."
OH PETER, I'M SO SCARED! HOLD ME!
BLIMEY, VALERIE, YOU CERTAINLY DO GET SCARED RATHER EASILY OF LATE.
"AND THEN IT BECAME SERIOUS."
EEEK! I'M FAINTING!
BLIMEY. I THINK I JUST FOUND AN ALIEN RAYGUN.
"IT SEEMED BEST THAT I INVESTIGATE WITHOUT THE OTHERS AROUND, SO I EXCUSED MYSELF.
GOTTA RUN, GUYS. AUNT MAY WILL BE LOOKING FOR ME.
OH! I'LL GO WITH YOU!
VALERIE!
"AND SO, AFTER I LOST SOME RATHER ENTHUSIASTIC PURSUIT, I DONNED MY TRUSTY SPIDER-MAN COSTUME."
KEEP A LOOKOUT, GUYS.
THEN I FOUND YOUR SMILODON.
OR HE FOUND ME.
THESE CHILDREN HEARD ABOUT A DINOSAUR ON THE MOORS? HMMM.

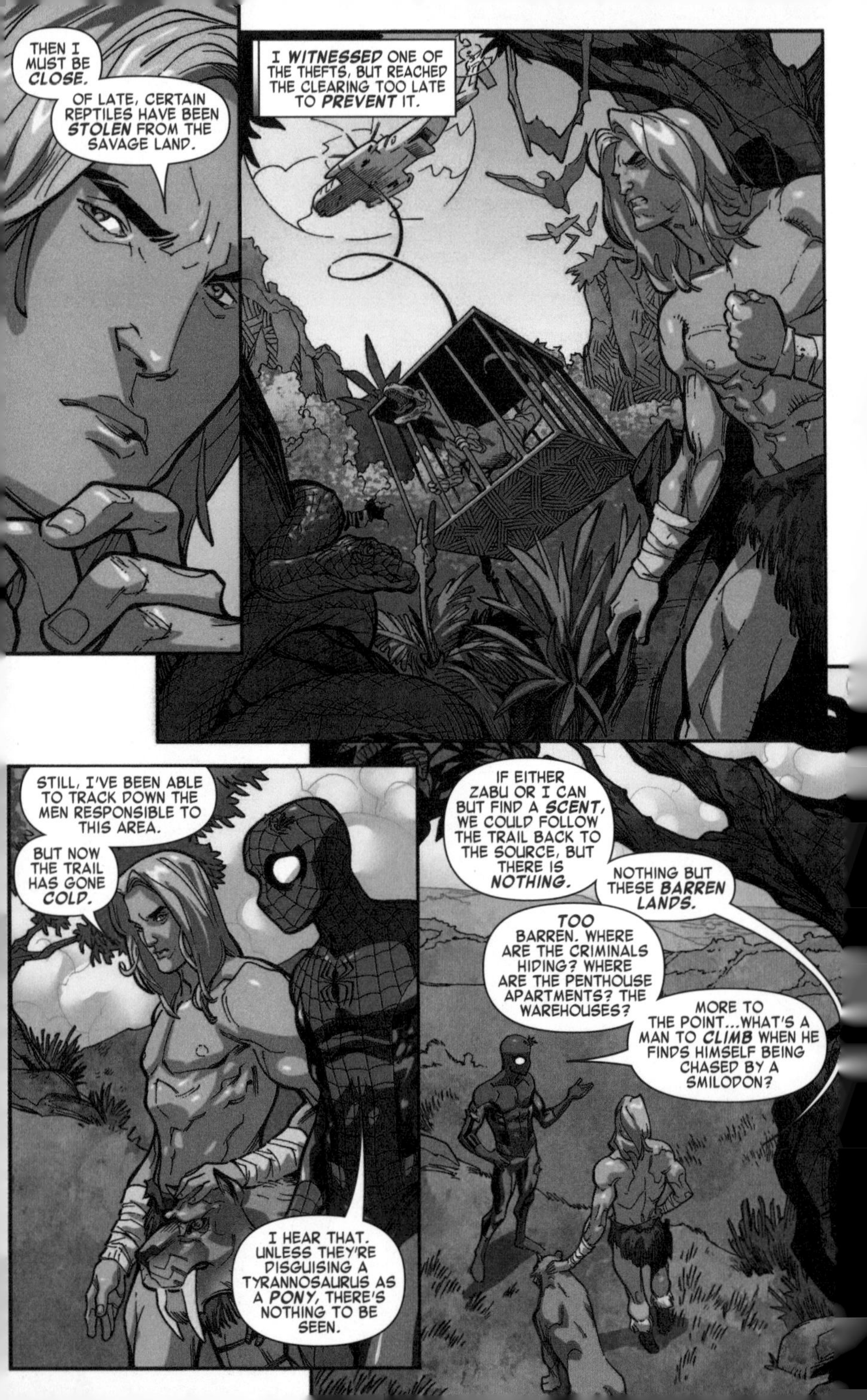
THEN I MUST BE CLOSE.
OF LATE, CERTAIN REPTILES HAVE BEEN STOLEN FROM THE SAVAGE LAND.
I WITNESSED ONE OF THE THEFTS, BUT REACHED THE CLEARING TOO LATE TO PREVENT IT.
STILL, I'VE BEEN ABLE TO TRACK DOWN THE MEN RESPONSIBLE TO THIS AREA.
BUT NOW THE TRAIL HAS GONE COLD.
I HEAR THAT. UNLESS THEY'RE DISGUISING A TYRANNOSAURUS AS A PONY, THERE'S NOTHING TO BE SEEN.
IF EITHER ZABU OR I CAN BUT FIND A SCENT, WE COULD FOLLOW THE TRAIL BACK TO THE SOURCE, BUT THERE IS NOTHING.
NOTHING BUT THESE BARREN LANDS.
TOO BARREN. WHERE ARE THE CRIMINALS HIDING? WHERE ARE THE PENTHOUSE APARTMENTS? THE WAREHOUSES?
MORE TO THE POINT...WHAT'S A MAN TO CLIMB WHEN HE FINDS HIMSELF BEING CHASED BY A SMILODON?

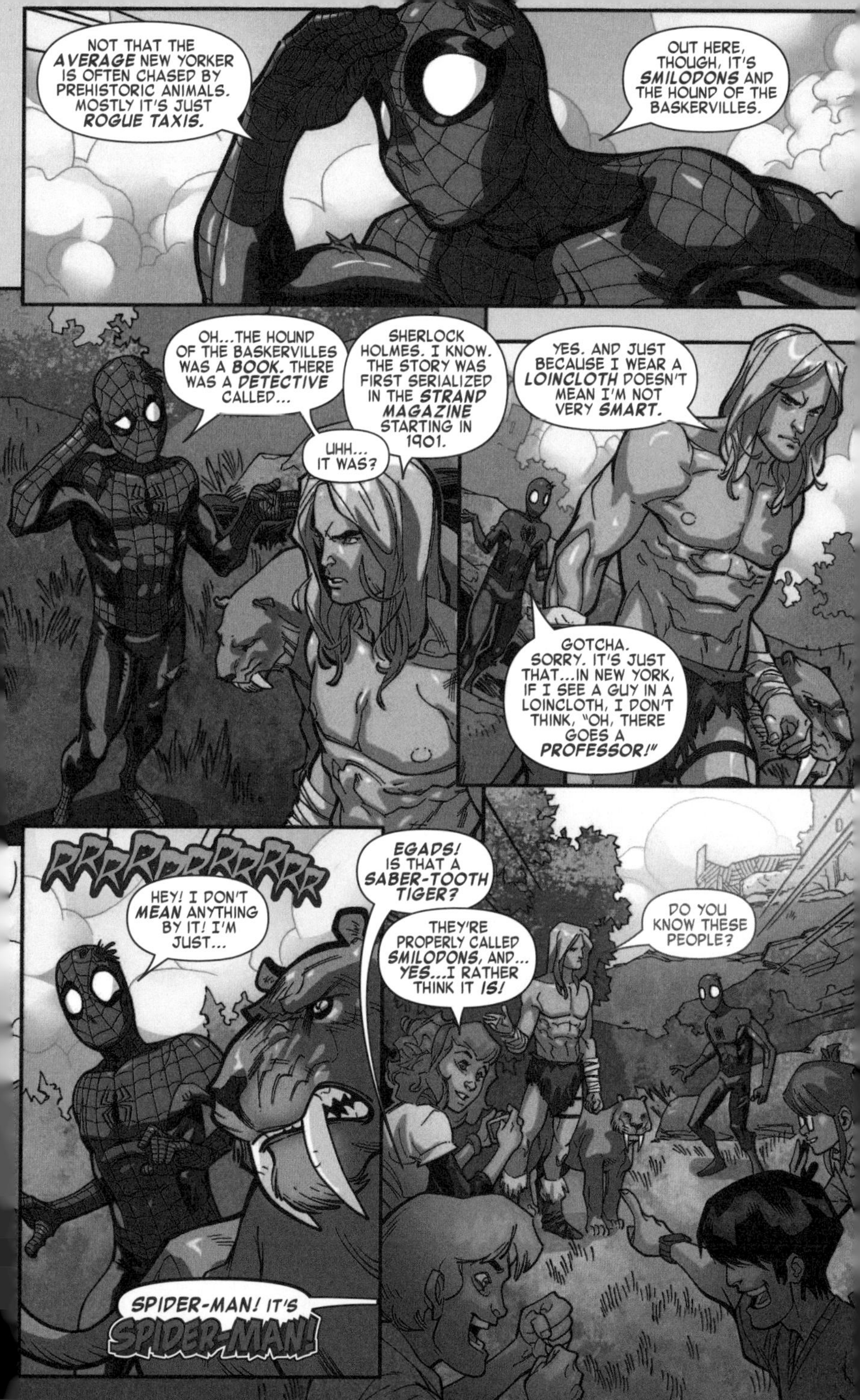
NOT THAT THE AVERAGE NEW YORKER IS OFTEN CHASED BY PREHISTORIC ANIMALS. MOSTLY IT'S JUST ROGUE TAXIS.
OUT HERE, THOUGH, IT'S SMILODONS AND THE HOUND OF THE BASKERVILLES.
OH...THE HOUND OF THE BASKERVILLES WAS A BOOK. THERE WAS A DETECTIVE CALLED...
SHERLOCK HOLMES. I KNOW. THE STORY WAS FIRST SERIALIZED IN THE STRAND MAGAZINE STARTING IN 1901.
UHH... IT WAS?
YES. AND JUST BECAUSE I WEAR A LOINCLOTH DOESN'T MEAN I'M NOT VERY SMART.
GOTCHA. SORRY. IT'S JUST THAT...IN NEW YORK, IF I SEE A GUY IN A LOINCLOTH, I DON'T THINK, "OH, THERE GOES A PROFESSOR!"
RRRRRRRRRRRRR
HEY! I DON'T MEAN ANYTHING BY IT! I'M JUST...
EGADS! IS THAT A SABER-TOOTH TIGER?
THEY'RE PROPERLY CALLED SMILODONS, AND... YES...I RATHER THINK IT IS!
DO YOU KNOW THESE PEOPLE?
SPIDER-MAN! IT'S SPIDER-MAN!

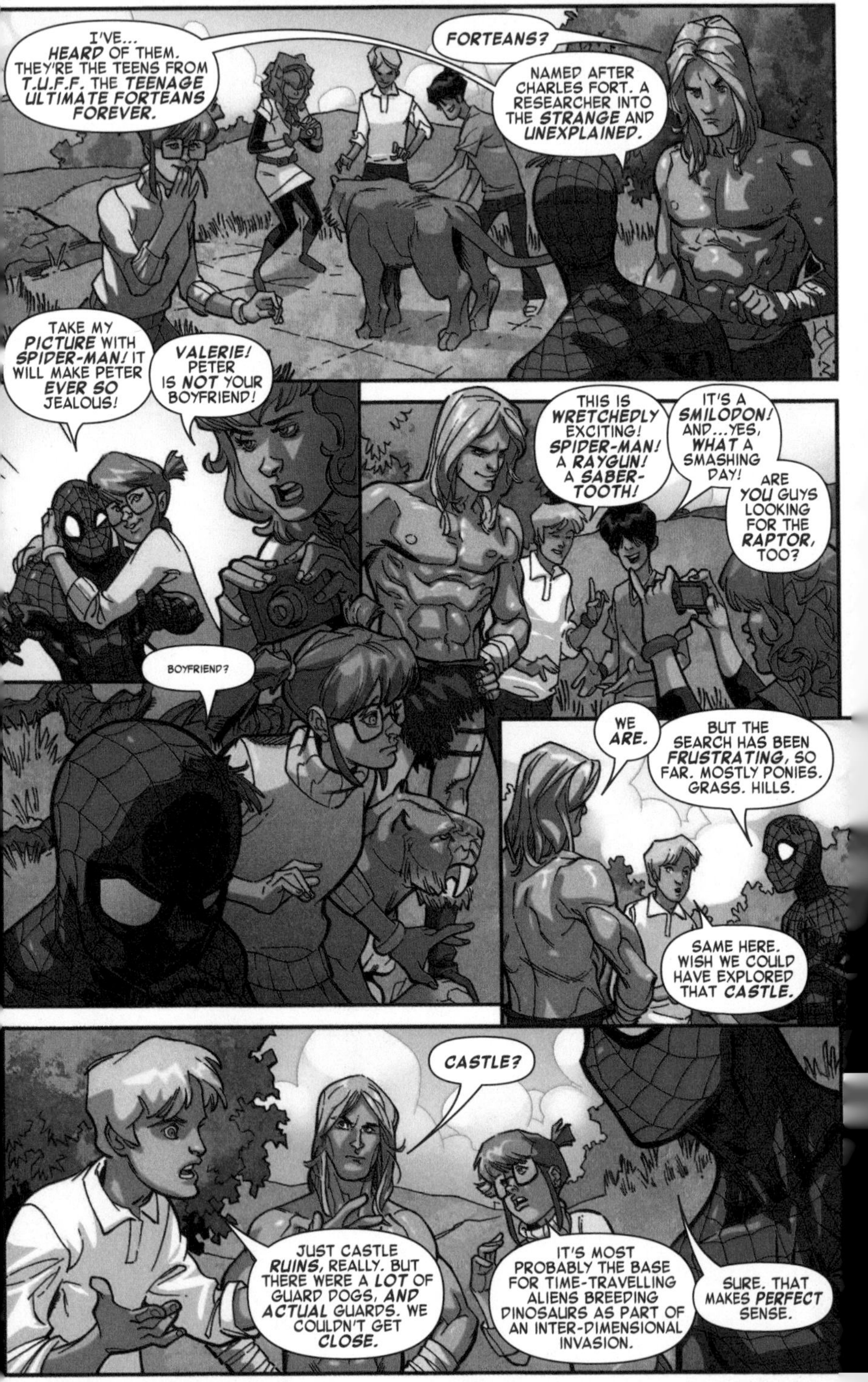

I'VE... HEARD OF THEM. THEY'RE THE TEENS FROM T.U.F.F. THE TEENAGE ULTIMATE FORTEANS FOREVER.
FORTEANS?
NAMED AFTER CHARLES FORT. A RESEARCHER INTO THE STRANGE AND UNEXPLAINED.
TAKE MY PICTURE WITH SPIDER-MAN! IT WILL MAKE PETER EVER SO JEALOUS!
VALERIE! PETER IS NOT YOUR BOYFRIEND!
THIS IS WRETCHEDLY EXCITING! SPIDER-MAN! A RAYGUN! A SABER-TOOTH!
IT'S A SMILODON! AND...YES, WHAT A SMASHING DAY!
ARE YOU GUYS LOOKING FOR THE RAPTOR, TOO?
BOYFRIEND?
WE ARE.
BUT THE SEARCH HAS BEEN FRUSTRATING, SO FAR. MOSTLY PONIES. GRASS. HILLS.
SAME HERE. WISH WE COULD HAVE EXPLORED THAT CASTLE.
CASTLE?
JUST CASTLE RUINS, REALLY. BUT THERE WERE A LOT OF GUARD DOGS, AND ACTUAL GUARDS. WE COULDN'T GET CLOSE.
IT'S MOST PROBABLY THE BASE FOR TIME-TRAVELLING ALIENS BREEDING DINOSAURS AS PART OF AN INTER-DIMENSIONAL INVASION.
SURE. THAT MAKES PERFECT SENSE.

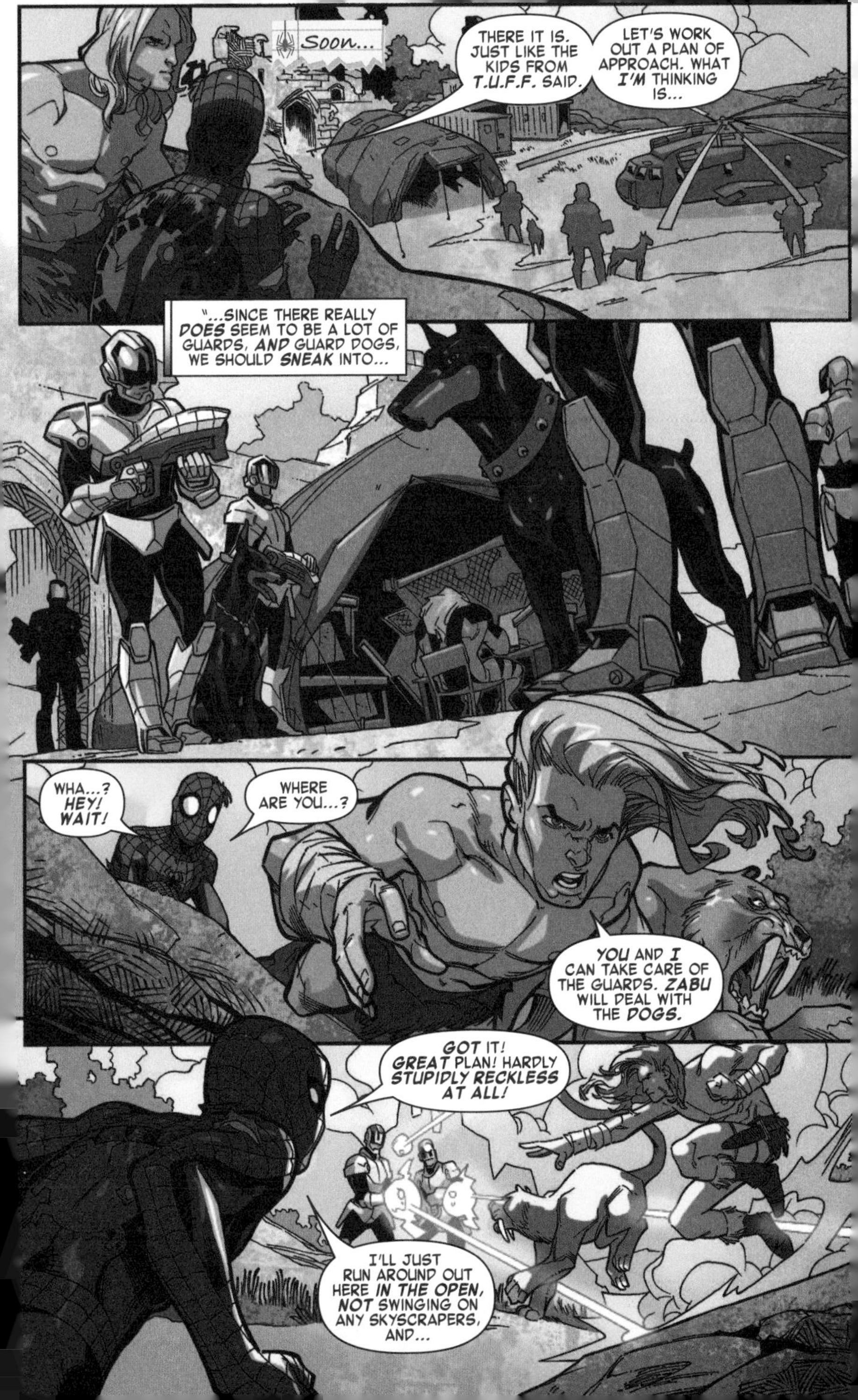
Soon...
THERE IT IS. JUST LIKE THE KIDS FROM T.U.F.F. SAID.
LET'S WORK OUT A PLAN OF APPROACH. WHAT I'M THINKING IS...
"...SINCE THERE REALLY DOES SEEM TO BE A LOT OF GUARDS, AND GUARD DOGS, WE SHOULD SNEAK INTO...
WHA...? HEY! WAIT!
WHERE ARE YOU...?
YOU AND I CAN TAKE CARE OF THE GUARDS. ZABU WILL DEAL WITH THE DOGS.
GOT IT! GREAT PLAN! HARDLY STUPIDLY RECKLESS AT ALL!
I'LL JUST RUN AROUND OUT HERE IN THE OPEN, NOT SWINGING ON ANY SKYSCRAPERS, AND...

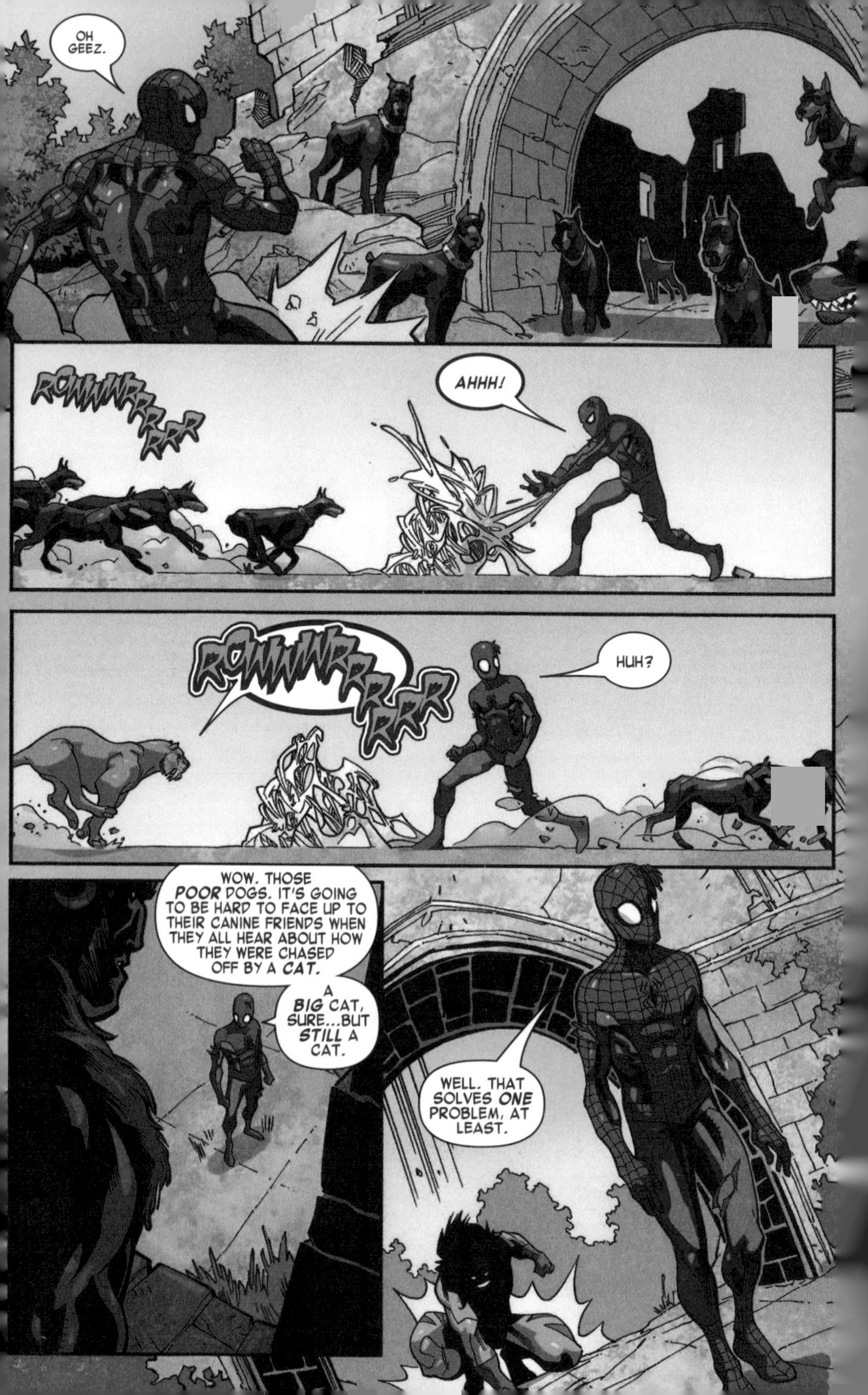
OH GEEZ.
RONWWRRRRR
AHHH!
RONWWRRRRRRR
HUH?
WOW. THOSE POOR DOGS. IT'S GOING TO BE HARD TO FACE UP TO THEIR CANINE FRIENDS WHEN THEY ALL HEAR ABOUT HOW THEY WERE CHASED OFF BY A CAT.
A BIG CAT, SURE...BUT STILL A CAT.
WELL. THAT SOLVES ONE PROBLEM, AT LEAST.

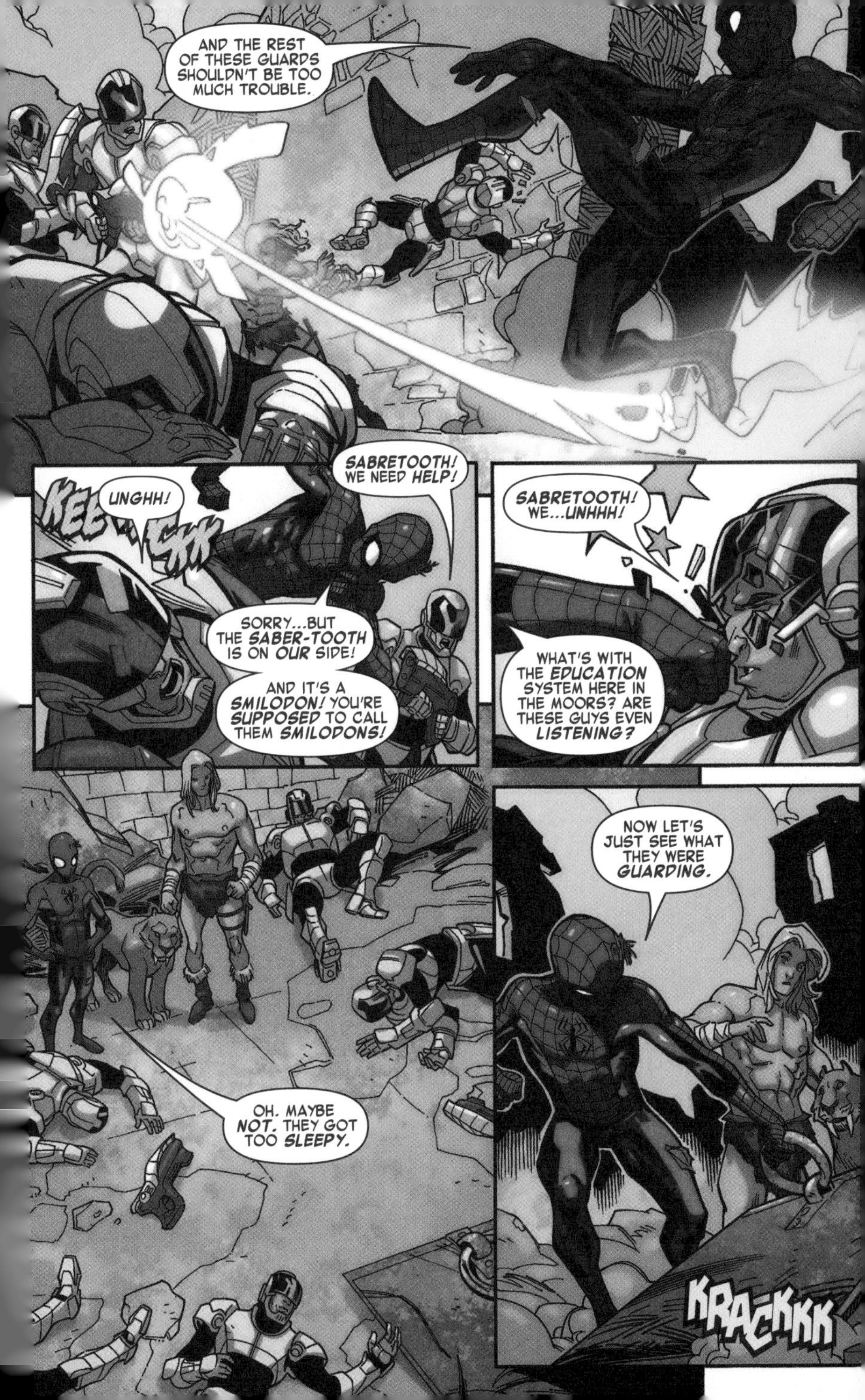
AND THE REST OF THESE GUARDS SHOULDN'T BE TOO MUCH TROUBLE.
UNGHH!
SABRETOOTH! WE NEED HELP!
SORRY...BUT THE SABER-TOOTH IS ON OUR SIDE!
AND IT'S A SMILODON! YOU'RE SUPPOSED TO CALL THEM SMILODONS!
SABRETOOTH! WE...UNHHH!
WHAT'S WITH THE EDUCATION SYSTEM HERE IN THE MOORS? ARE THESE GUYS EVEN LISTENING?
OH. MAYBE NOT. THEY GOT TOO SLEEPY.
NOW LET'S JUST SEE WHAT THEY WERE GUARDING.
KRACKKK

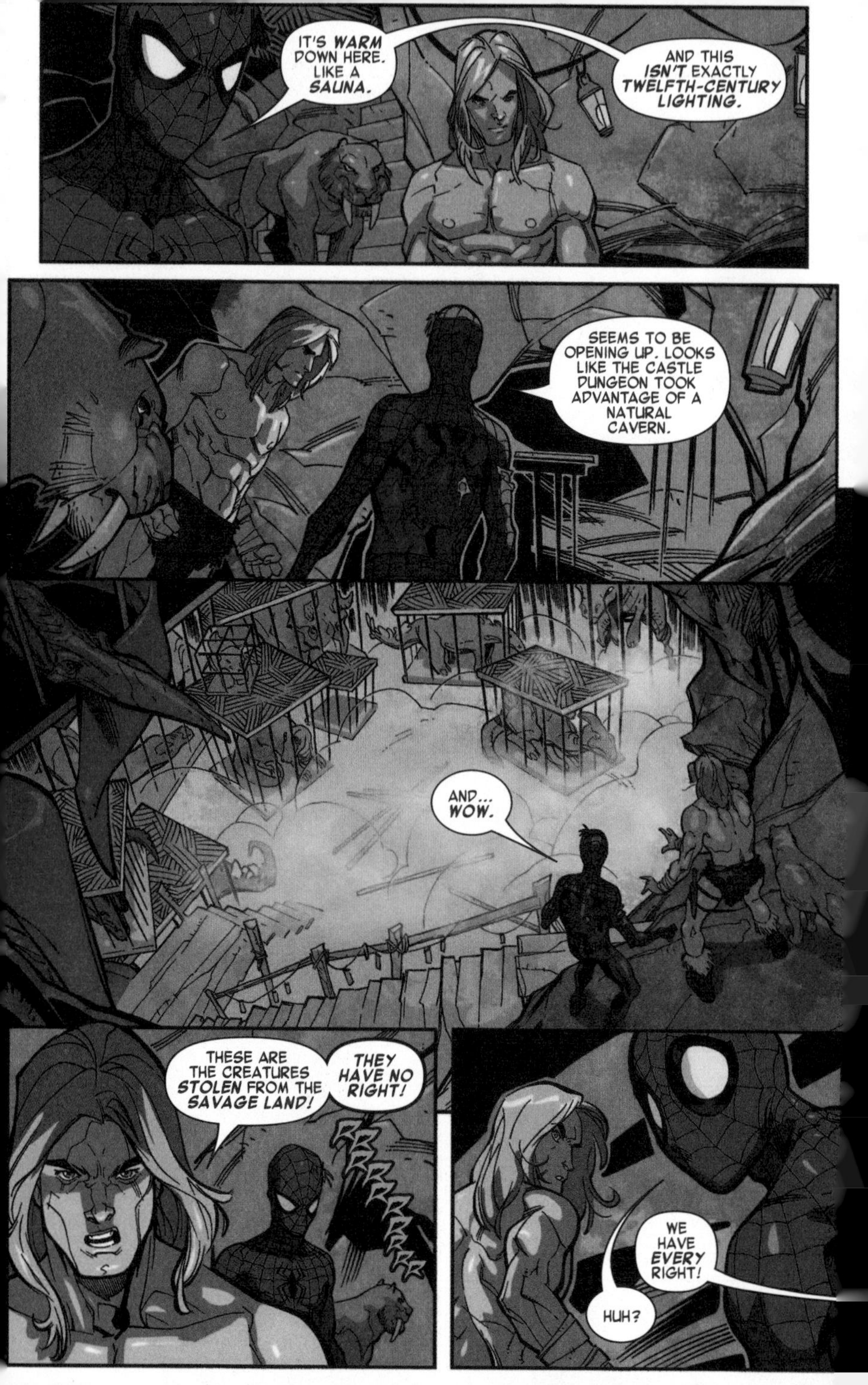
IT'S WARM DOWN HERE. LIKE A SAUNA.
AND THIS ISN'T EXACTLY TWELFTH-CENTURY LIGHTING.
SEEMS TO BE OPENING UP. LOOKS LIKE THE CASTLE DUNGEON TOOK ADVANTAGE OF A NATURAL CAVERN.
AND... WOW.
THESE ARE THE CREATURES STOLEN FROM THE SAVAGE LAND!
THEY HAVE NO RIGHT!
RRRRRRRRRR
WE HAVE EVERY RIGHT!
HUH?

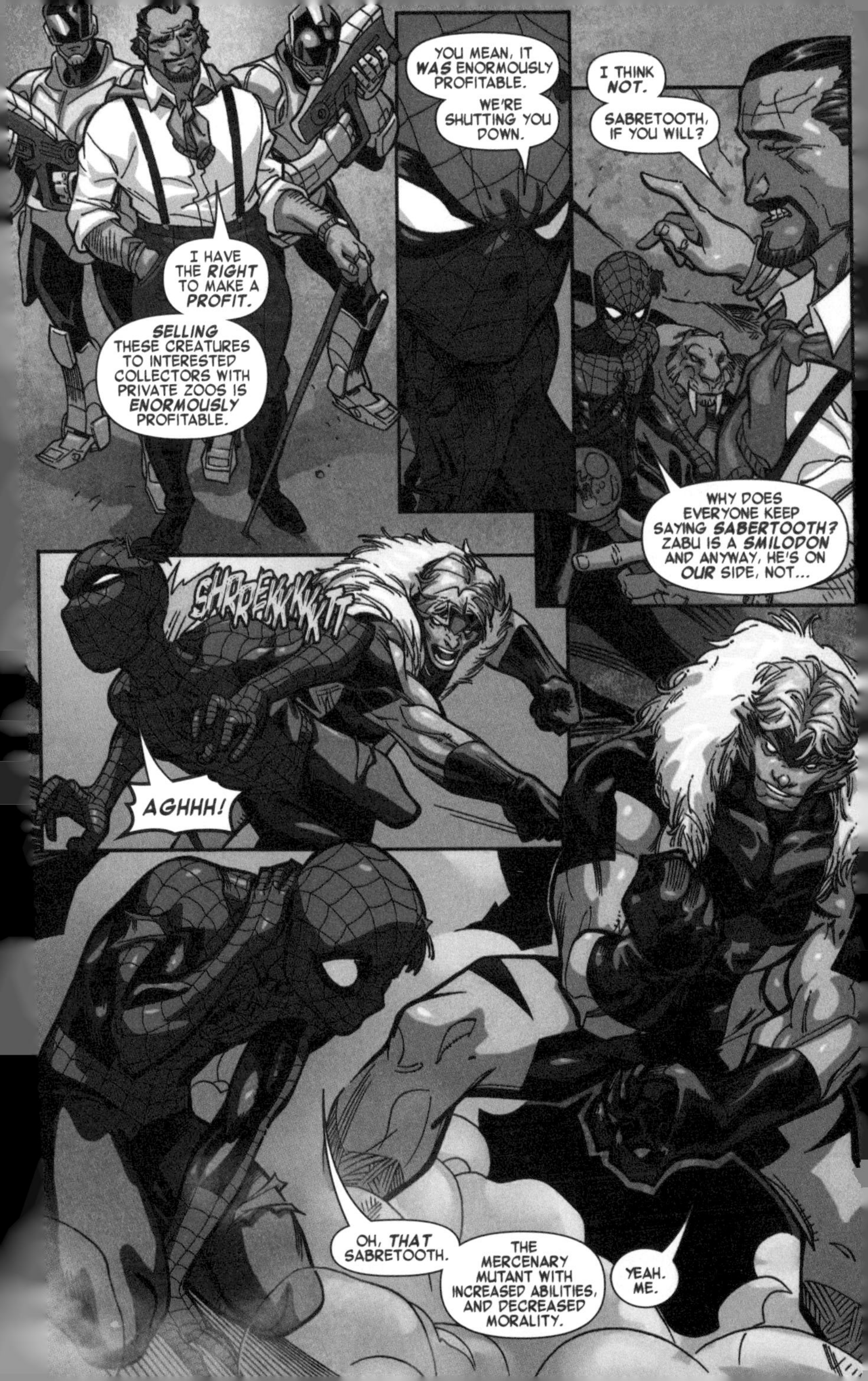
I HAVE THE RIGHT TO MAKE A PROFIT.
SELLING THESE CREATURES TO INTERESTED COLLECTORS WITH PRIVATE ZOOS IS ENORMOUSLY PROFITABLE.
YOU MEAN, IT WAS ENORMOUSLY PROFITABLE.
WE'RE SHUTTING YOU DOWN.
I THINK NOT.
SABRETOOTH, IF YOU WILL?
WHY DOES EVERYONE KEEP SAYING SABERTOOTH? ZABU IS A SMILODON AND ANYWAY, HE'S ON OUR SIDE, NOT...
SHREKKKKTT
AGHHH!
OH, THAT SABRETOOTH.
THE MERCENARY MUTANT WITH INCREASED ABILITIES, AND DECREASED MORALITY.
YEAH. ME.

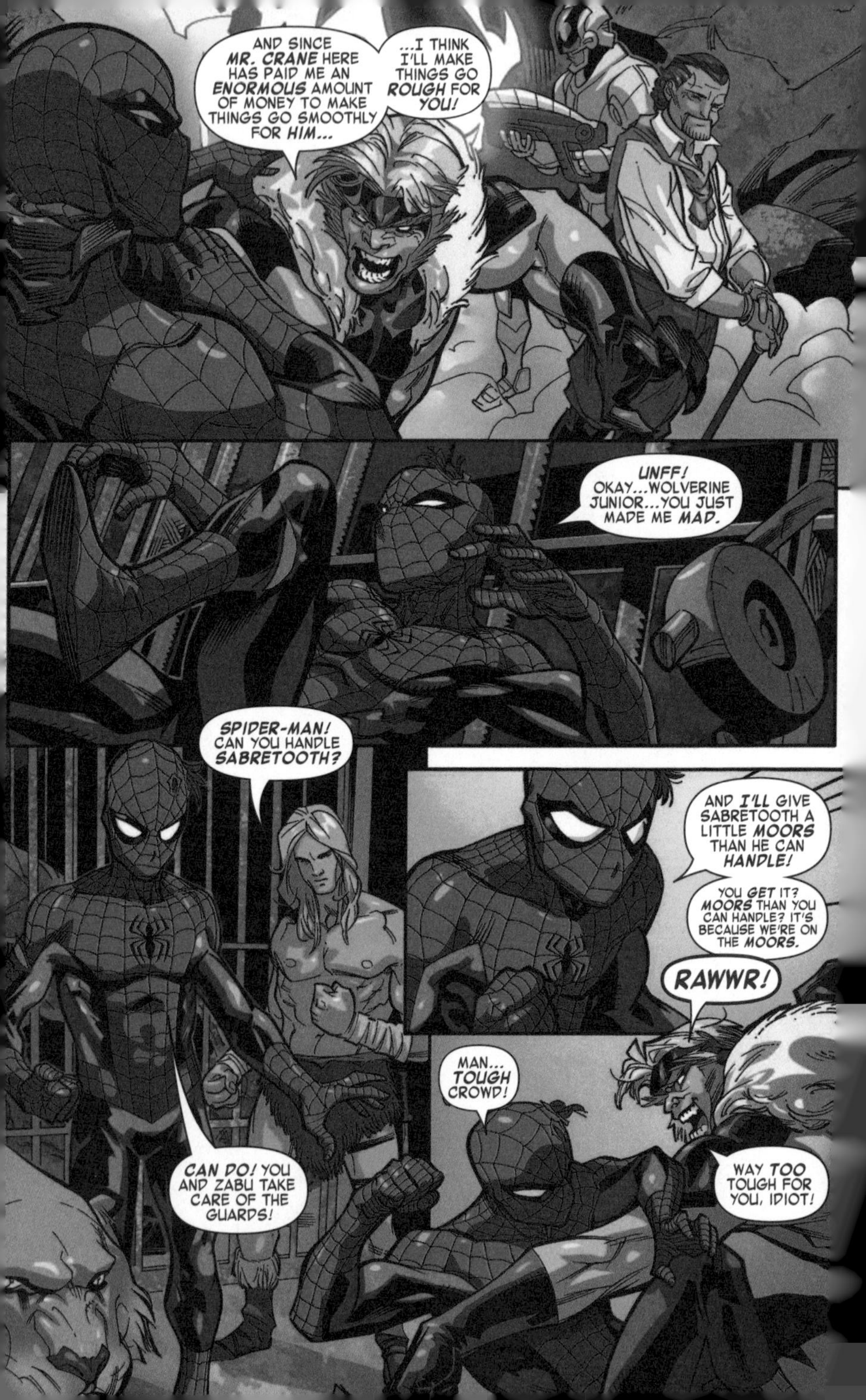
AND SINCE MR. CRANE HERE HAS PAID ME AN ENORMOUS AMOUNT OF MONEY TO MAKE THINGS GO SMOOTHLY FOR HIM...
...I THINK I'LL MAKE THINGS GO ROUGH FOR YOU!
UNFF! OKAY...WOLVERINE JUNIOR...YOU JUST MADE ME MAD.
SPIDER-MAN! CAN YOU HANDLE SABRETOOTH?
CAN DO! YOU AND ZABU TAKE CARE OF THE GUARDS!
AND I'LL GIVE SABRETOOTH A LITTLE MOORS THAN HE CAN HANDLE!
YOU GET IT? MOORS THAN YOU CAN HANDLE? IT'S BECAUSE WE'RE ON THE MOORS.
RAWWR!
MAN... TOUGH CROWD!
WAY TOO TOUGH FOR YOU, IDIOT!

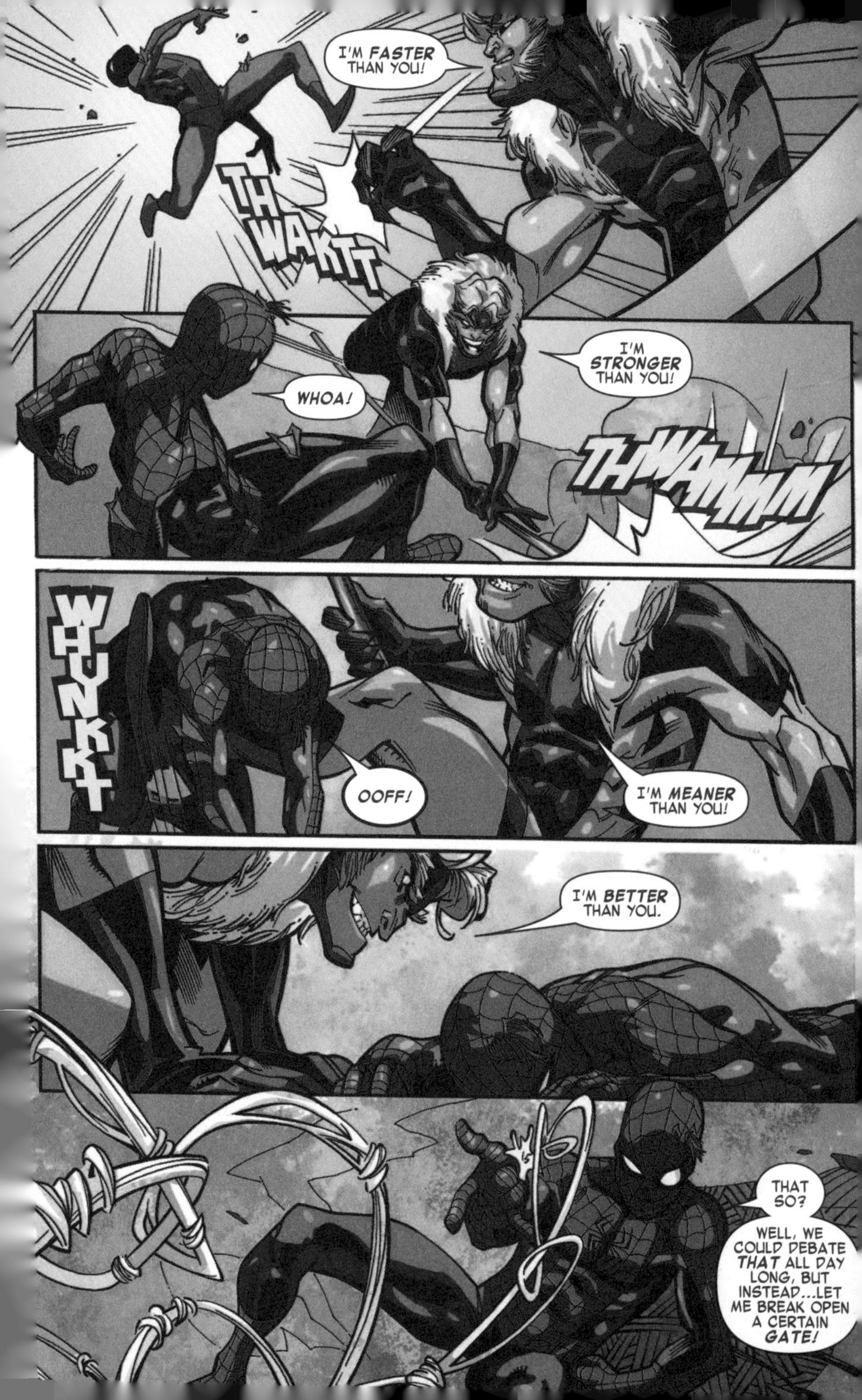
I'M FASTER THAN YOU!
THWAKTT
WHOA!
I'M STRONGER THAN YOU!
THWAMMM
WHUNKT
OOFF!
I'M MEANER THAN YOU!
I'M BETTER THAN YOU.
THAT SO?
WELL, WE COULD DEBATE THAT ALL DAY LONG, BUT INSTEAD...LET ME BREAK OPEN A CERTAIN GATE!

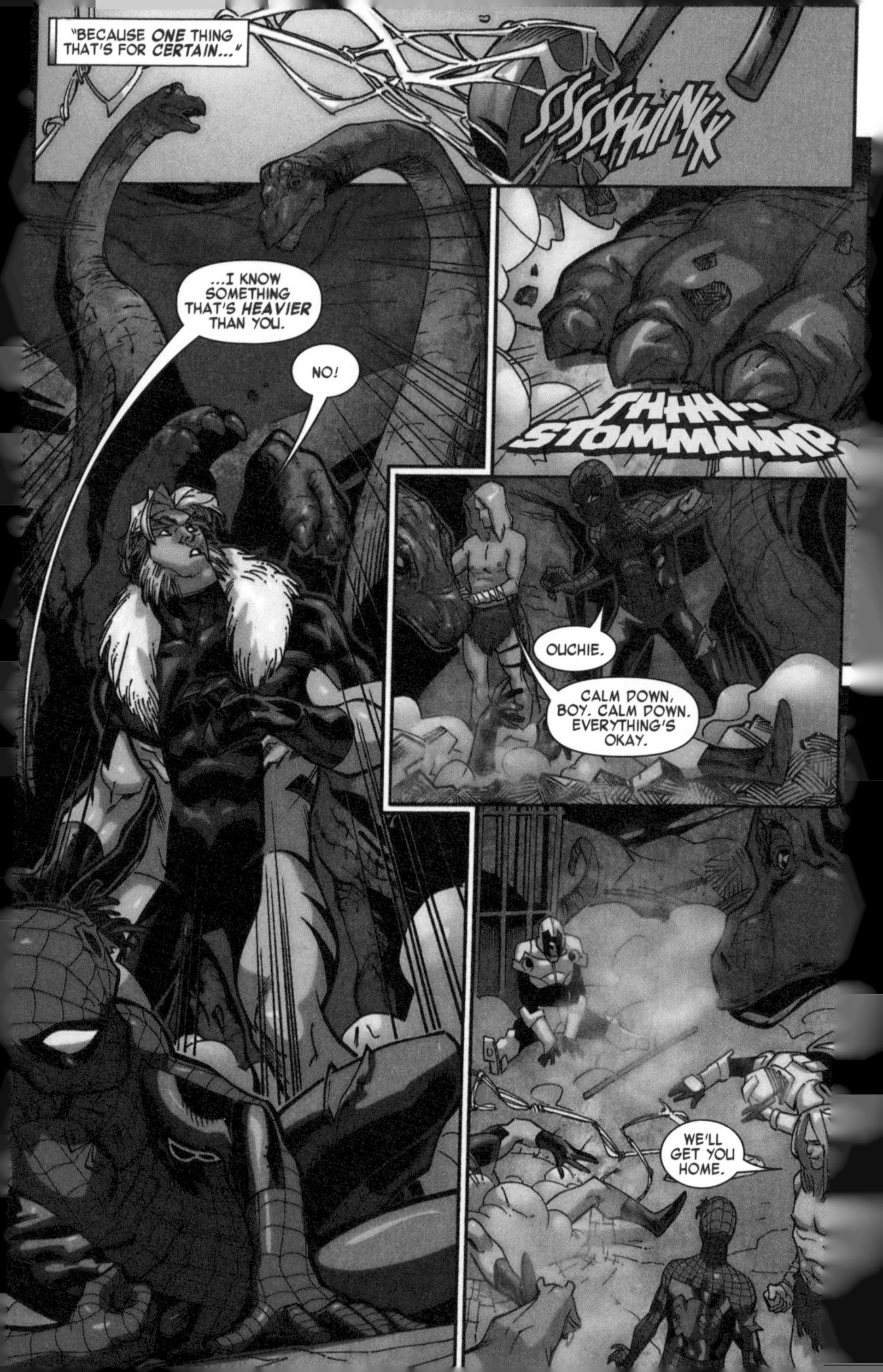

"BECAUSE ONE THING THAT'S FOR CERTAIN..."
SSSSCHHUNKK
...I KNOW SOMETHING THAT'S HEAVIER THAN YOU.
NO!
THHH-STOMMMMMP
OUCHIE.
CALM DOWN, BOY. CALM DOWN. EVERYTHING'S OKAY.
WE'LL GET YOU HOME.

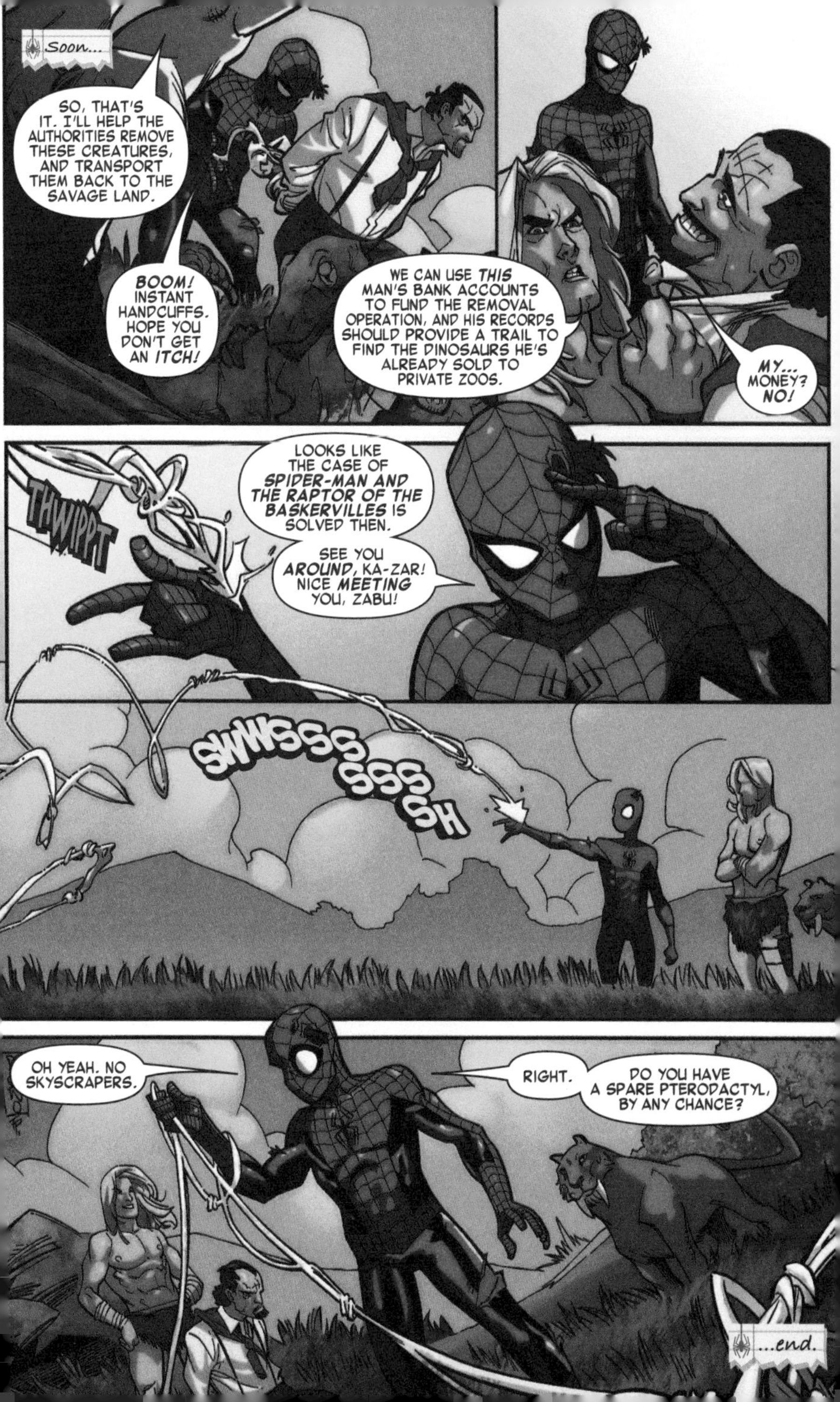
Soon...
SO, THAT'S IT. I'LL HELP THE AUTHORITIES REMOVE THESE CREATURES, AND TRANSPORT THEM BACK TO THE SAVAGE LAND.
BOOM! INSTANT HANDCUFFS. HOPE YOU DON'T GET AN ITCH!
WE CAN USE THIS MAN'S BANK ACCOUNTS TO FUND THE REMOVAL OPERATION, AND HIS RECORDS SHOULD PROVIDE A TRAIL TO FIND THE DINOSAURS HE'S ALREADY SOLD TO PRIVATE ZOOS.
MY... MONEY? NO!
THWIPPT
LOOKS LIKE THE CASE OF SPIDER-MAN AND THE RAPTOR OF THE BASKERVILLES IS SOLVED THEN.
SEE YOU AROUND, KA-ZAR! NICE MEETING YOU, ZABU!
SWWSSSSSSSSH
OH YEAH. NO SKYSCRAPERS.
RIGHT.
DO YOU HAVE A SPARE PTERODACTYL, BY ANY CHANCE?
...end.

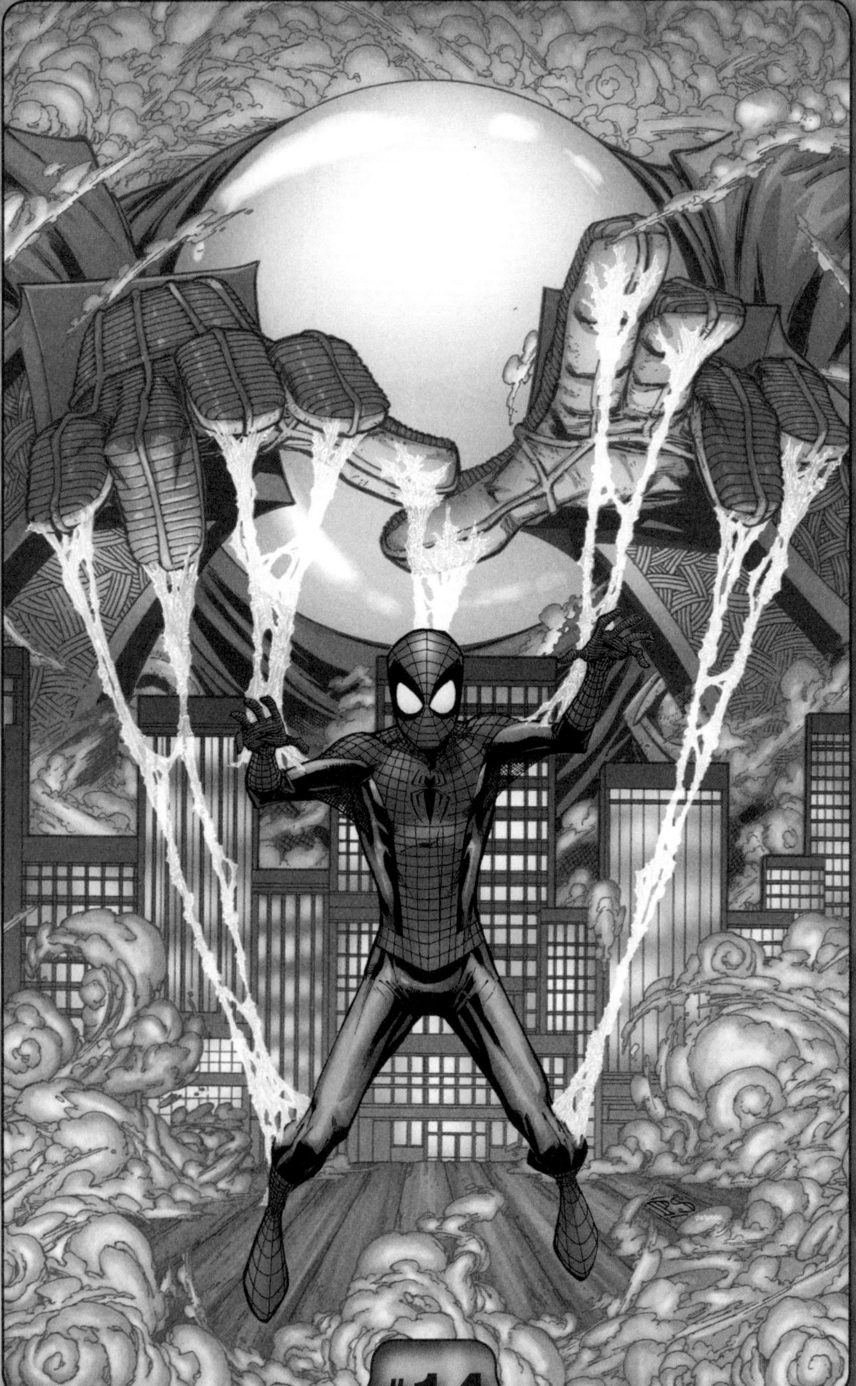

#14

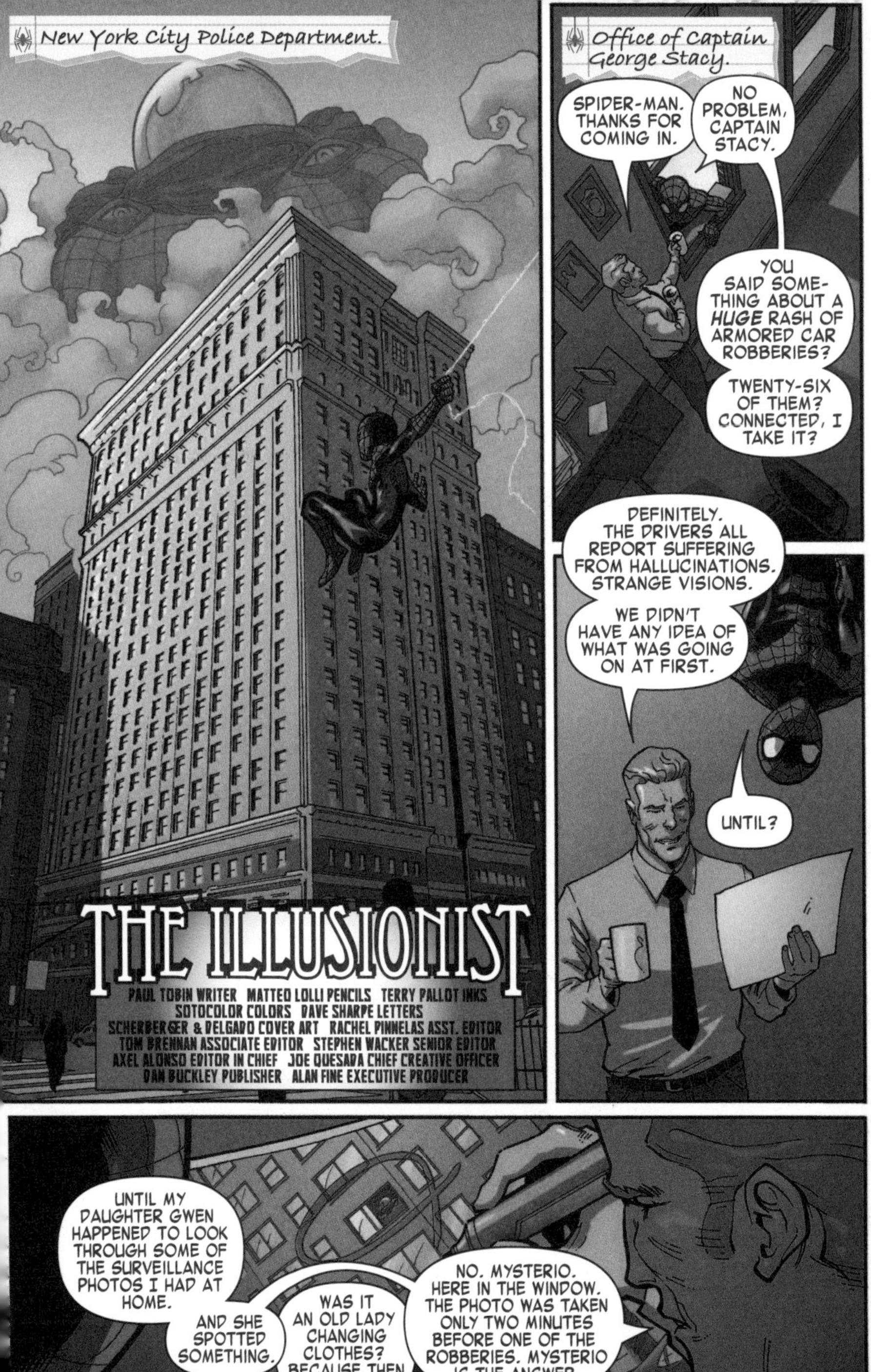
New York City Police Department.
THE ILLUSIONIST
PAUL TOBIN WRITER MATTEO LOLLI PENCILS TERRY PALLOT INKS
SOTOCOLOR COLORS DAVE SHARPE LETTERS
SCHERBERGER & DELGADO COVER ART RACHEL PINNELAS ASST. EDITOR
TOM BRENNAN ASSOCIATE EDITOR STEPHEN WACKER SENIOR EDITOR
AXEL ALONSO EDITOR IN CHIEF JOE QUESADA CHIEF CREATIVE OFFICER
DAN BUCKLEY PUBLISHER ALAN FINE EXECUTIVE PRODUCER
Office of Captain George Stacy.
SPIDER-MAN. THANKS FOR COMING IN.
NO PROBLEM, CAPTAIN STACY.
YOU SAID SOME-THING ABOUT A HUGE RASH OF ARMORED CAR ROBBERIES?
TWENTY-SIX OF THEM? CONNECTED, I TAKE IT?
DEFINITELY. THE DRIVERS ALL REPORT SUFFERING FROM HALLUCINATIONS. STRANGE VISIONS.
WE DIDN'T HAVE ANY IDEA OF WHAT WAS GOING ON AT FIRST.
UNTIL?
UNTIL MY DAUGHTER GWEN HAPPENED TO LOOK THROUGH SOME OF THE SURVEILLANCE PHOTOS I HAD AT HOME.
AND SHE SPOTTED SOMETHING.
WAS IT AN OLD LADY CHANGING CLOTHES? BECAUSE THEN I DON'T...
NO. MYSTERIO. HERE IN THE WINDOW. THE PHOTO WAS TAKEN ONLY TWO MINUTES BEFORE ONE OF THE ROBBERIES. MYSTERIO IS THE ANSWER.

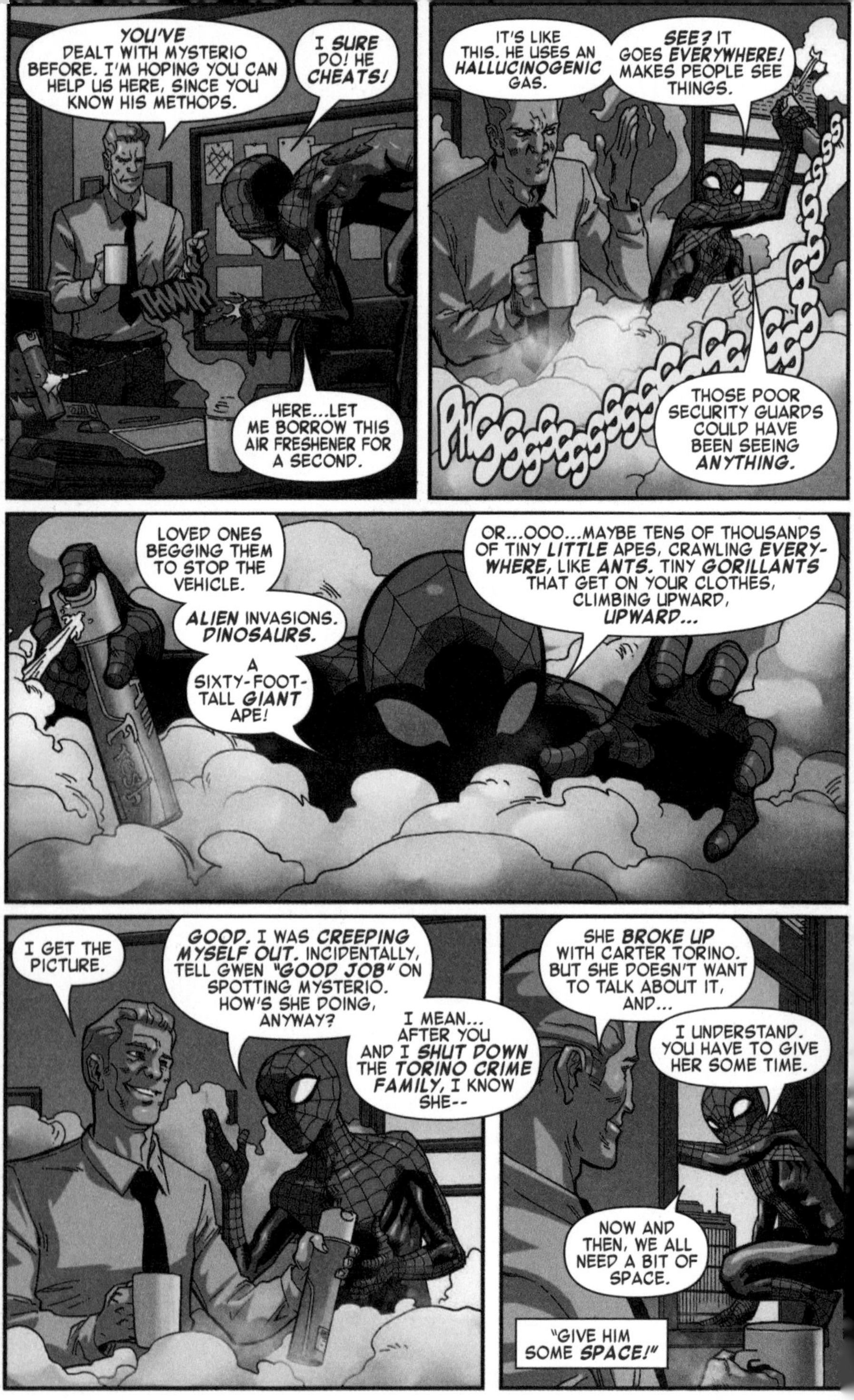
YOU'VE DEALT WITH MYSTERIO BEFORE. I'M HOPING YOU CAN HELP US HERE, SINCE YOU KNOW HIS METHODS.
I SURE DO! HE CHEATS!
THWIPP
HERE...LET ME BORROW THIS AIR FRESHENER FOR A SECOND.
IT'S LIKE THIS. HE USES AN HALLUCINOGENIC GAS.
SEE? IT GOES EVERYWHERE! MAKES PEOPLE SEE THINGS.
PHSSSSSSSSSSSSSSSSSSSSSSS
THOSE POOR SECURITY GUARDS COULD HAVE BEEN SEEING ANYTHING.
LOVED ONES BEGGING THEM TO STOP THE VEHICLE.
ALIEN INVASIONS. DINOSAURS.
A SIXTY-FOOT-TALL GIANT APE!
OR...OOO...MAYBE TENS OF THOUSANDS OF TINY LITTLE APES, CRAWLING EVERYWHERE, LIKE ANTS. TINY GORILLANTS THAT GET ON YOUR CLOTHES, CLIMBING UPWARD, UPWARD...
I GET THE PICTURE.
GOOD. I WAS CREEPING MYSELF OUT. INCIDENTALLY, TELL GWEN "GOOD JOB" ON SPOTTING MYSTERIO. HOW'S SHE DOING, ANYWAY?
I MEAN... AFTER YOU AND I SHUT DOWN THE TORINO CRIME FAMILY, I KNOW SHE--
SHE BROKE UP WITH CARTER TORINO. BUT SHE DOESN'T WANT TO TALK ABOUT IT, AND...
I UNDERSTAND. YOU HAVE TO GIVE HER SOME TIME.
NOW AND THEN, WE ALL NEED A BIT OF SPACE.
"GIVE HIM SOME SPACE!"

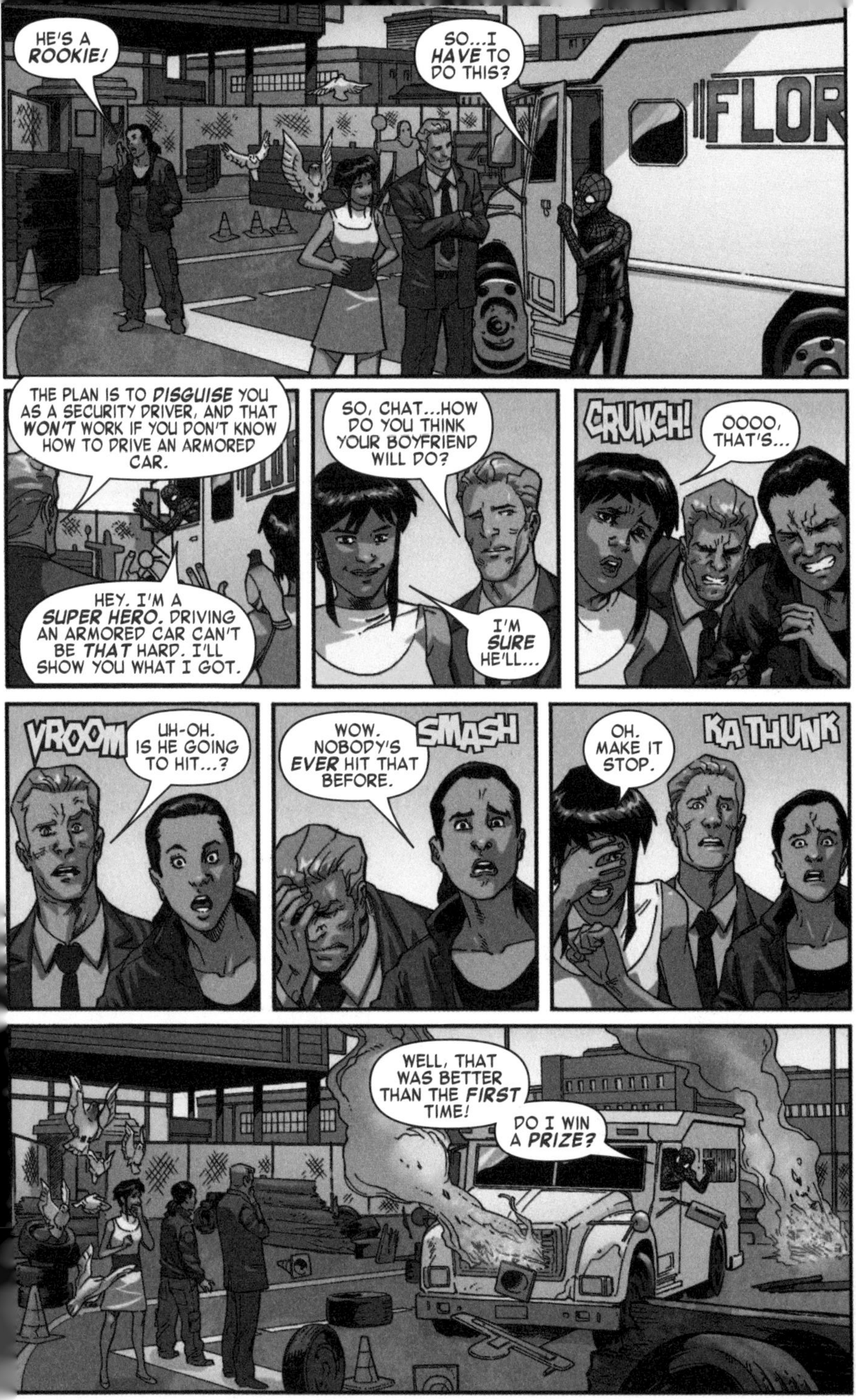
HE'S A ROOKIE!
SO...I HAVE TO DO THIS?
FLOR
THE PLAN IS TO DISGUISE YOU AS A SECURITY DRIVER, AND THAT WON'T WORK IF YOU DON'T KNOW HOW TO DRIVE AN ARMORED CAR.
HEY. I'M A SUPER HERO. DRIVING AN ARMORED CAR CAN'T BE THAT HARD. I'LL SHOW YOU WHAT I GOT.
SO, CHAT...HOW DO YOU THINK YOUR BOYFRIEND WILL DO?
I'M SURE HE'LL...
CRUNCH!
OOOO, THAT'S...
VROOM
UH-OH. IS HE GOING TO HIT...?
WOW. NOBODY'S EVER HIT THAT BEFORE.
SMASH
OH. MAKE IT STOP.
KATHUNK
WELL, THAT WAS BETTER THAN THE FIRST TIME!
DO I WIN A PRIZE?

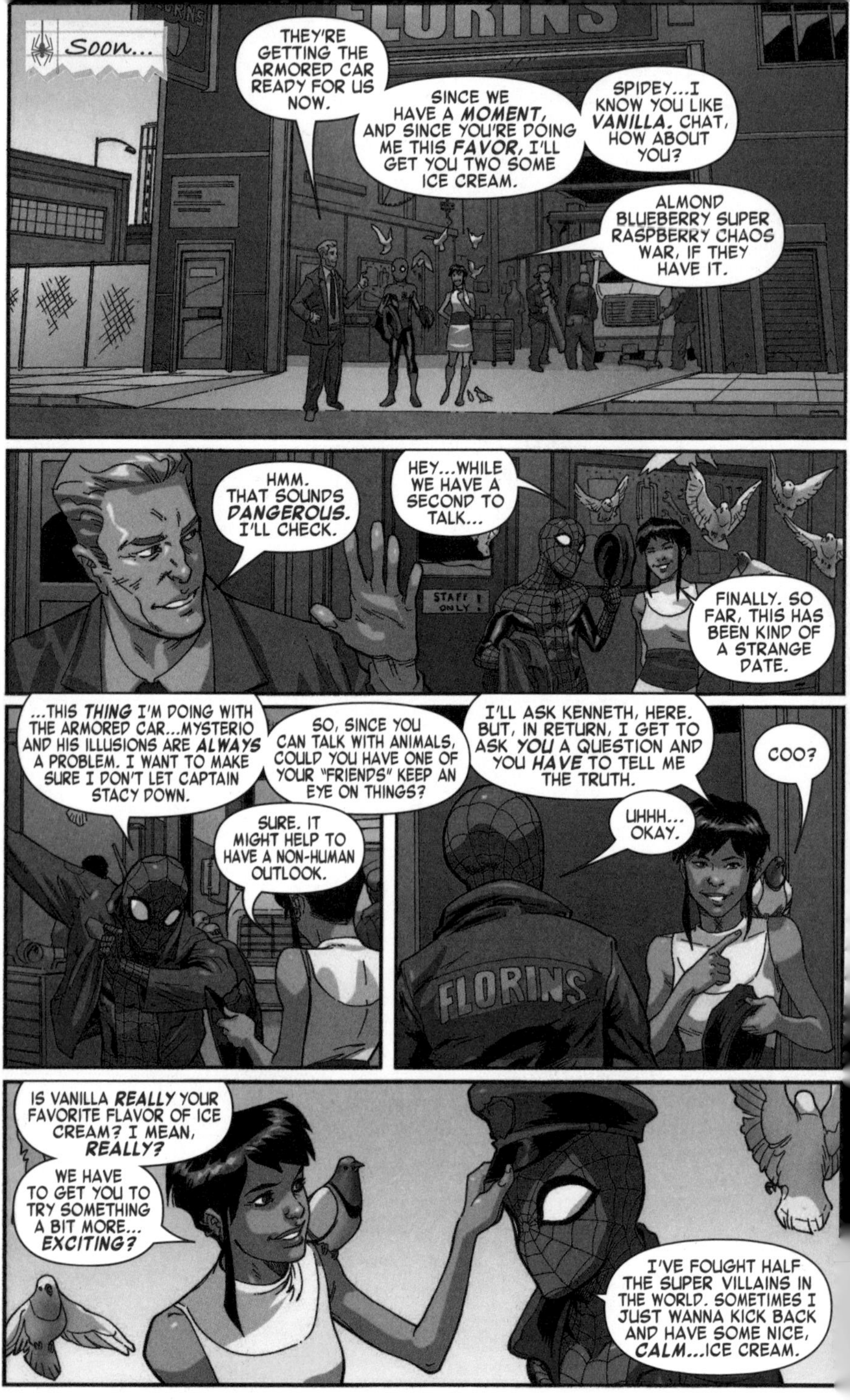
Soon...
FLORINS
THEY'RE GETTING THE ARMORED CAR READY FOR US NOW.
SINCE WE HAVE A MOMENT, AND SINCE YOU'RE DOING ME THIS FAVOR, I'LL GET YOU TWO SOME ICE CREAM.
SPIDEY...I KNOW YOU LIKE VANILLA. CHAT, HOW ABOUT YOU?
ALMOND BLUEBERRY SUPER RASPBERRY CHAOS WAR, IF THEY HAVE IT.
HMM. THAT SOUNDS DANGEROUS. I'LL CHECK.
HEY...WHILE WE HAVE A SECOND TO TALK...
STAFF ONLY
FINALLY. SO FAR, THIS HAS BEEN KIND OF A STRANGE DATE.
...THIS THING I'M DOING WITH THE ARMORED CAR...MYSTERIO AND HIS ILLUSIONS ARE ALWAYS A PROBLEM. I WANT TO MAKE SURE I DON'T LET CAPTAIN STACY DOWN.
SO, SINCE YOU CAN TALK WITH ANIMALS, COULD YOU HAVE ONE OF YOUR "FRIENDS" KEEP AN EYE ON THINGS?
SURE. IT MIGHT HELP TO HAVE A NON-HUMAN OUTLOOK.
I'LL ASK KENNETH, HERE. BUT, IN RETURN, I GET TO ASK YOU A QUESTION AND YOU HAVE TO TELL ME THE TRUTH.
COO?
UHHH... OKAY.
FLORINS
IS VANILLA REALLY YOUR FAVORITE FLAVOR OF ICE CREAM? I MEAN, REALLY?
WE HAVE TO GET YOU TO TRY SOMETHING A BIT MORE... EXCITING?
I'VE FOUGHT HALF THE SUPER VILLAINS IN THE WORLD. SOMETIMES I JUST WANNA KICK BACK AND HAVE SOME NICE, CALM...ICE CREAM.

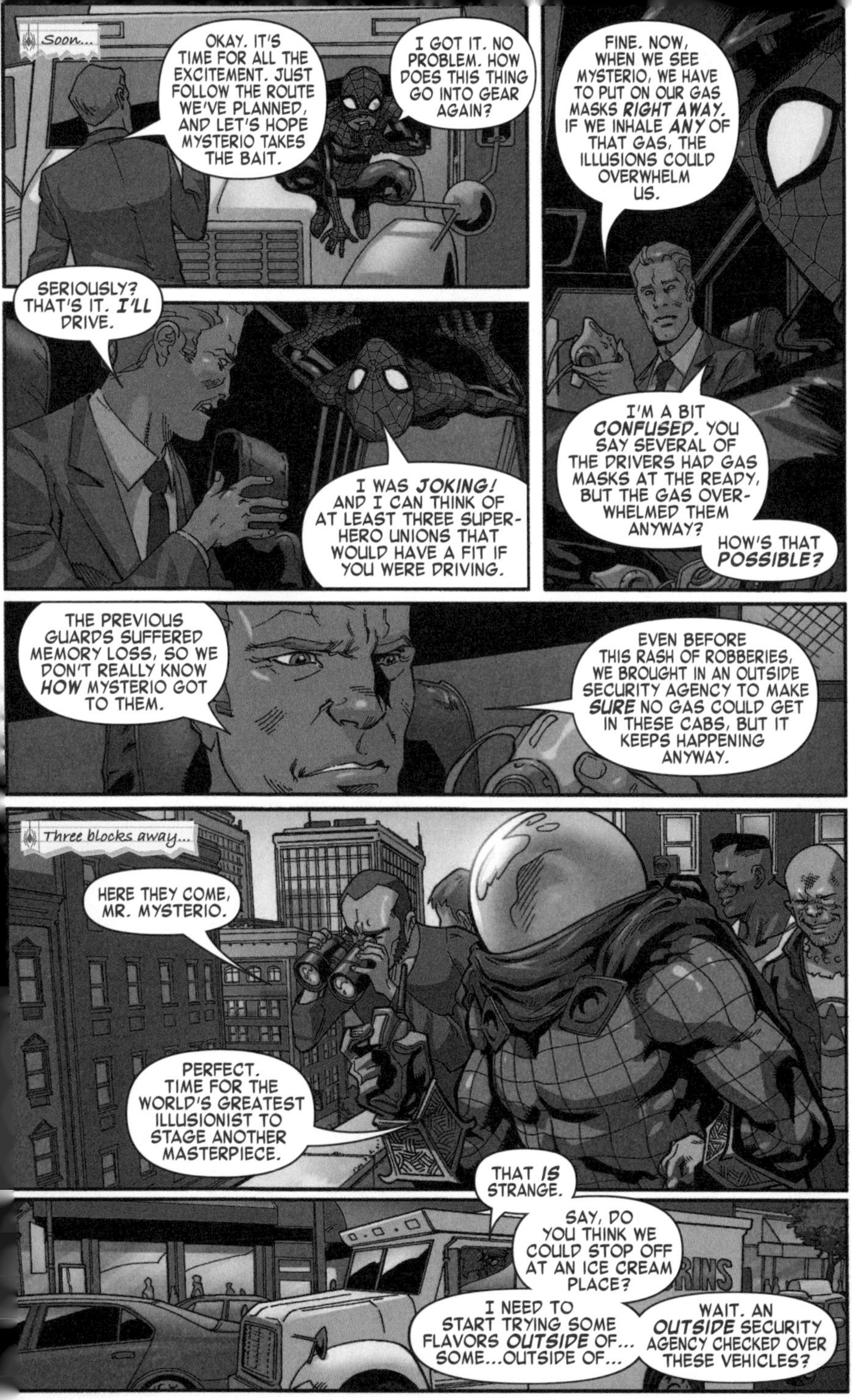
Soon...
OKAY. IT'S TIME FOR ALL THE EXCITEMENT. JUST FOLLOW THE ROUTE WE'VE PLANNED, AND LET'S HOPE MYSTERIO TAKES THE BAIT.
I GOT IT. NO PROBLEM. HOW DOES THIS THING GO INTO GEAR AGAIN?
SERIOUSLY? THAT'S IT. I'LL DRIVE.
I WAS JOKING! AND I CAN THINK OF AT LEAST THREE SUPER-HERO UNIONS THAT WOULD HAVE A FIT IF YOU WERE DRIVING.
FINE. NOW, WHEN WE SEE MYSTERIO, WE HAVE TO PUT ON OUR GAS MASKS RIGHT AWAY. IF WE INHALE ANY OF THAT GAS, THE ILLUSIONS COULD OVERWHELM US.
I'M A BIT CONFUSED. YOU SAY SEVERAL OF THE DRIVERS HAD GAS MASKS AT THE READY, BUT THE GAS OVER-WHELMED THEM ANYWAY?
HOW'S THAT POSSIBLE?
THE PREVIOUS GUARDS SUFFERED MEMORY LOSS, SO WE DON'T REALLY KNOW HOW MYSTERIO GOT TO THEM.
EVEN BEFORE THIS RASH OF ROBBERIES, WE BROUGHT IN AN OUTSIDE SECURITY AGENCY TO MAKE SURE NO GAS COULD GET IN THESE CABS, BUT IT KEEPS HAPPENING ANYWAY.
Three blocks away...
HERE THEY COME, MR. MYSTERIO.
PERFECT. TIME FOR THE WORLD'S GREATEST ILLUSIONIST TO STAGE ANOTHER MASTERPIECE.
THAT IS STRANGE.
SAY, DO YOU THINK WE COULD STOP OFF AT AN ICE CREAM PLACE?
I NEED TO START TRYING SOME FLAVORS OUTSIDE OF... SOME...OUTSIDE OF...
WAIT. AN OUTSIDE SECURITY AGENCY CHECKED OVER THESE VEHICLES?

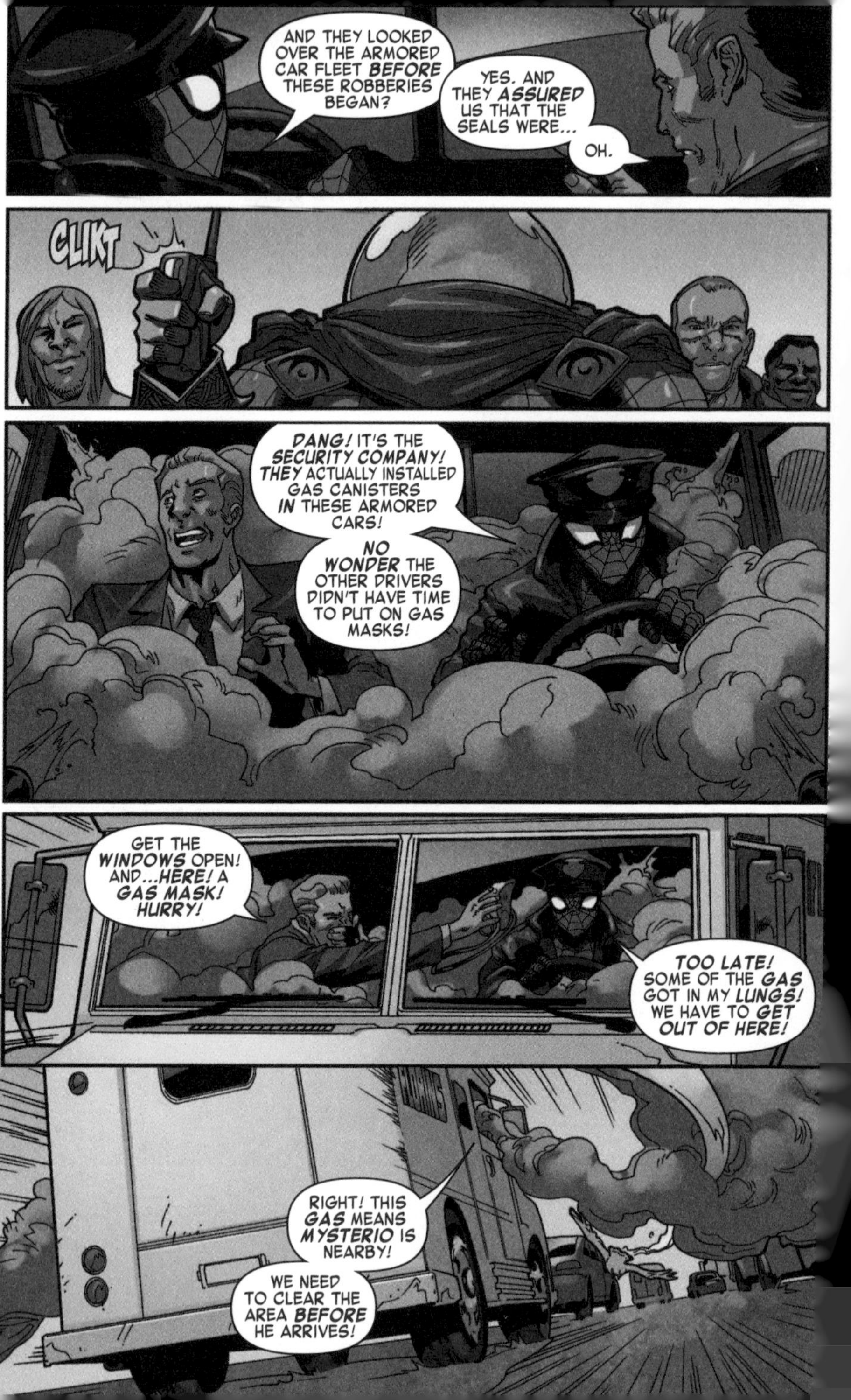
AND THEY LOOKED OVER THE ARMORED CAR FLEET BEFORE THESE ROBBERIES BEGAN?
YES. AND THEY ASSURED US THAT THE SEALS WERE...
OH.
CLIKT
DANG! IT'S THE SECURITY COMPANY! THEY ACTUALLY INSTALLED GAS CANISTERS IN THESE ARMORED CARS!
NO WONDER THE OTHER DRIVERS DIDN'T HAVE TIME TO PUT ON GAS MASKS!
GET THE WINDOWS OPEN! AND...HERE! A GAS MASK! HURRY!
TOO LATE! SOME OF THE GAS GOT IN MY LUNGS! WE HAVE TO GET OUT OF HERE!
RIGHT! THIS GAS MEANS MYSTERIO IS NEARBY!
WE NEED TO CLEAR THE AREA BEFORE HE ARRIVES!

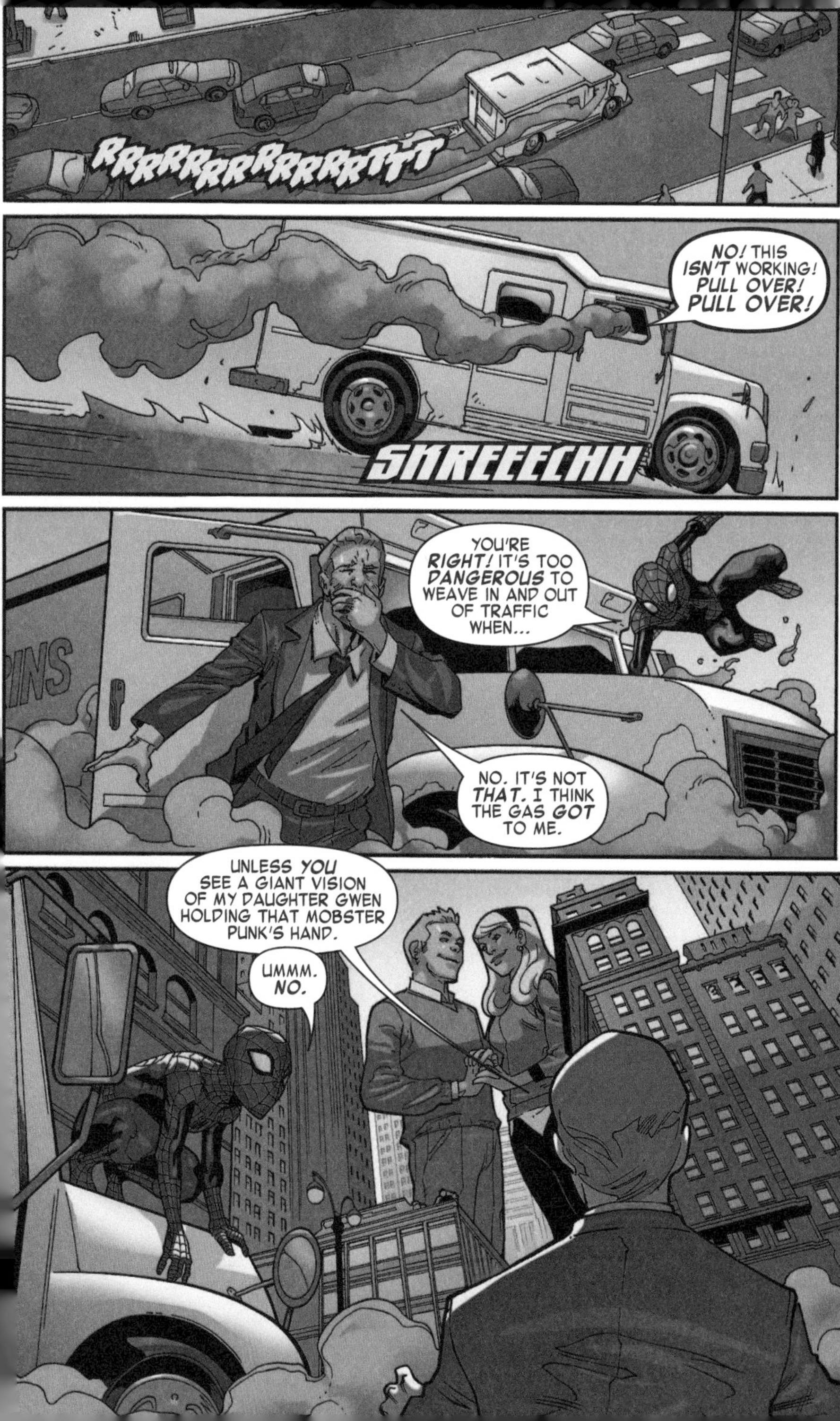
RRRRRRRRRRRRRTTTT
NO! THIS ISN'T WORKING! PULL OVER! PULL OVER!
SKREEECHH
YOU'RE RIGHT! IT'S TOO DANGEROUS TO WEAVE IN AND OUT OF TRAFFIC WHEN...
NO. IT'S NOT THAT. I THINK THE GAS GOT TO ME.
UNLESS YOU SEE A GIANT VISION OF MY DAUGHTER GWEN HOLDING THAT MOBSTER PUNK'S HAND.
UMMM. NO.

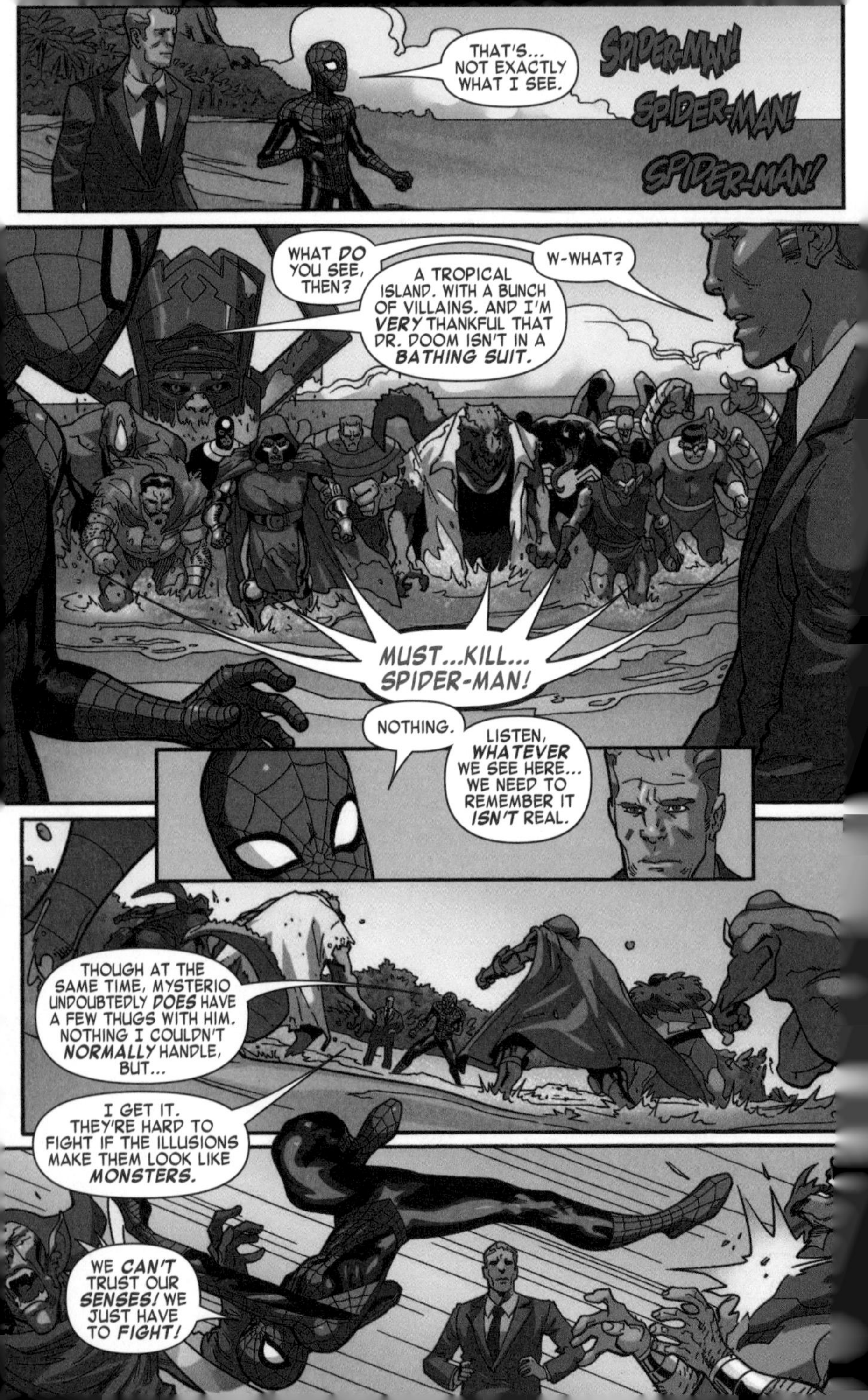
THAT'S... NOT EXACTLY WHAT I SEE.
SPIDER-MAN!
SPIDER-MAN!
SPIDER-MAN!
WHAT DO YOU SEE, THEN?
A TROPICAL ISLAND. WITH A BUNCH OF VILLAINS. AND I'M VERY THANKFUL THAT DR. DOOM ISN'T IN A BATHING SUIT.
W-WHAT?
MUST...KILL... SPIDER-MAN!
NOTHING.
LISTEN, WHATEVER WE SEE HERE... WE NEED TO REMEMBER IT ISN'T REAL.
THOUGH AT THE SAME TIME, MYSTERIO UNDOUBTEDLY DOES HAVE A FEW THUGS WITH HIM. NOTHING I COULDN'T NORMALLY HANDLE, BUT...
I GET IT. THEY'RE HARD TO FIGHT IF THE ILLUSIONS MAKE THEM LOOK LIKE MONSTERS.
WE CAN'T TRUST OUR SENSES! WE JUST HAVE TO FIGHT!

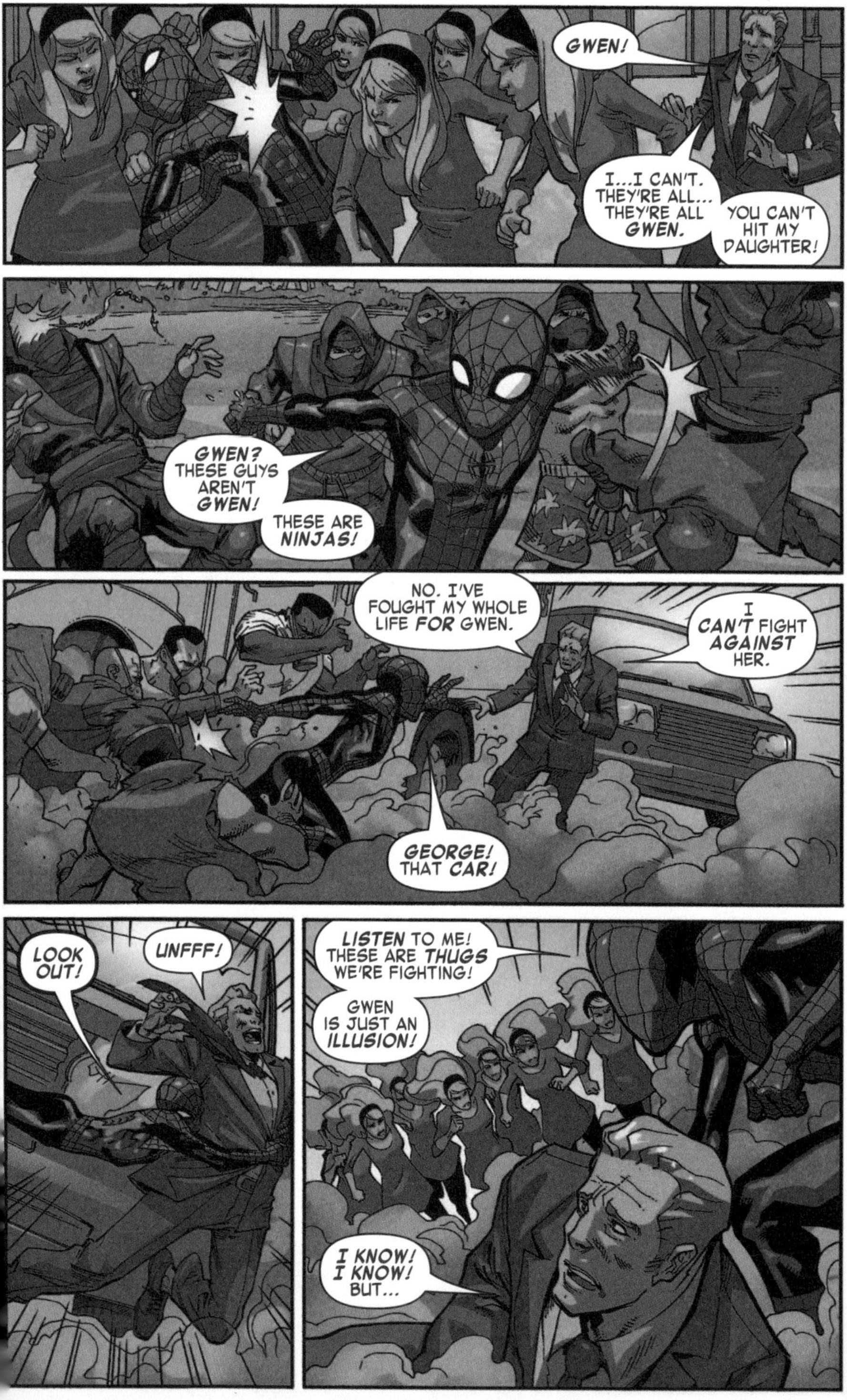
GWEN!
I...I CAN'T. THEY'RE ALL... THEY'RE ALL GWEN.
YOU CAN'T HIT MY DAUGHTER!
GWEN? THESE GUYS AREN'T GWEN!
THESE ARE NINJAS!
NO. I'VE FOUGHT MY WHOLE LIFE FOR GWEN.
I CAN'T FIGHT AGAINST HER.
GEORGE! THAT CAR!
LOOK OUT!
UNFFF!
LISTEN TO ME! THESE ARE THUGS WE'RE FIGHTING!
GWEN IS JUST AN ILLUSION!
I KNOW! I KNOW! BUT...

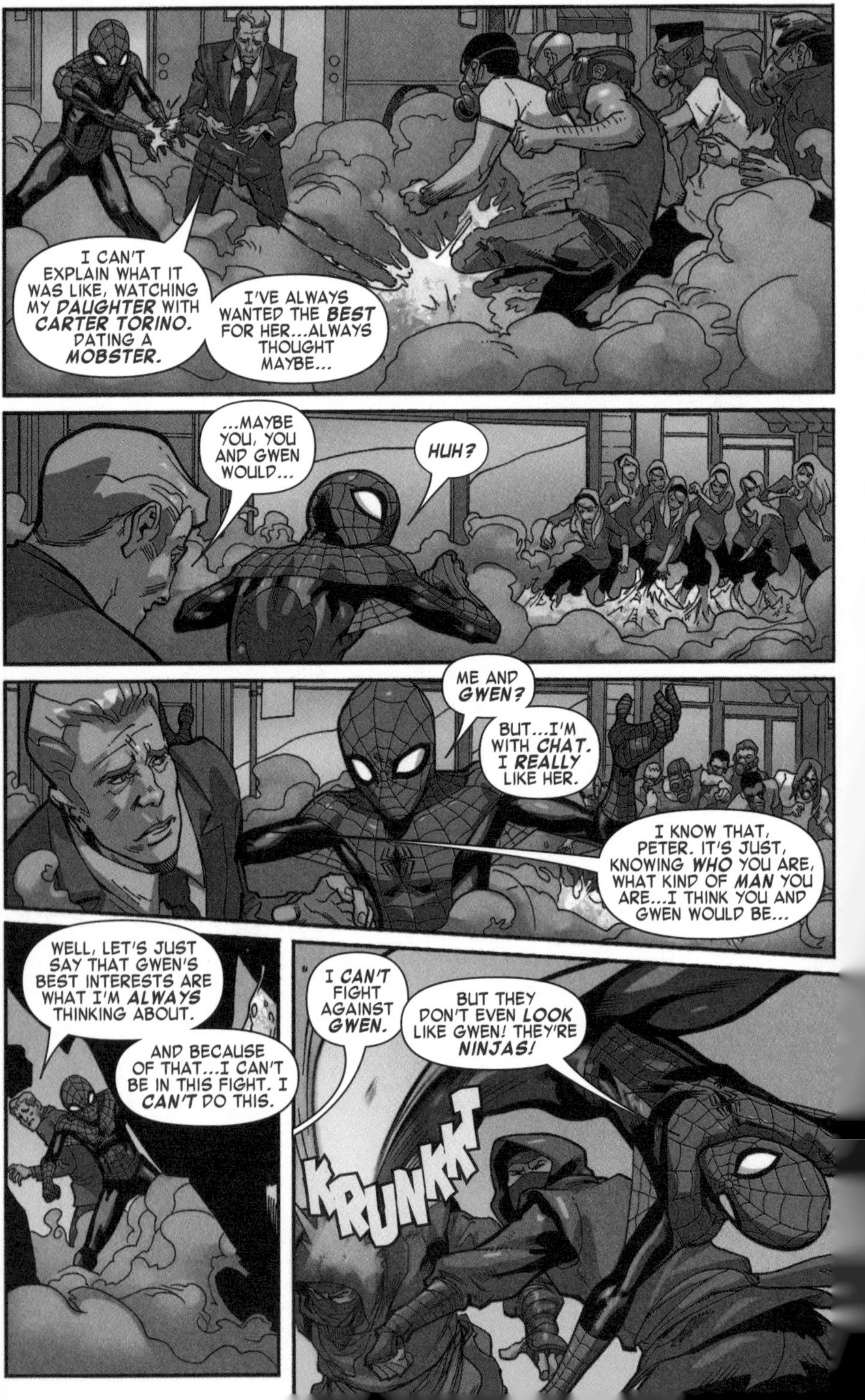
I CAN'T EXPLAIN WHAT IT WAS LIKE, WATCHING MY DAUGHTER WITH CARTER TORINO. DATING A MOBSTER.
I'VE ALWAYS WANTED THE BEST FOR HER...ALWAYS THOUGHT MAYBE...
...MAYBE YOU, YOU AND GWEN WOULD...
HUH?
ME AND GWEN?
BUT...I'M WITH CHAT. I REALLY LIKE HER.
I KNOW THAT, PETER. IT'S JUST, KNOWING WHO YOU ARE, WHAT KIND OF MAN YOU ARE...I THINK YOU AND GWEN WOULD BE...
WELL, LET'S JUST SAY THAT GWEN'S BEST INTERESTS ARE WHAT I'M ALWAYS THINKING ABOUT.
AND BECAUSE OF THAT...I CAN'T BE IN THIS FIGHT. I CAN'T DO THIS.
I CAN'T FIGHT AGAINST GWEN.
BUT THEY DON'T EVEN LOOK LIKE GWEN! THEY'RE NINJAS!
KRUNKKT

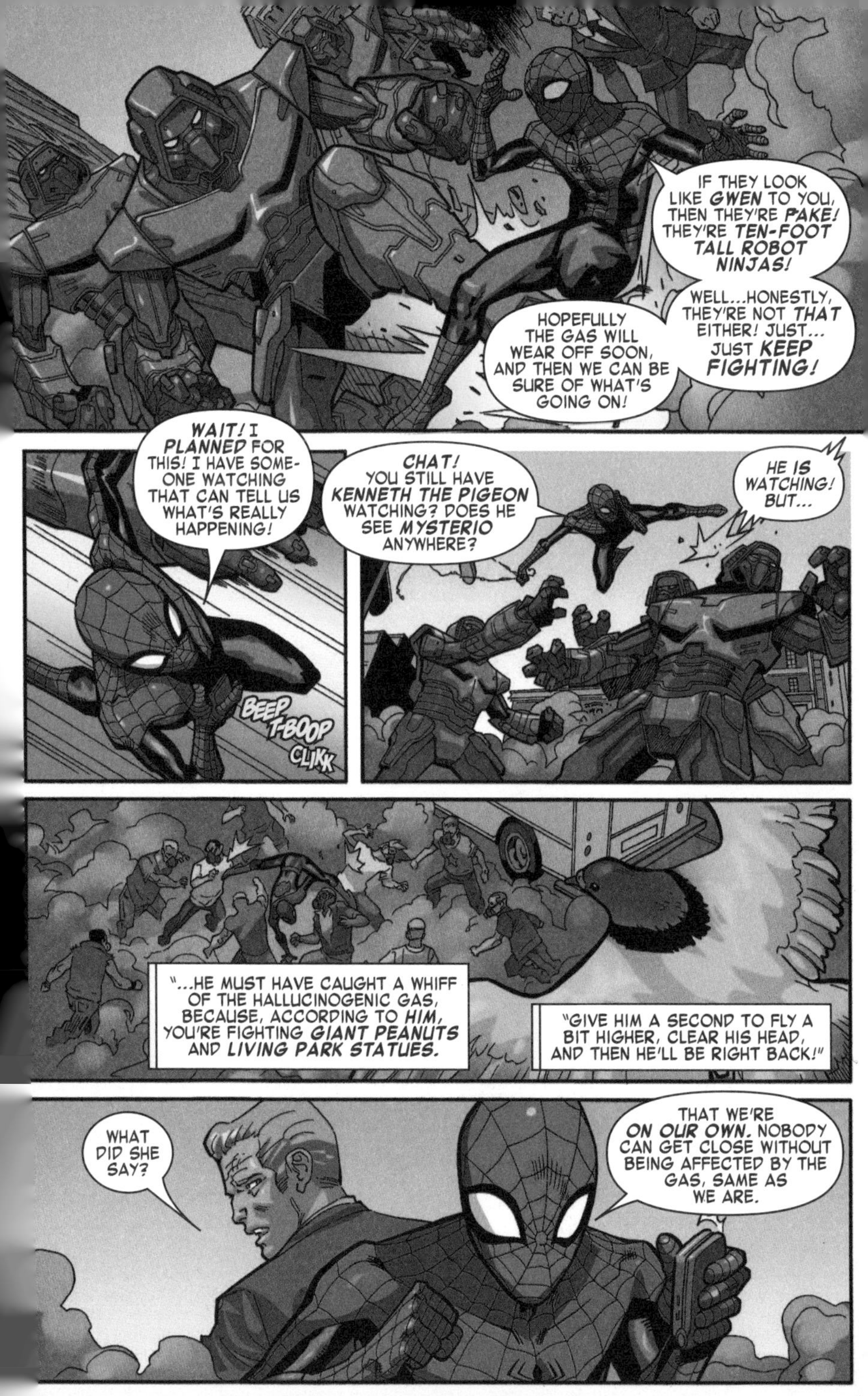
IF THEY LOOK LIKE GWEN TO YOU, THEN THEY'RE FAKE! THEY'RE TEN-FOOT TALL ROBOT NINJAS!
WELL...HONESTLY, THEY'RE NOT THAT EITHER! JUST... JUST KEEP FIGHTING!
HOPEFULLY THE GAS WILL WEAR OFF SOON, AND THEN WE CAN BE SURE OF WHAT'S GOING ON!
WAIT! I PLANNED FOR THIS! I HAVE SOME-ONE WATCHING THAT CAN TELL US WHAT'S REALLY HAPPENING!
BEEP T-BOOP CLIKK
CHAT! YOU STILL HAVE KENNETH THE PIGEON WATCHING? DOES HE SEE MYSTERIO ANYWHERE?
HE IS WATCHING! BUT...
"...HE MUST HAVE CAUGHT A WHIFF OF THE HALLUCINOGENIC GAS, BECAUSE, ACCORDING TO HIM, YOU'RE FIGHTING GIANT PEANUTS AND LIVING PARK STATUES.
"GIVE HIM A SECOND TO FLY A BIT HIGHER, CLEAR HIS HEAD, AND THEN HE'LL BE RIGHT BACK!"
WHAT DID SHE SAY?
THAT WE'RE ON OUR OWN. NOBODY CAN GET CLOSE WITHOUT BEING AFFECTED BY THE GAS, SAME AS WE ARE.

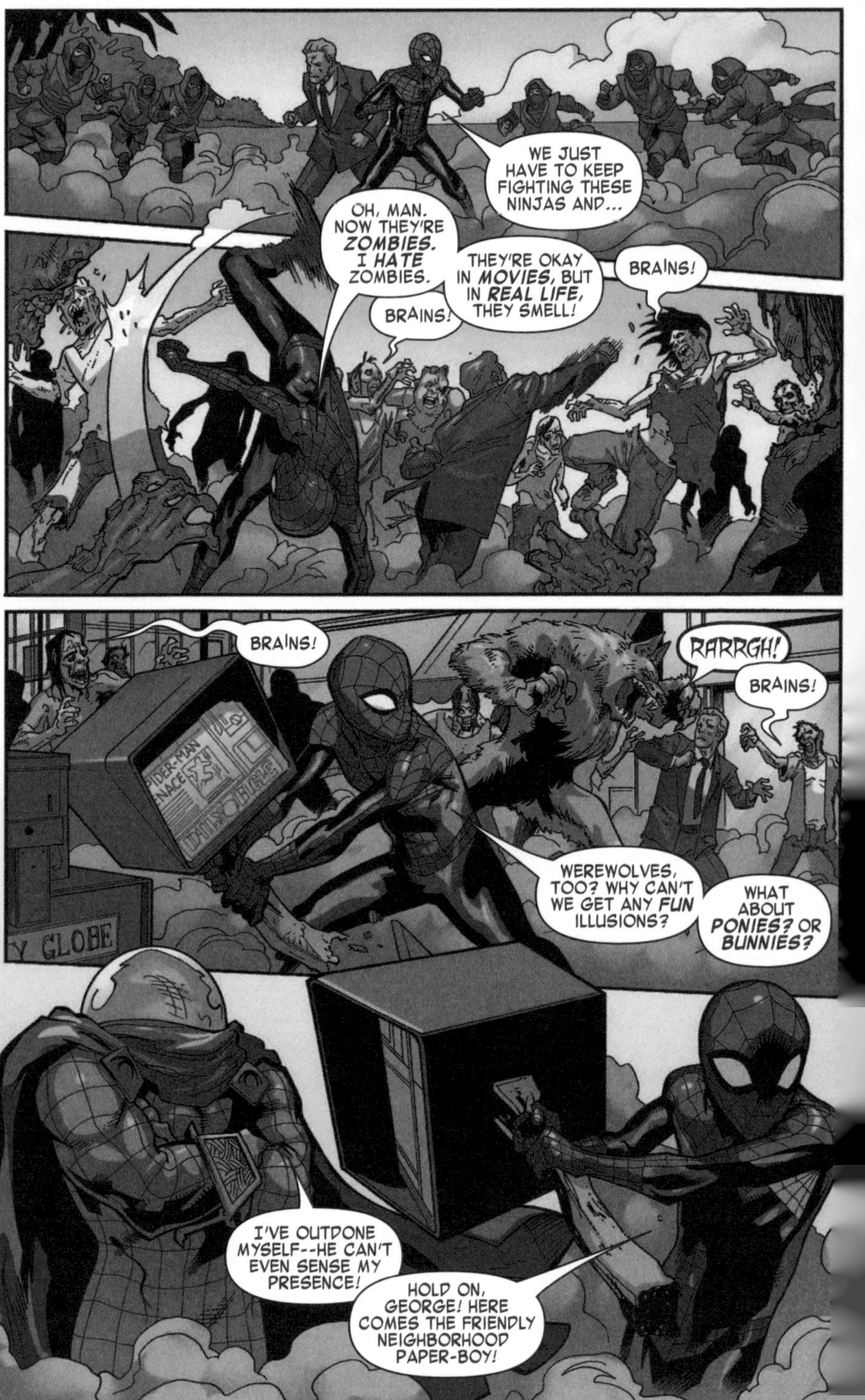
WE JUST HAVE TO KEEP FIGHTING THESE NINJAS AND...
OH, MAN. NOW THEY'RE ZOMBIES. I HATE ZOMBIES.
THEY'RE OKAY IN MOVIES, BUT IN REAL LIFE, THEY SMELL!
BRAINS!
BRAINS!
BRAINS!
RARRGH!
BRAINS!
SPIDER-MAN MENACE
DAILY BUGLE
Y GLOBE
WEREWOLVES, TOO? WHY CAN'T WE GET ANY FUN ILLUSIONS?
WHAT ABOUT PONIES? OR BUNNIES?
I'VE OUTDONE MYSELF--HE CAN'T EVEN SENSE MY PRESENCE!
HOLD ON, GEORGE! HERE COMES THE FRIENDLY NEIGHBORHOOD PAPER-BOY!

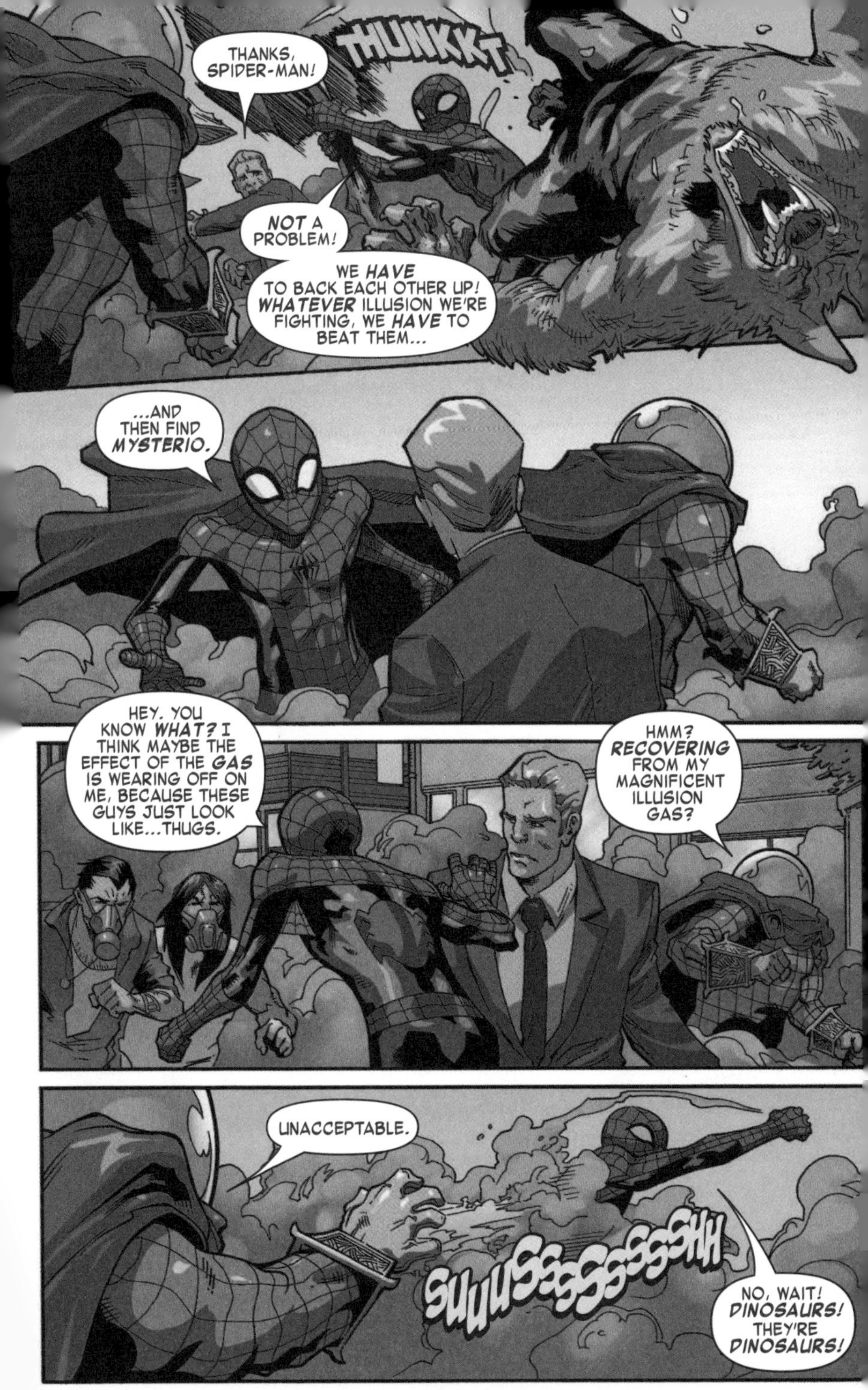
THANKS, SPIDER-MAN!
THUNKKT
NOT A PROBLEM!
WE HAVE TO BACK EACH OTHER UP! WHATEVER ILLUSION WE'RE FIGHTING, WE HAVE TO BEAT THEM...
...AND THEN FIND MYSTERIO.
HEY. YOU KNOW WHAT? I THINK MAYBE THE EFFECT OF THE GAS IS WEARING OFF ON ME, BECAUSE THESE GUYS JUST LOOK LIKE...THUGS.
HMM? RECOVERING FROM MY MAGNIFICENT ILLUSION GAS?
UNACCEPTABLE.
SUUUSSSSSSSSSHH
NO, WAIT! DINOSAURS! THEY'RE DINOSAURS!

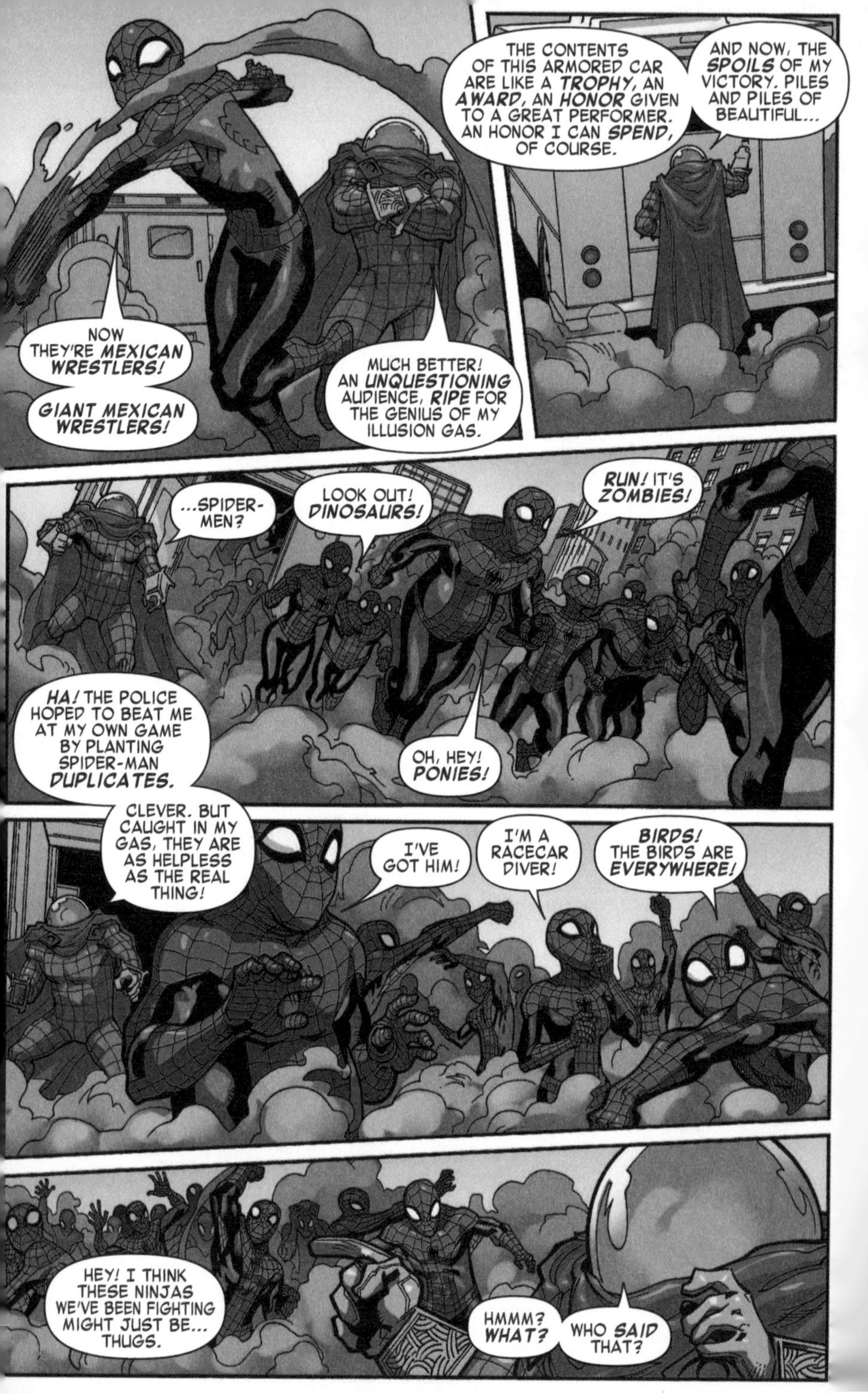

NOW THEY'RE *MEXICAN WRESTLERS!*
GIANT MEXICAN WRESTLERS!
MUCH BETTER! AN *UNQUESTIONING* AUDIENCE, *RIPE* FOR THE GENIUS OF MY ILLUSION GAS.
THE CONTENTS OF THIS ARMORED CAR ARE LIKE A *TROPHY*, AN *AWARD*, AN *HONOR* GIVEN TO A GREAT PERFORMER. AN HONOR I CAN *SPEND*, OF COURSE.
AND NOW, THE *SPOILS* OF MY VICTORY. PILES AND PILES OF BEAUTIFUL...
...SPIDER-MEN?
LOOK OUT! *DINOSAURS!*
RUN! IT'S *ZOMBIES!*
HA! THE POLICE HOPED TO BEAT ME AT MY OWN GAME BY PLANTING SPIDER-MAN *DUPLICATES.*
OH, HEY! *PONIES!*
CLEVER. BUT CAUGHT IN MY GAS, THEY ARE AS HELPLESS AS THE REAL THING!
I'VE GOT HIM!
I'M A RACECAR DIVER!
BIRDS! THE BIRDS ARE *EVERYWHERE!*
HEY! I THINK THESE NINJAS WE'VE BEEN FIGHTING MIGHT JUST BE... THUGS.
HMMM? *WHAT?*
WHO *SAID* THAT?

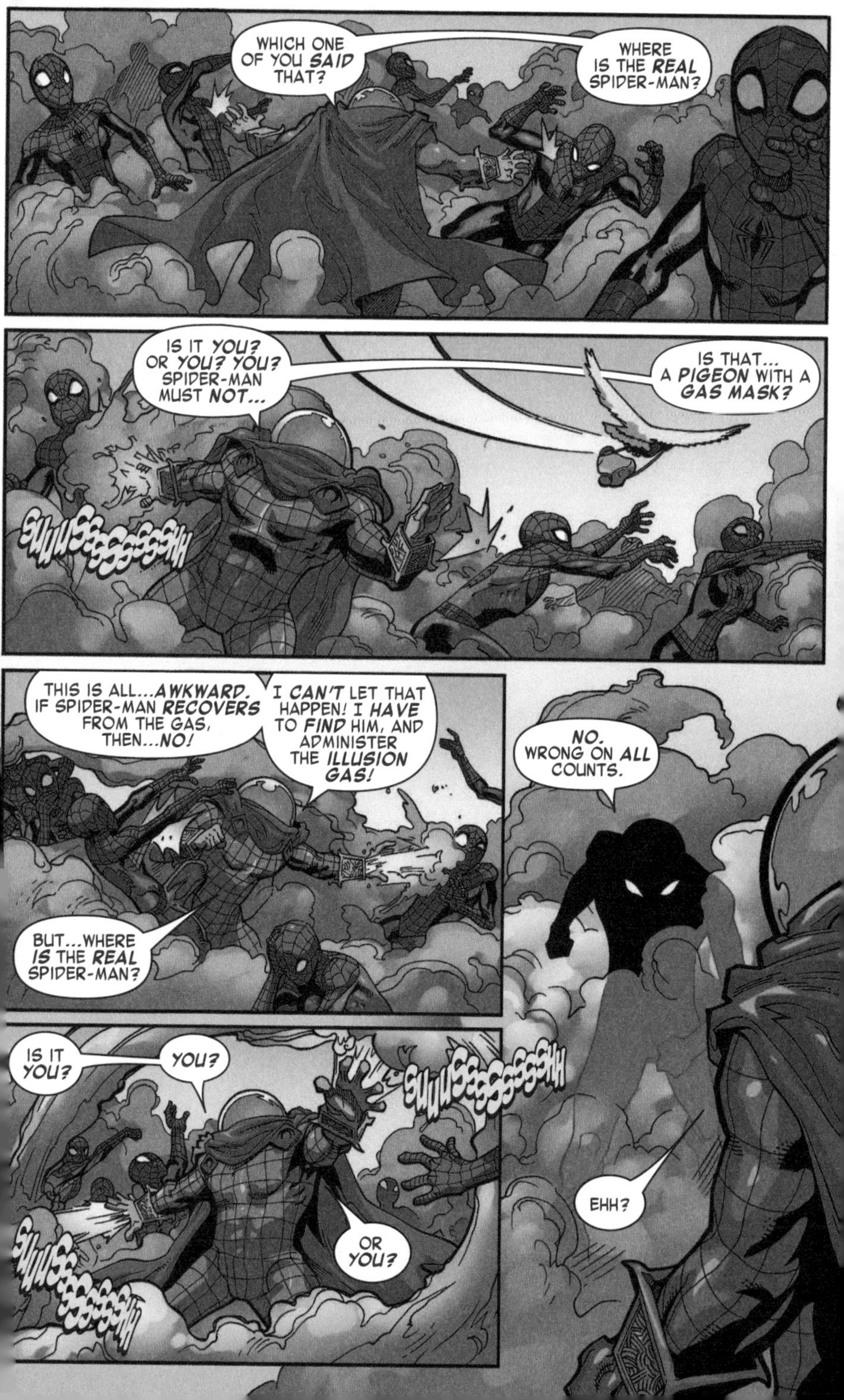
WHICH ONE OF YOU SAID THAT?
WHERE IS THE REAL SPIDER-MAN?
IS IT YOU? OR YOU? YOU? SPIDER-MAN MUST NOT...
IS THAT... A PIGEON WITH A GAS MASK?
THIS IS ALL...AWKWARD. IF SPIDER-MAN RECOVERS FROM THE GAS, THEN...NO!
I CAN'T LET THAT HAPPEN! I HAVE TO FIND HIM, AND ADMINISTER THE ILLUSION GAS!
BUT...WHERE IS THE REAL SPIDER-MAN?
IS IT YOU?
YOU?
OR YOU?
NO. WRONG ON ALL COUNTS.
EHH?

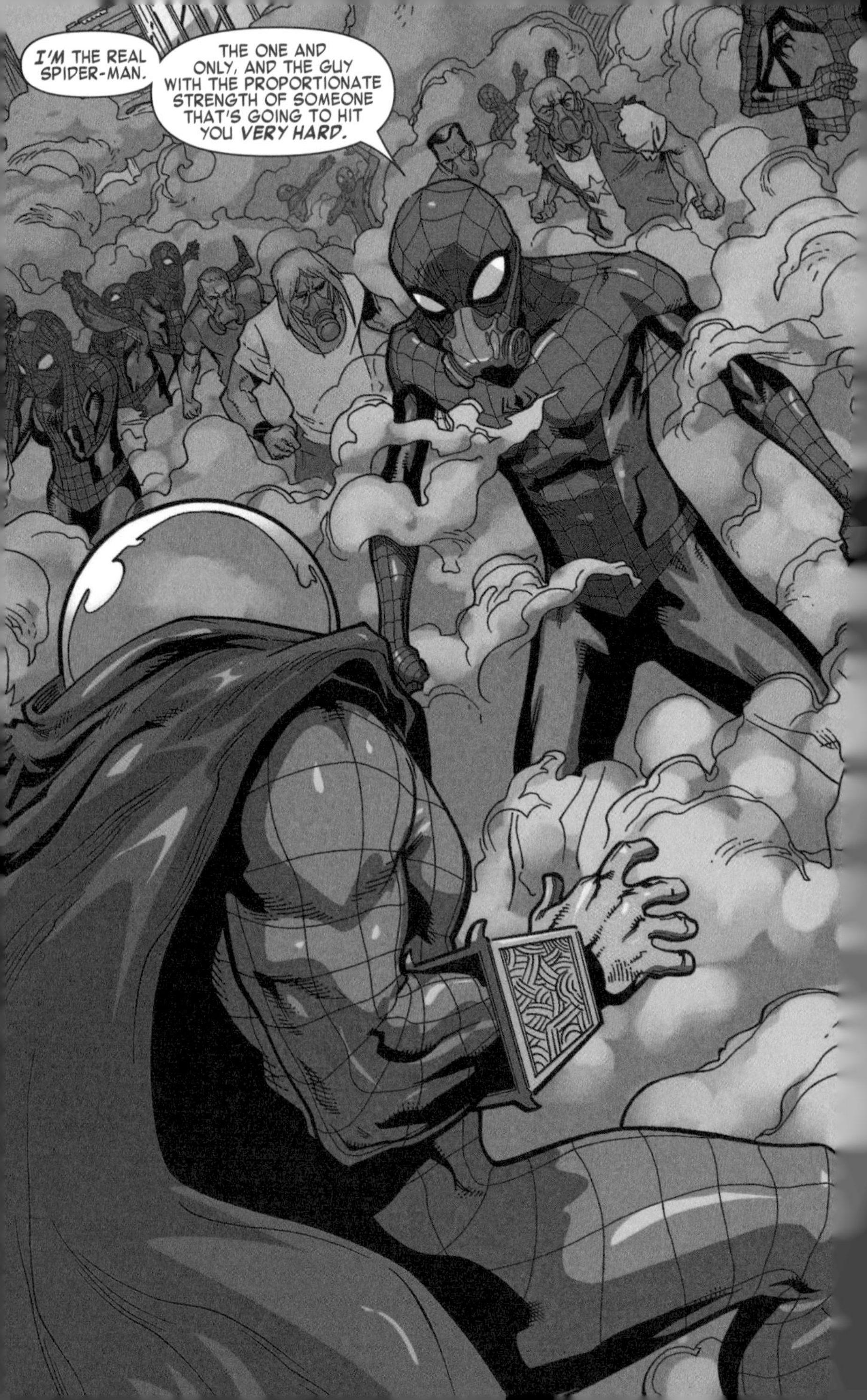
I'M THE REAL SPIDER-MAN.
THE ONE AND ONLY, AND THE GUY WITH THE PROPORTIONATE STRENGTH OF SOMEONE THAT'S GOING TO HIT YOU VERY HARD.

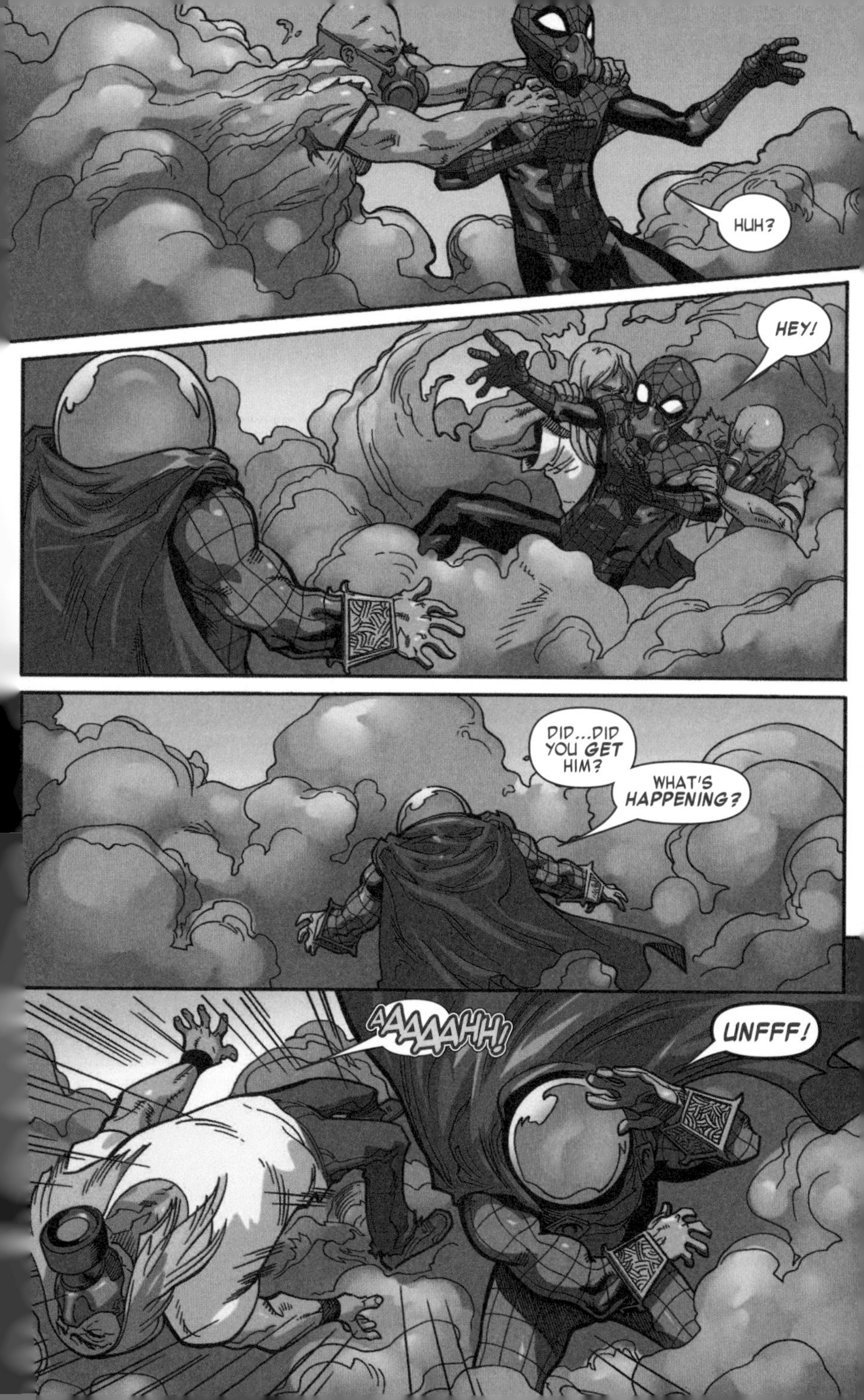
HUH?
HEY!
DID...DID YOU GET HIM?
WHAT'S HAPPENING?
AAAAAHH!
UNFFF!

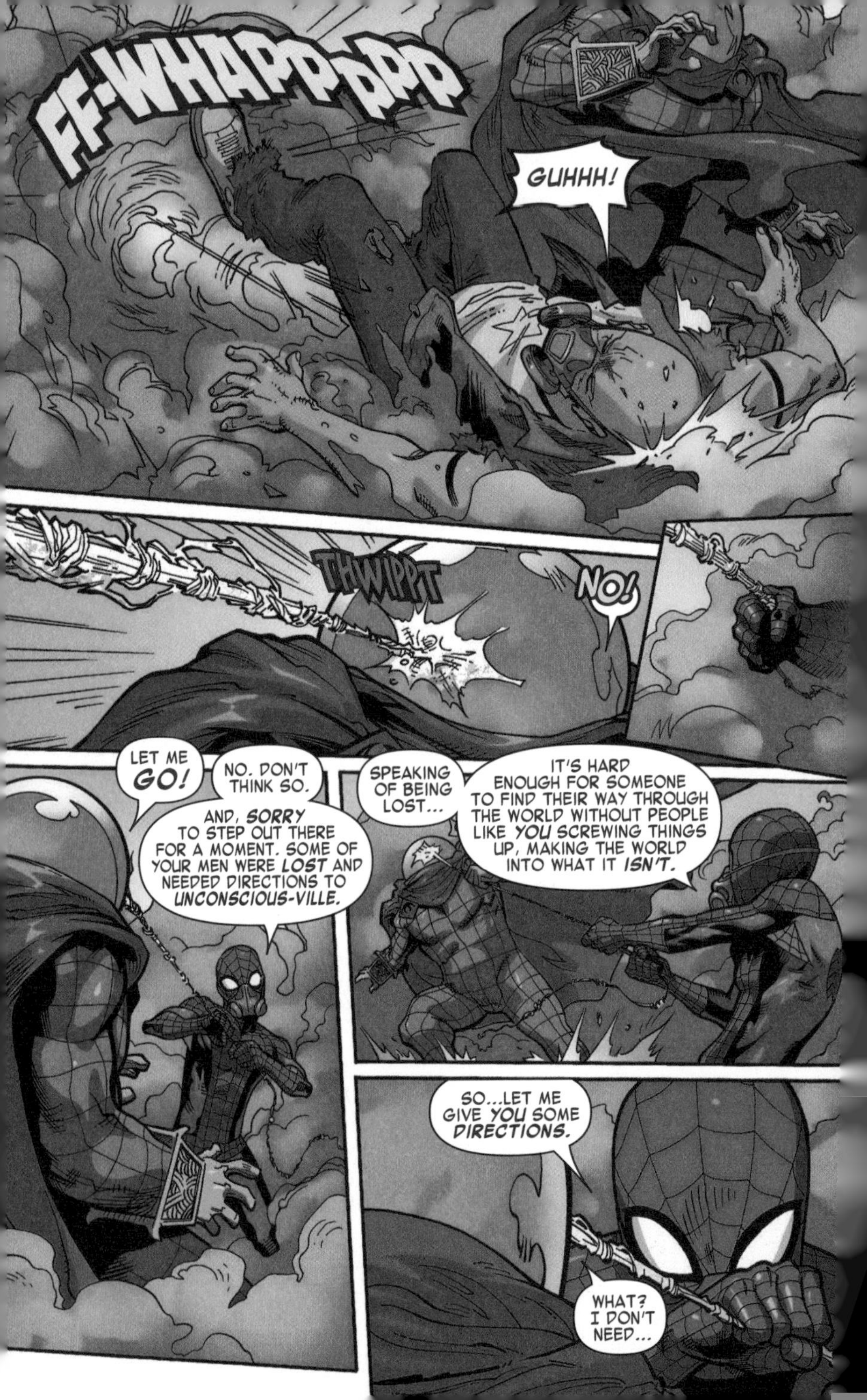
FF-WHAPPPPP
GUHHH!
THWIPPT
NO!
LET ME GO!
NO. DON'T THINK SO.
AND, SORRY TO STEP OUT THERE FOR A MOMENT. SOME OF YOUR MEN WERE LOST AND NEEDED DIRECTIONS TO UNCONSCIOUS-VILLE.
SPEAKING OF BEING LOST...
IT'S HARD ENOUGH FOR SOMEONE TO FIND THEIR WAY THROUGH THE WORLD WITHOUT PEOPLE LIKE YOU SCREWING THINGS UP, MAKING THE WORLD INTO WHAT IT ISN'T.
SO...LET ME GIVE YOU SOME DIRECTIONS.
WHAT? I DON'T NEED...

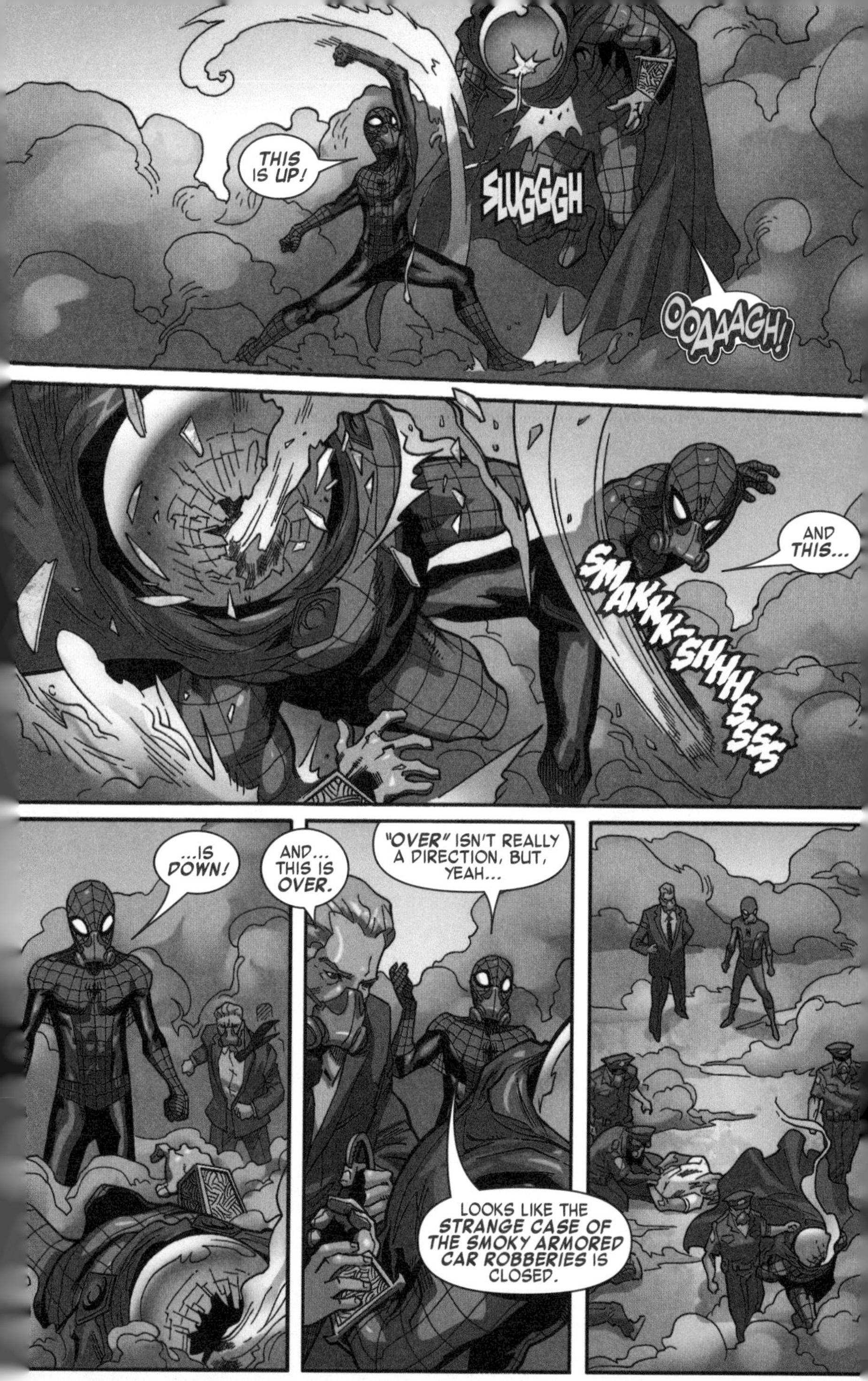

THIS IS UP!
SLUGGGH
OODAAAGH!
AND THIS...
SMAKKK-SHHHSSSS
...IS DOWN!
AND... THIS IS OVER.
"OVER" ISN'T REALLY A DIRECTION, BUT, YEAH...
LOOKS LIKE THE STRANGE CASE OF THE SMOKY ARMORED CAR ROBBERIES IS CLOSED.

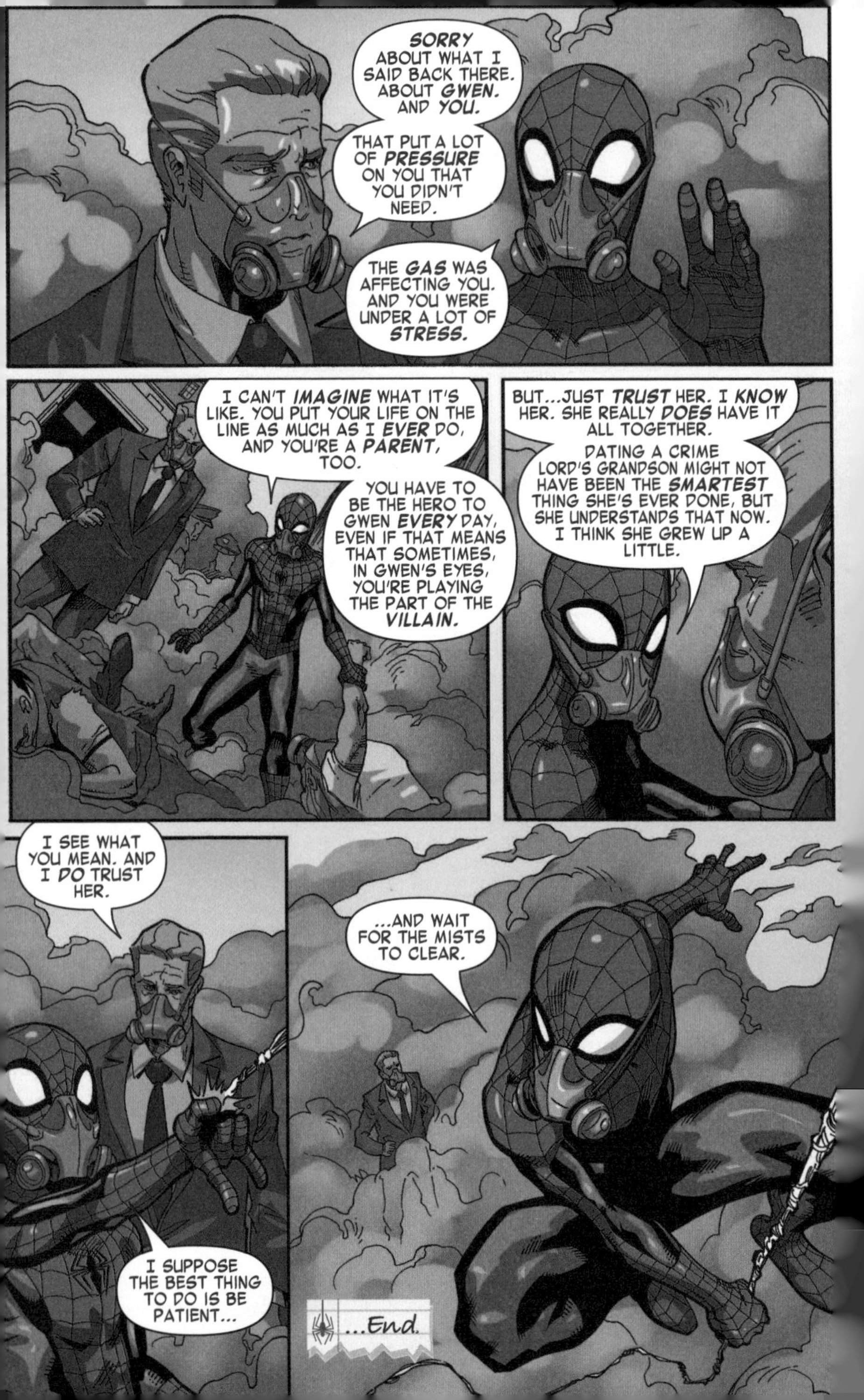
SORRY ABOUT WHAT I SAID BACK THERE. ABOUT GWEN. AND YOU.
THAT PUT A LOT OF PRESSURE ON YOU THAT YOU DIDN'T NEED.
THE GAS WAS AFFECTING YOU. AND YOU WERE UNDER A LOT OF STRESS.
I CAN'T IMAGINE WHAT IT'S LIKE. YOU PUT YOUR LIFE ON THE LINE AS MUCH AS I EVER DO, AND YOU'RE A PARENT, TOO.
YOU HAVE TO BE THE HERO TO GWEN EVERY DAY, EVEN IF THAT MEANS THAT SOMETIMES, IN GWEN'S EYES, YOU'RE PLAYING THE PART OF THE VILLAIN.
BUT...JUST TRUST HER. I KNOW HER. SHE REALLY DOES HAVE IT ALL TOGETHER.
DATING A CRIME LORD'S GRANDSON MIGHT NOT HAVE BEEN THE SMARTEST THING SHE'S EVER DONE, BUT SHE UNDERSTANDS THAT NOW. I THINK SHE GREW UP A LITTLE.
I SEE WHAT YOU MEAN. AND I DO TRUST HER.
I SUPPOSE THE BEST THING TO DO IS BE PATIENT...
...AND WAIT FOR THE MISTS TO CLEAR.
...End.

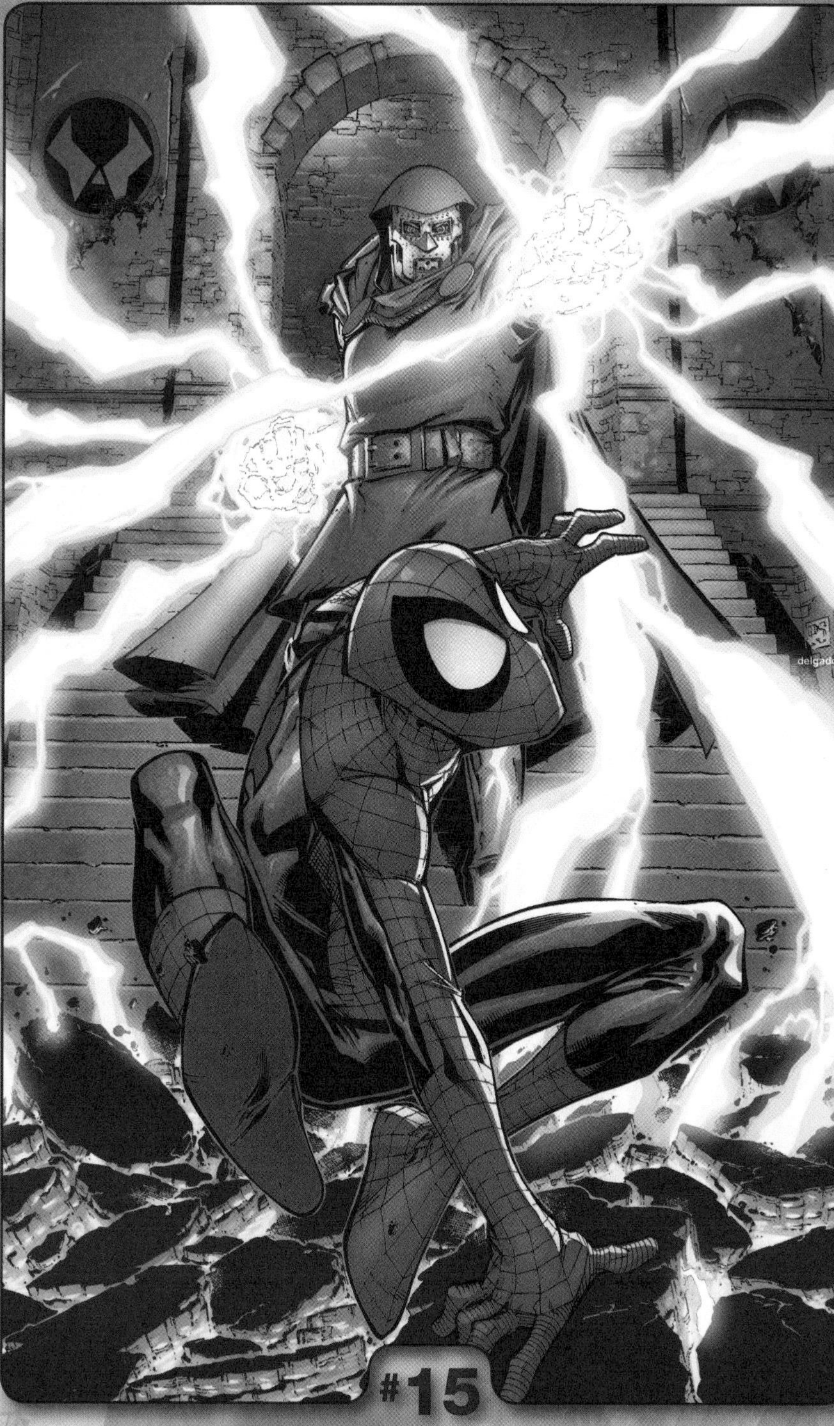
delgado
#15

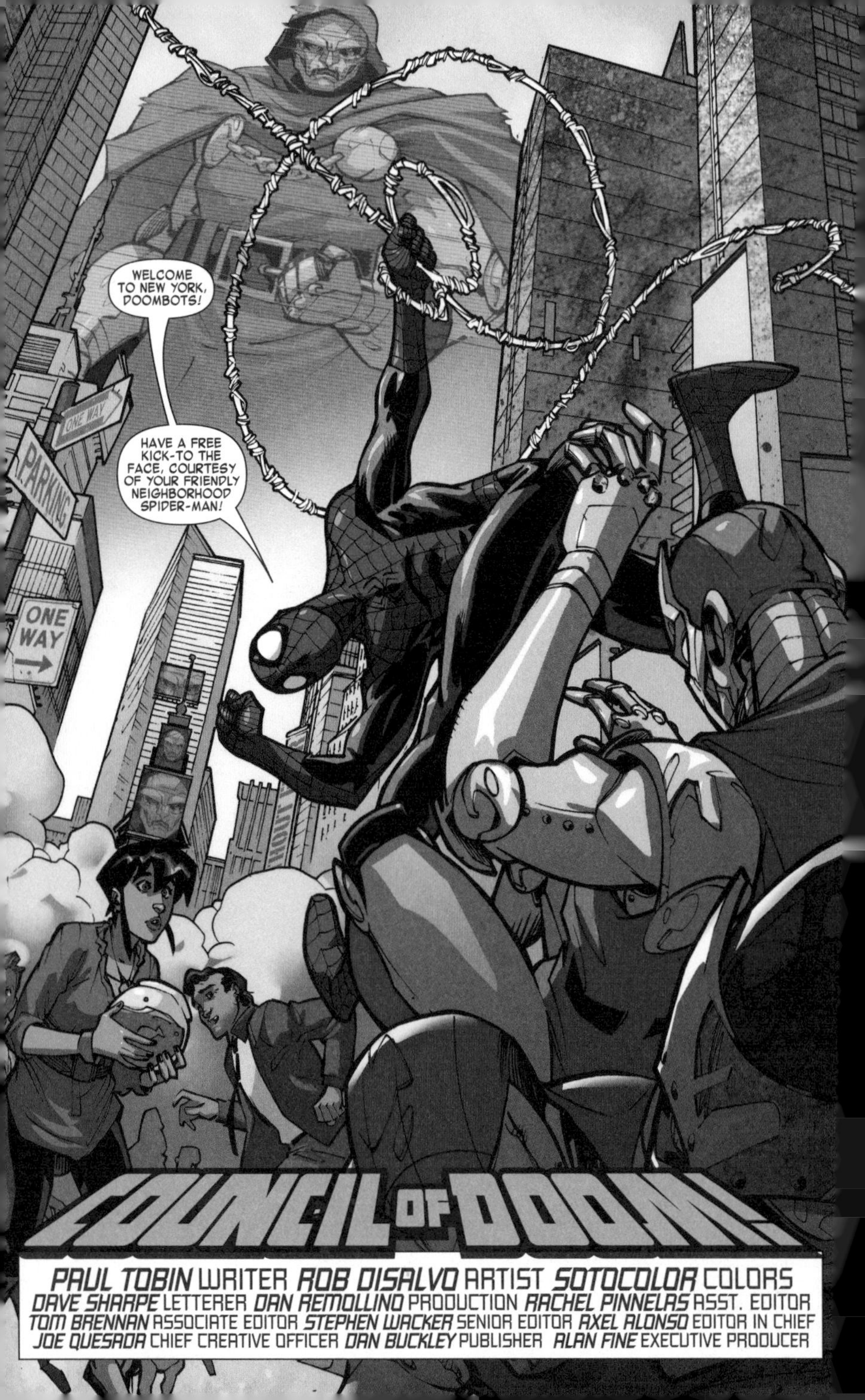
WELCOME TO NEW YORK, DOOMBOTS!
HAVE A FREE KICK-TO THE FACE, COURTESY OF YOUR FRIENDLY NEIGHBORHOOD SPIDER-MAN!
ONE WAY
PARKING
ONE WAY
COUNCIL OF DOOM!
PAUL TOBIN WRITER ROB DISALVO ARTIST SOTOCOLOR COLORS
DAVE SHARPE LETTERER DAN REMOLLINO PRODUCTION RACHEL PINNELAS ASST. EDITOR
TOM BRENNAN ASSOCIATE EDITOR STEPHEN WACKER SENIOR EDITOR AXEL ALONSO EDITOR IN CHIEF
JOE QUESADA CHIEF CREATIVE OFFICER DAN BUCKLEY PUBLISHER ALAN FINE EXECUTIVE PRODUCER

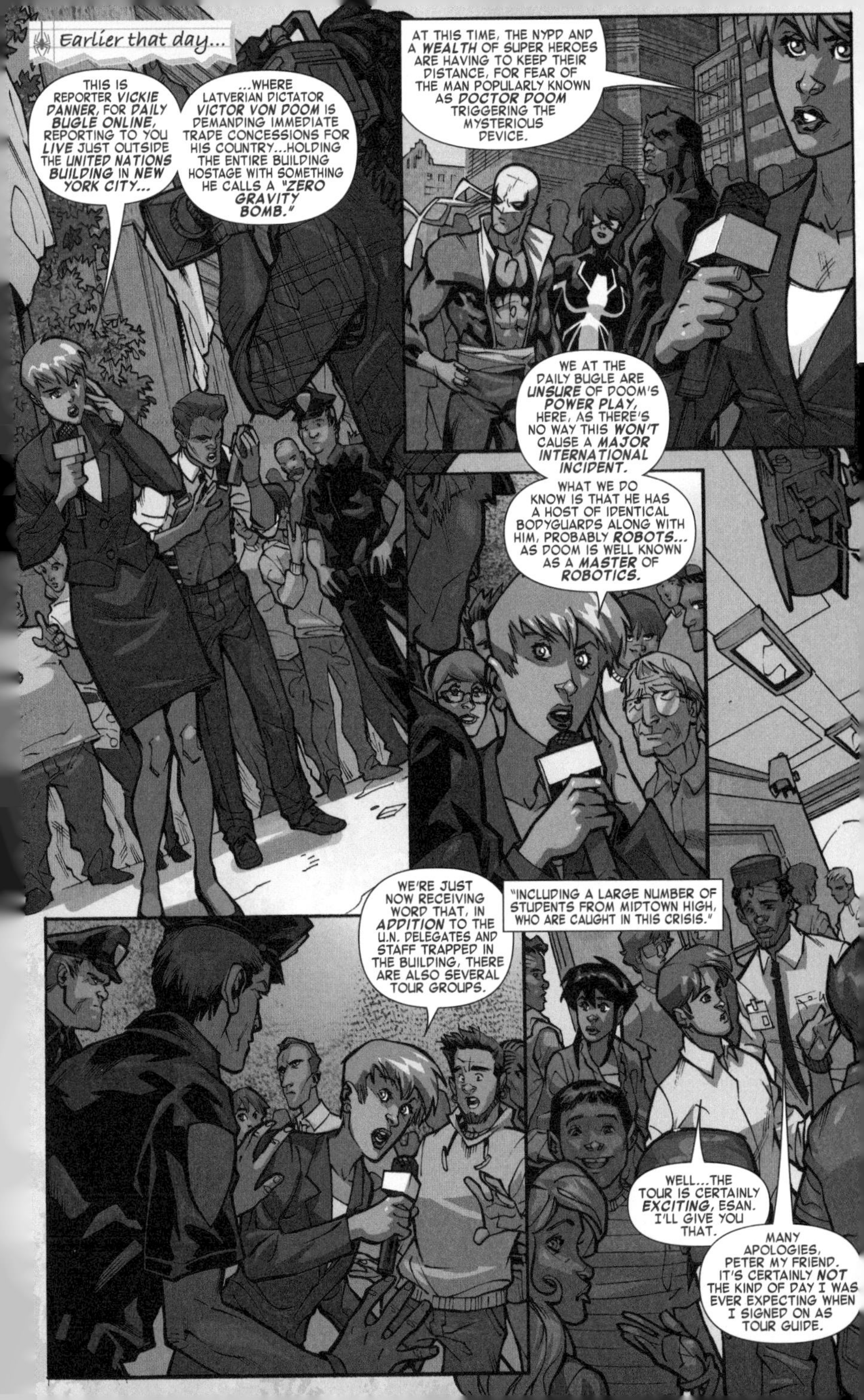
Earlier that day...
THIS IS REPORTER VICKIE DANNER, FOR DAILY BUGLE ONLINE, REPORTING TO YOU LIVE JUST OUTSIDE THE UNITED NATIONS BUILDING IN NEW YORK CITY...
...WHERE LATVERIAN DICTATOR VICTOR VON DOOM IS DEMANDING IMMEDIATE TRADE CONCESSIONS FOR HIS COUNTRY...HOLDING THE ENTIRE BUILDING HOSTAGE WITH SOMETHING HE CALLS A "ZERO GRAVITY BOMB."
AT THIS TIME, THE NYPD AND A WEALTH OF SUPER HEROES ARE HAVING TO KEEP THEIR DISTANCE, FOR FEAR OF THE MAN POPULARLY KNOWN AS DOCTOR DOOM TRIGGERING THE MYSTERIOUS DEVICE.
WE AT THE DAILY BUGLE ARE UNSURE OF DOOM'S POWER PLAY, HERE, AS THERE'S NO WAY THIS WON'T CAUSE A MAJOR INTERNATIONAL INCIDENT.
WHAT WE DO KNOW IS THAT HE HAS A HOST OF IDENTICAL BODYGUARDS ALONG WITH HIM, PROBABLY ROBOTS... AS DOOM IS WELL KNOWN AS A MASTER OF ROBOTICS.
WE'RE JUST NOW RECEIVING WORD THAT, IN ADDITION TO THE U.N. DELEGATES AND STAFF TRAPPED IN THE BUILDING, THERE ARE ALSO SEVERAL TOUR GROUPS.
"INCLUDING A LARGE NUMBER OF STUDENTS FROM MIDTOWN HIGH, WHO ARE CAUGHT IN THIS CRISIS."
WELL...THE TOUR IS CERTAINLY EXCITING, ESAN. I'LL GIVE YOU THAT.
MANY APOLOGIES, PETER MY FRIEND. IT'S CERTAINLY NOT THE KIND OF DAY I WAS EVER EXPECTING WHEN I SIGNED ON AS TOUR GUIDE.

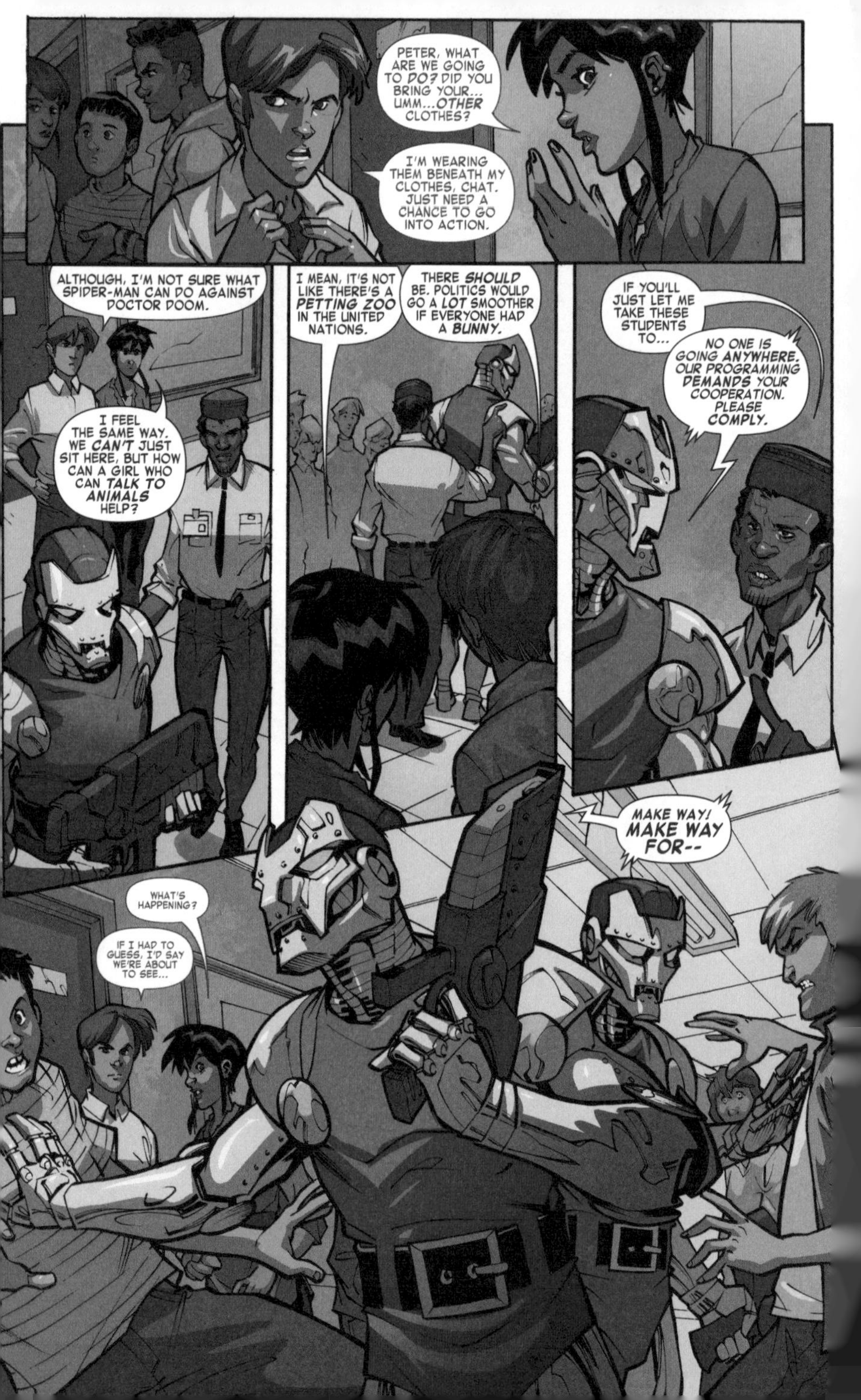
PETER, WHAT ARE WE GOING TO DO? DID YOU BRING YOUR... UMM...OTHER CLOTHES?
I'M WEARING THEM BENEATH MY CLOTHES, CHAT. JUST NEED A CHANCE TO GO INTO ACTION.
ALTHOUGH, I'M NOT SURE WHAT SPIDER-MAN CAN DO AGAINST DOCTOR DOOM.
I FEEL THE SAME WAY. WE CAN'T JUST SIT HERE, BUT HOW CAN A GIRL WHO CAN TALK TO ANIMALS HELP?
I MEAN, IT'S NOT LIKE THERE'S A PETTING ZOO IN THE UNITED NATIONS.
THERE SHOULD BE. POLITICS WOULD GO A LOT SMOOTHER IF EVERYONE HAD A BUNNY.
IF YOU'LL JUST LET ME TAKE THESE STUDENTS TO...
NO ONE IS GOING ANYWHERE. OUR PROGRAMMING DEMANDS YOUR COOPERATION. PLEASE COMPLY.
MAKE WAY! MAKE WAY FOR--
WHAT'S HAPPENING?
IF I HAD TO GUESS, I'D SAY WE'RE ABOUT TO SEE...

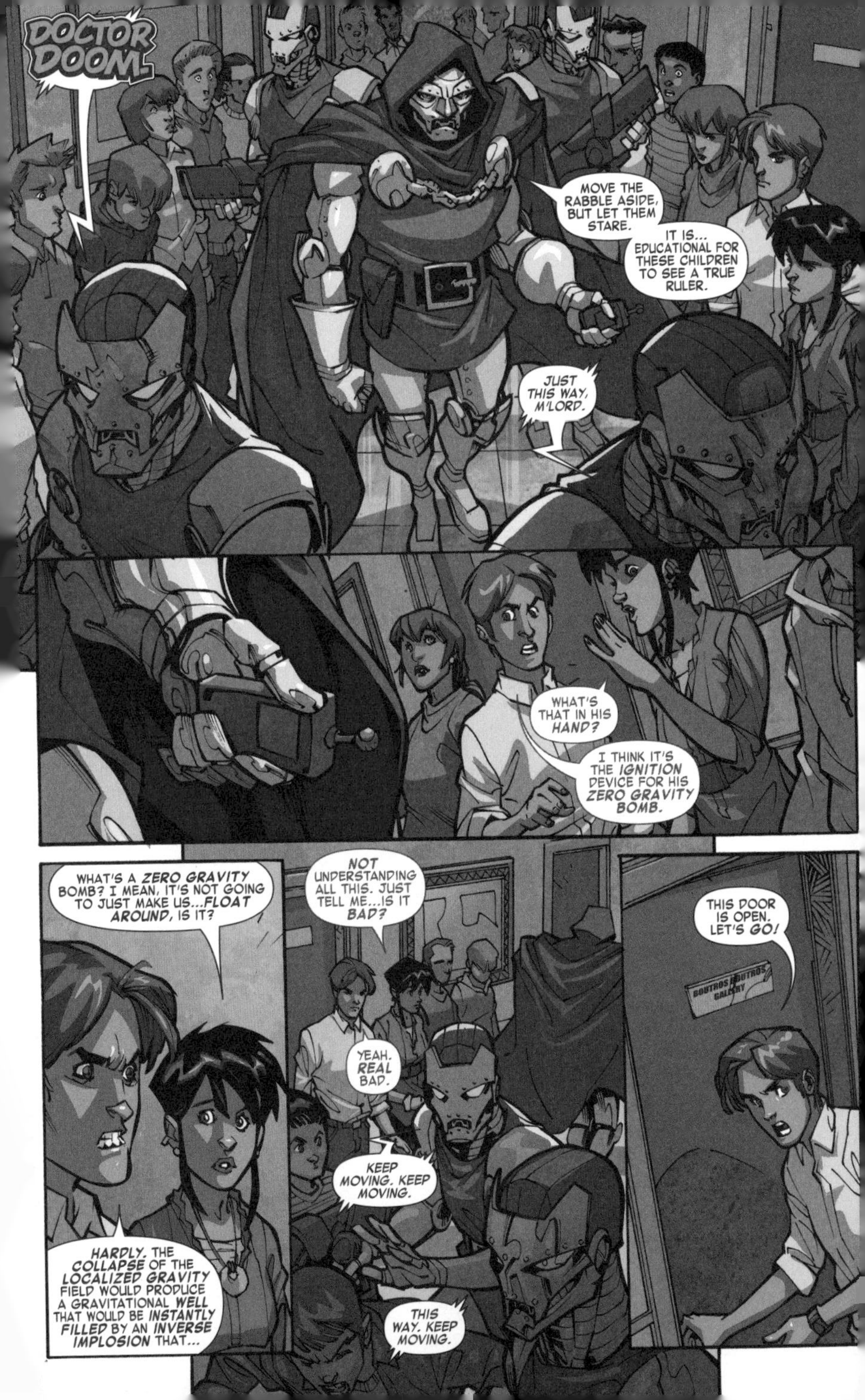
DOCTOR DOOM!
MOVE THE RABBLE ASIDE, BUT LET THEM STARE.
IT IS... EDUCATIONAL FOR THESE CHILDREN TO SEE A TRUE RULER.
JUST THIS WAY, M'LORD.
WHAT'S THAT IN HIS HAND?
I THINK IT'S THE IGNITION DEVICE FOR HIS ZERO GRAVITY BOMB.
WHAT'S A ZERO GRAVITY BOMB? I MEAN, IT'S NOT GOING TO JUST MAKE US...FLOAT AROUND, IS IT?
HARDLY. THE COLLAPSE OF THE LOCALIZED GRAVITY FIELD WOULD PRODUCE A GRAVITATIONAL WELL THAT WOULD BE INSTANTLY FILLED BY AN INVERSE IMPLOSION THAT...
NOT UNDERSTANDING ALL THIS. JUST TELL ME...IS IT BAD?
YEAH. REAL BAD.
KEEP MOVING. KEEP MOVING.
THIS WAY. KEEP MOVING.
THIS DOOR IS OPEN. LET'S GO!
BOUTROS BOUTROS GALLERY

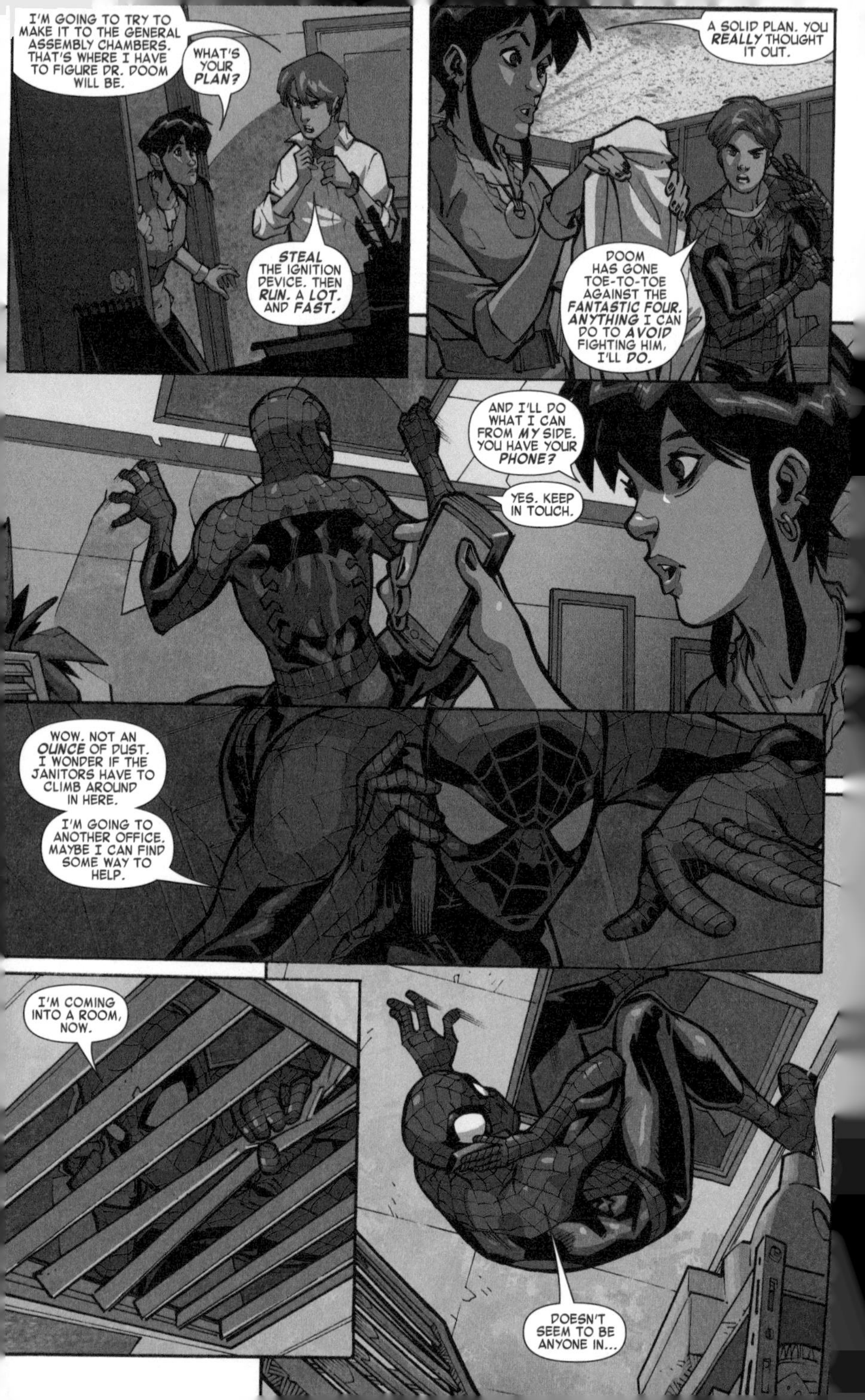
I'M GOING TO TRY TO MAKE IT TO THE GENERAL ASSEMBLY CHAMBERS. THAT'S WHERE I HAVE TO FIGURE DR. DOOM WILL BE.
WHAT'S YOUR PLAN?
STEAL THE IGNITION DEVICE. THEN RUN. A LOT. AND FAST.
A SOLID PLAN. YOU REALLY THOUGHT IT OUT.
DOOM HAS GONE TOE-TO-TOE AGAINST THE FANTASTIC FOUR. ANYTHING I CAN DO TO AVOID FIGHTING HIM, I'LL DO.
AND I'LL DO WHAT I CAN FROM MY SIDE. YOU HAVE YOUR PHONE?
YES. KEEP IN TOUCH.
WOW. NOT AN OUNCE OF DUST. I WONDER IF THE JANITORS HAVE TO CLIMB AROUND IN HERE.
I'M GOING TO ANOTHER OFFICE. MAYBE I CAN FIND SOME WAY TO HELP.
I'M COMING INTO A ROOM, NOW.
DOESN'T SEEM TO BE ANYONE IN...

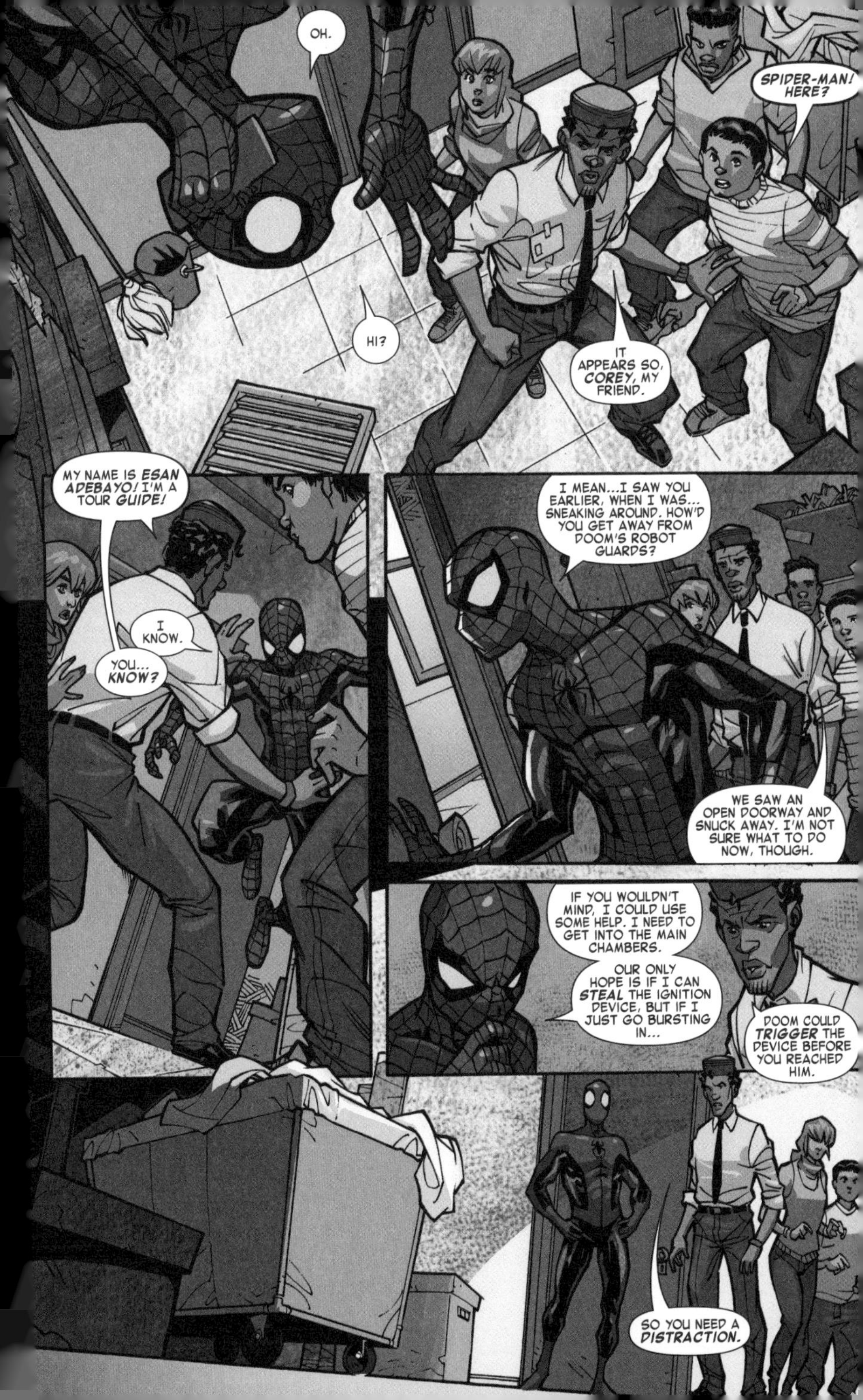
OH.
SPIDER-MAN! HERE?
HI?
IT APPEARS SO, COREY, MY FRIEND.
MY NAME IS ESAN ADEBAYO! I'M A TOUR GUIDE!
I KNOW.
YOU... KNOW?
I MEAN...I SAW YOU EARLIER, WHEN I WAS... SNEAKING AROUND. HOW'D YOU GET AWAY FROM DOOM'S ROBOT GUARDS?
WE SAW AN OPEN DOORWAY AND SNUCK AWAY. I'M NOT SURE WHAT TO DO NOW, THOUGH.
IF YOU WOULDN'T MIND, I COULD USE SOME HELP. I NEED TO GET INTO THE MAIN CHAMBERS.
OUR ONLY HOPE IS IF I CAN STEAL THE IGNITION DEVICE, BUT IF I JUST GO BURSTING IN...
DOOM COULD TRIGGER THE DEVICE BEFORE YOU REACHED HIM.
SO YOU NEED A DISTRACTION.

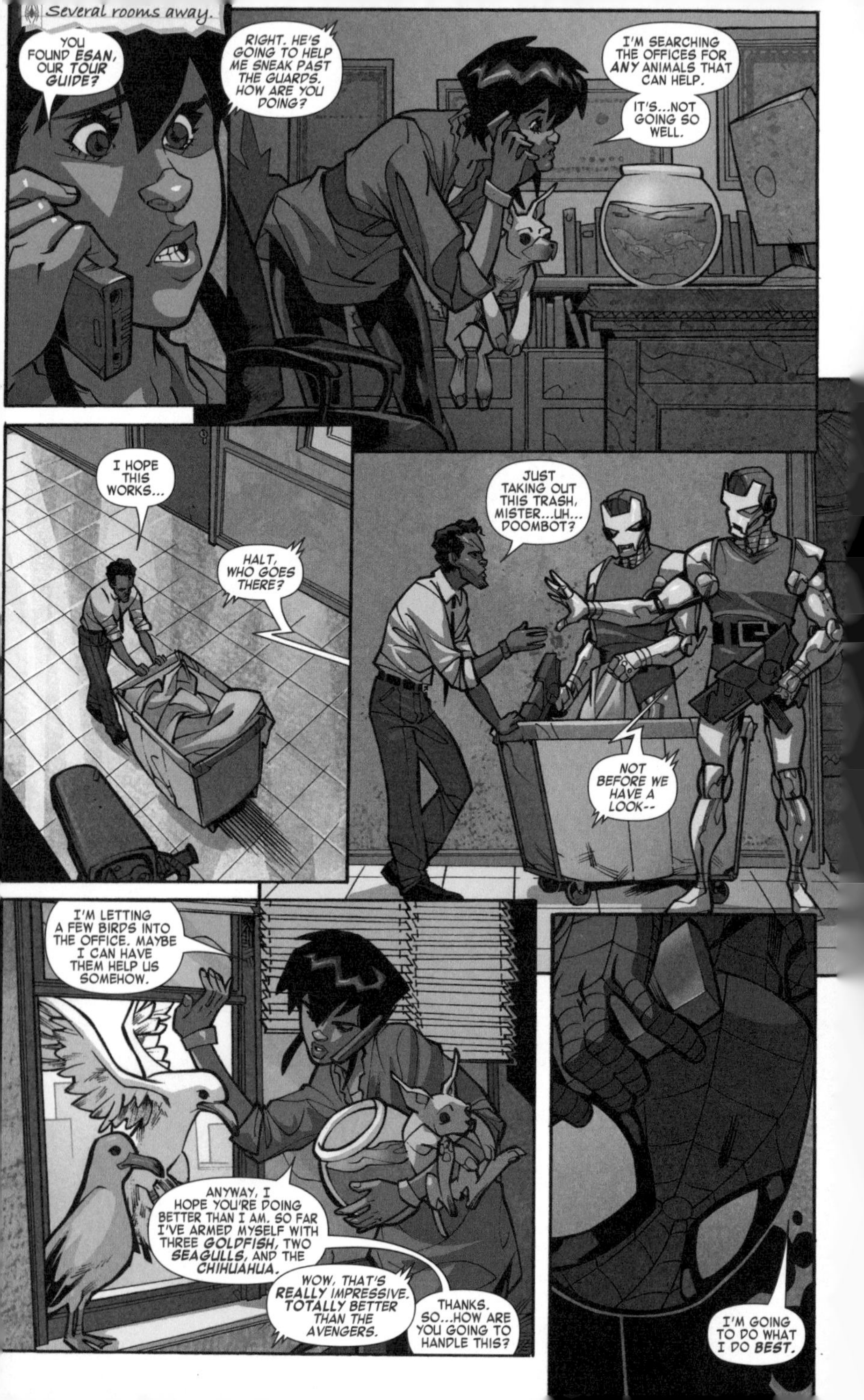

Several rooms away.
YOU FOUND ESAN, OUR TOUR GUIDE?
RIGHT. HE'S GOING TO HELP ME SNEAK PAST THE GUARDS. HOW ARE YOU DOING?
I'M SEARCHING THE OFFICES FOR ANY ANIMALS THAT CAN HELP.
IT'S...NOT GOING SO WELL.
I HOPE THIS WORKS...
HALT, WHO GOES THERE?
JUST TAKING OUT THIS TRASH, MISTER...UH... DOOMBOT?
NOT BEFORE WE HAVE A LOOK--
I'M LETTING A FEW BIRDS INTO THE OFFICE. MAYBE I CAN HAVE THEM HELP US SOMEHOW.
ANYWAY, I HOPE YOU'RE DOING BETTER THAN I AM. SO FAR I'VE ARMED MYSELF WITH THREE GOLDFISH, TWO SEAGULLS, AND THE CHIHUAHUA.
WOW, THAT'S REALLY IMPRESSIVE. TOTALLY BETTER THAN THE AVENGERS.
THANKS. SO...HOW ARE YOU GOING TO HANDLE THIS?
I'M GOING TO DO WHAT I DO BEST.

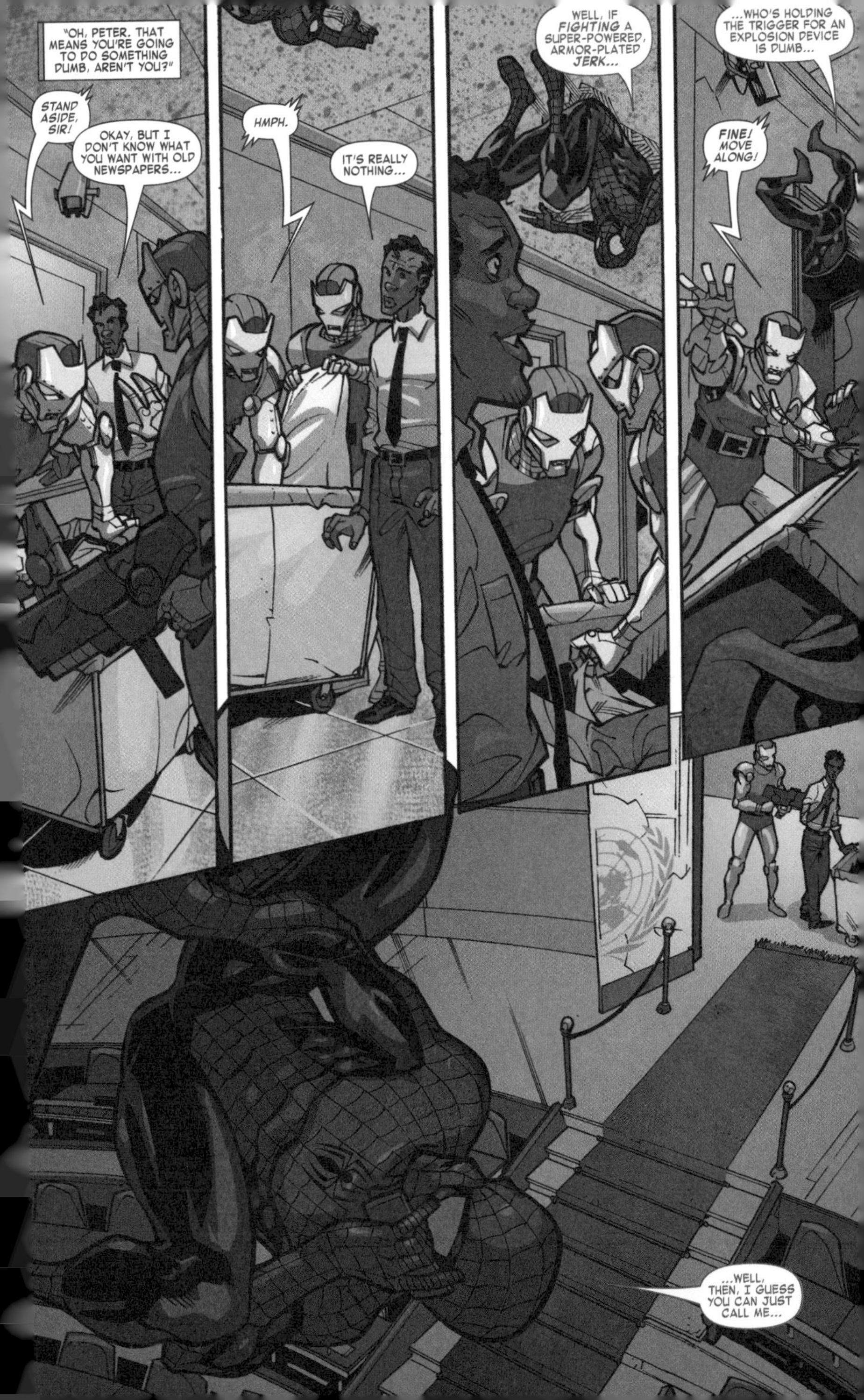
"OH, PETER. THAT MEANS YOU'RE GOING TO DO SOMETHING DUMB, AREN'T YOU?"
STAND ASIDE, SIR!
OKAY, BUT I DON'T KNOW WHAT YOU WANT WITH OLD NEWSPAPERS...
HMPH.
IT'S REALLY NOTHING...
WELL, IF FIGHTING A SUPER-POWERED, ARMOR-PLATED JERK...
...WHO'S HOLDING THE TRIGGER FOR AN EXPLOSION DEVICE IS DUMB...
FINE! MOVE ALONG!
...WELL, THEN, I GUESS YOU CAN JUST CALL ME...

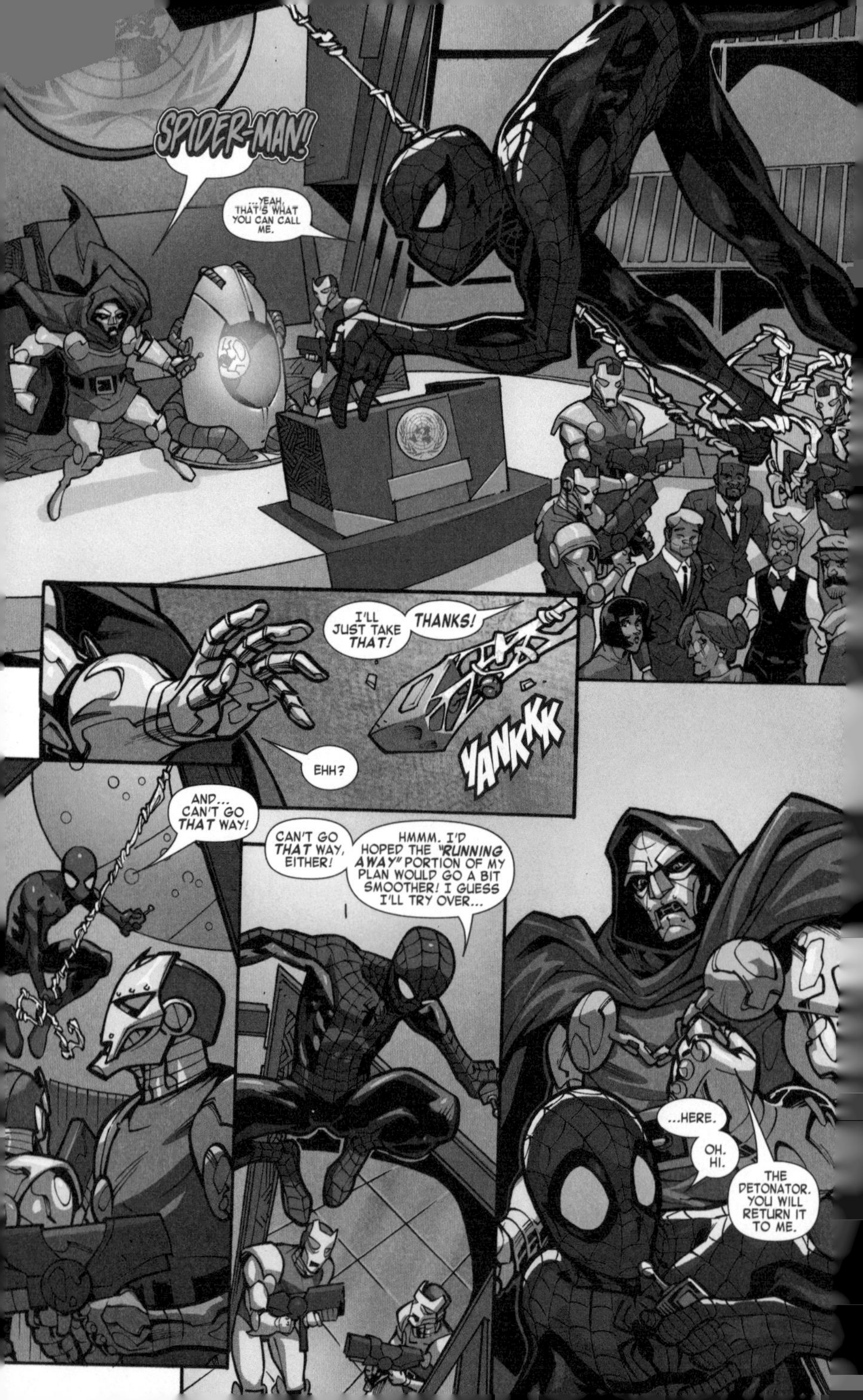
SPIDER-MAN!
...YEAH, THAT'S WHAT YOU CAN CALL ME.
I'LL JUST TAKE THAT!
THANKS!
YANKKK
EHH?
AND... CAN'T GO THAT WAY!
CAN'T GO THAT WAY, EITHER!
HMMM. I'D HOPED THE "RUNNING AWAY" PORTION OF MY PLAN WOULD GO A BIT SMOOTHER! I GUESS I'LL TRY OVER...
...HERE.
OH. HI.
THE DETONATOR. YOU WILL RETURN IT TO ME.

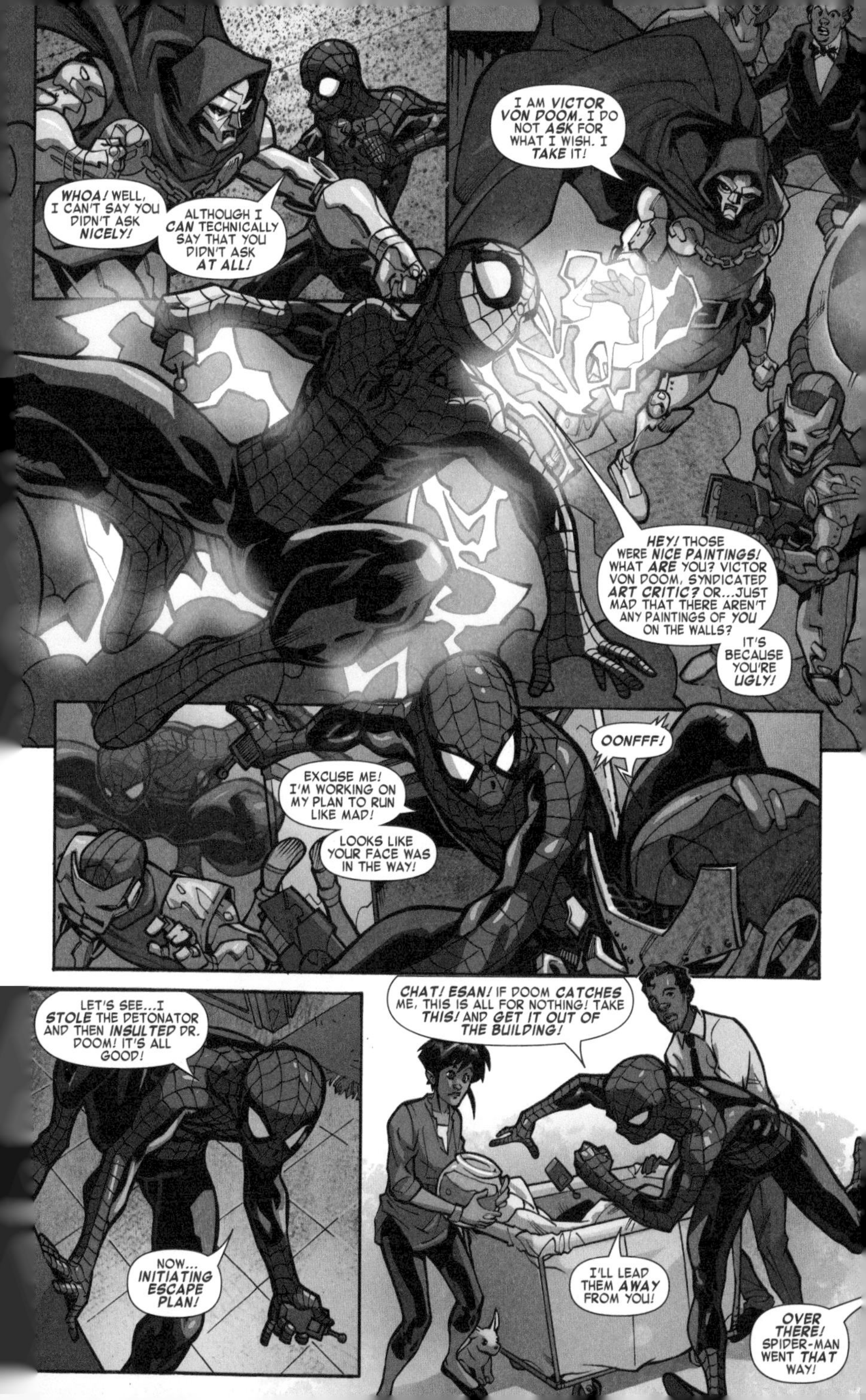
WHOA! WELL, I CAN'T SAY YOU DIDN'T ASK NICELY!
ALTHOUGH I CAN TECHNICALLY SAY THAT YOU DIDN'T ASK AT ALL!
I AM VICTOR VON DOOM. I DO NOT ASK FOR WHAT I WISH. I TAKE IT!
HEY! THOSE WERE NICE PAINTINGS! WHAT ARE YOU? VICTOR VON DOOM, SYNDICATED ART CRITIC? OR...JUST MAD THAT THERE AREN'T ANY PAINTINGS OF YOU ON THE WALLS?
IT'S BECAUSE YOU'RE UGLY!
OONFFF!
EXCUSE ME! I'M WORKING ON MY PLAN TO RUN LIKE MAD!
LOOKS LIKE YOUR FACE WAS IN THE WAY!
LET'S SEE...I STOLE THE DETONATOR AND THEN INSULTED DR. DOOM! IT'S ALL GOOD!
NOW... INITIATING ESCAPE PLAN!
CHAT! ESAN! IF DOOM CATCHES ME, THIS IS ALL FOR NOTHING! TAKE THIS! AND GET IT OUT OF THE BUILDING!
I'LL LEAD THEM AWAY FROM YOU!
OVER THERE! SPIDER-MAN WENT THAT WAY!

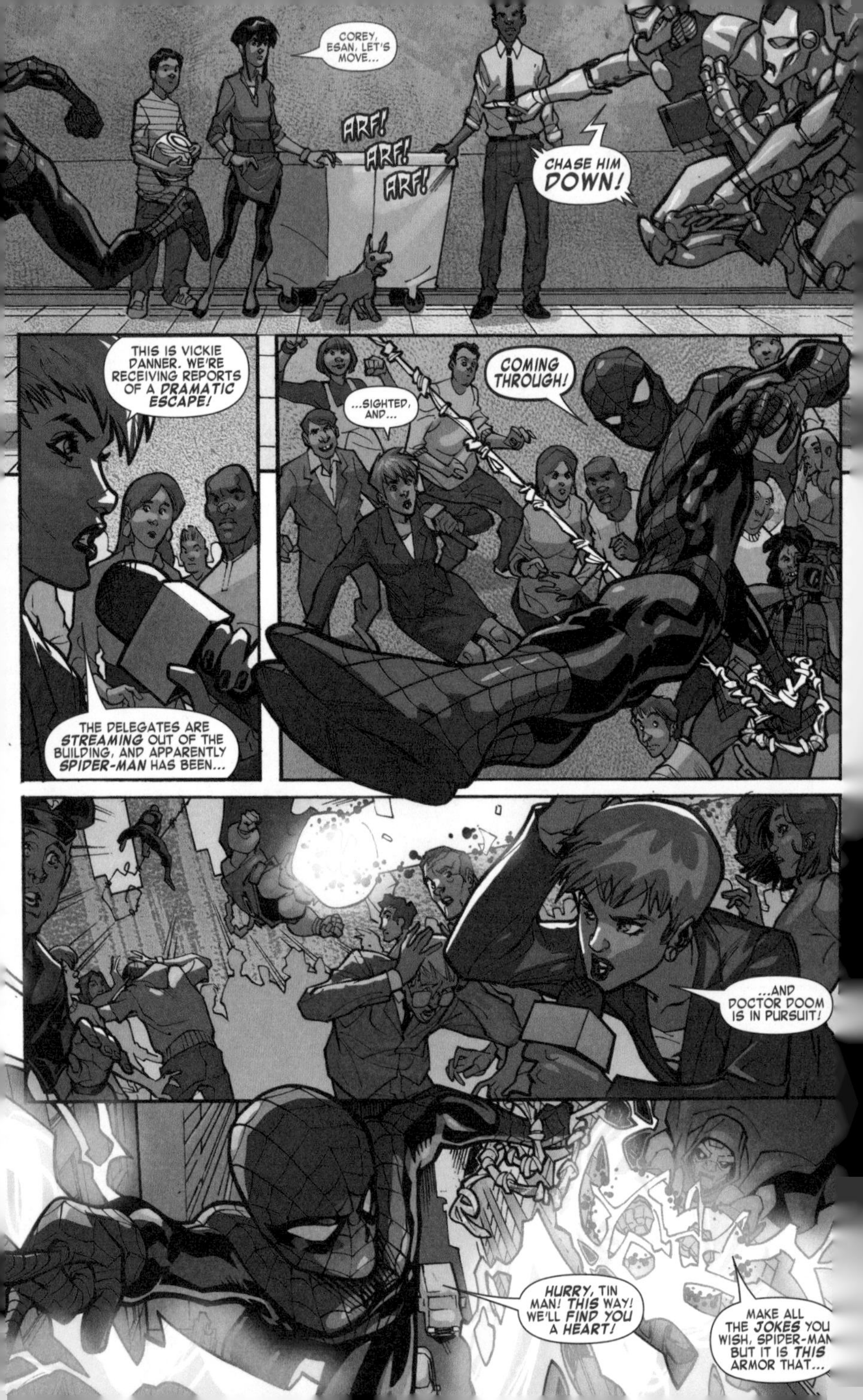
COREY, ESAN, LET'S MOVE...
ARF! ARF! ARF!
CHASE HIM DOWN!
THIS IS VICKIE DANNER. WE'RE RECEIVING REPORTS OF A DRAMATIC ESCAPE!
THE DELEGATES ARE STREAMING OUT OF THE BUILDING, AND APPARENTLY SPIDER-MAN HAS BEEN...
...SIGHTED, AND...
COMING THROUGH!
...AND DOCTOR DOOM IS IN PURSUIT!
HURRY, TIN MAN! THIS WAY! WE'LL FIND YOU A HEART!
MAKE ALL THE JOKES YOU WISH, SPIDER-MAN BUT IT IS THIS ARMOR THAT...

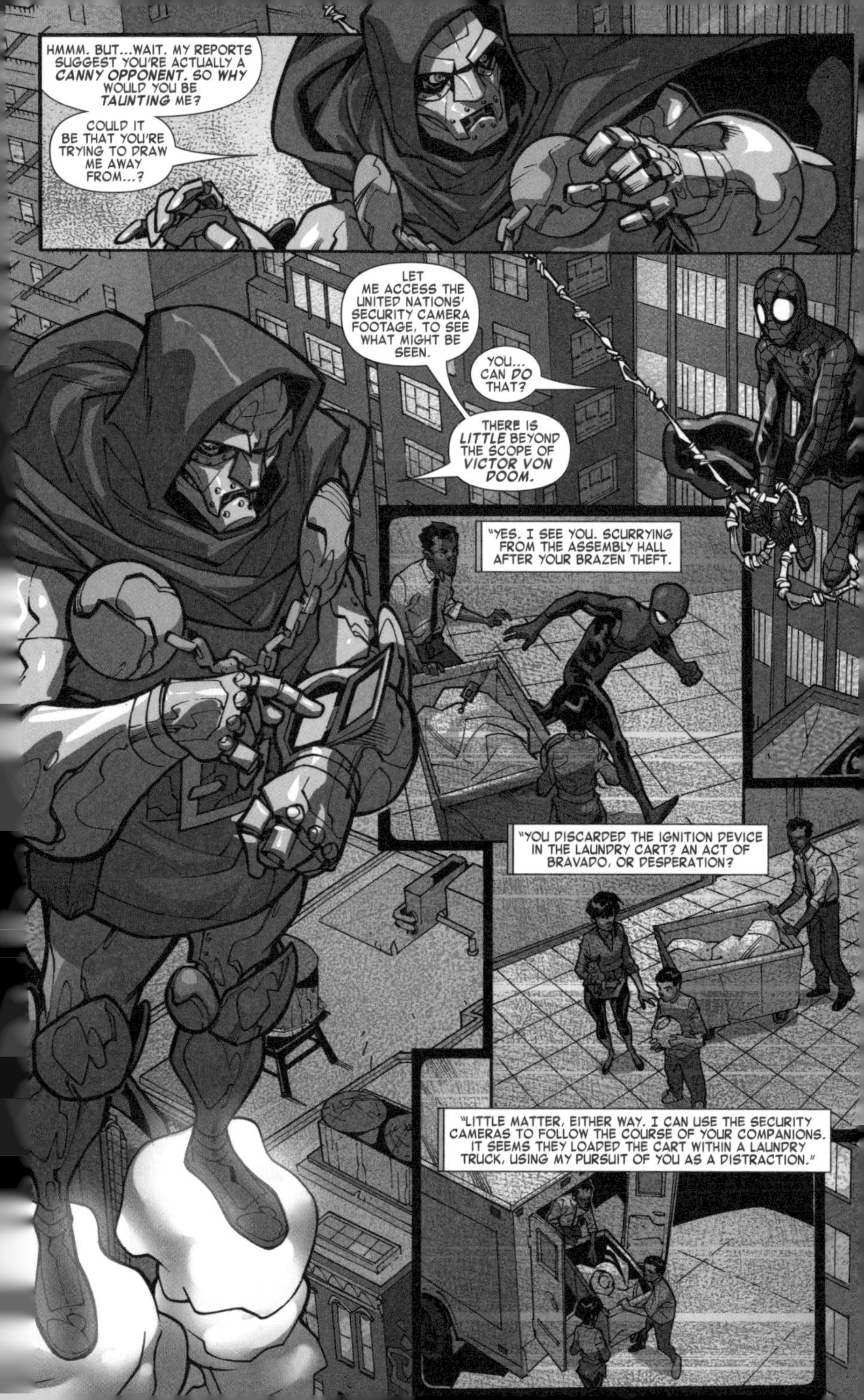
HMMM. BUT...WAIT. MY REPORTS SUGGEST YOU'RE ACTUALLY A *CANNY OPPONENT.* SO *WHY* WOULD YOU BE *TAUNTING* ME?
COULD IT BE THAT YOU'RE TRYING TO DRAW ME AWAY FROM...?
LET ME ACCESS THE UNITED NATIONS' SECURITY CAMERA FOOTAGE, TO SEE WHAT MIGHT BE SEEN.
YOU... CAN *DO* THAT?
THERE IS *LITTLE* BEYOND THE SCOPE OF *VICTOR VON DOOM.*
"YES. I SEE YOU. SCURRYING FROM THE ASSEMBLY HALL AFTER YOUR BRAZEN THEFT.
"YOU DISCARDED THE IGNITION DEVICE IN THE LAUNDRY CART? AN ACT OF BRAVADO, OR DESPERATION?
"LITTLE MATTER, EITHER WAY. I CAN USE THE SECURITY CAMERAS TO FOLLOW THE COURSE OF YOUR COMPANIONS. IT SEEMS THEY LOADED THE CART WITHIN A LAUNDRY TRUCK, USING MY PURSUIT OF YOU AS A DISTRACTION."

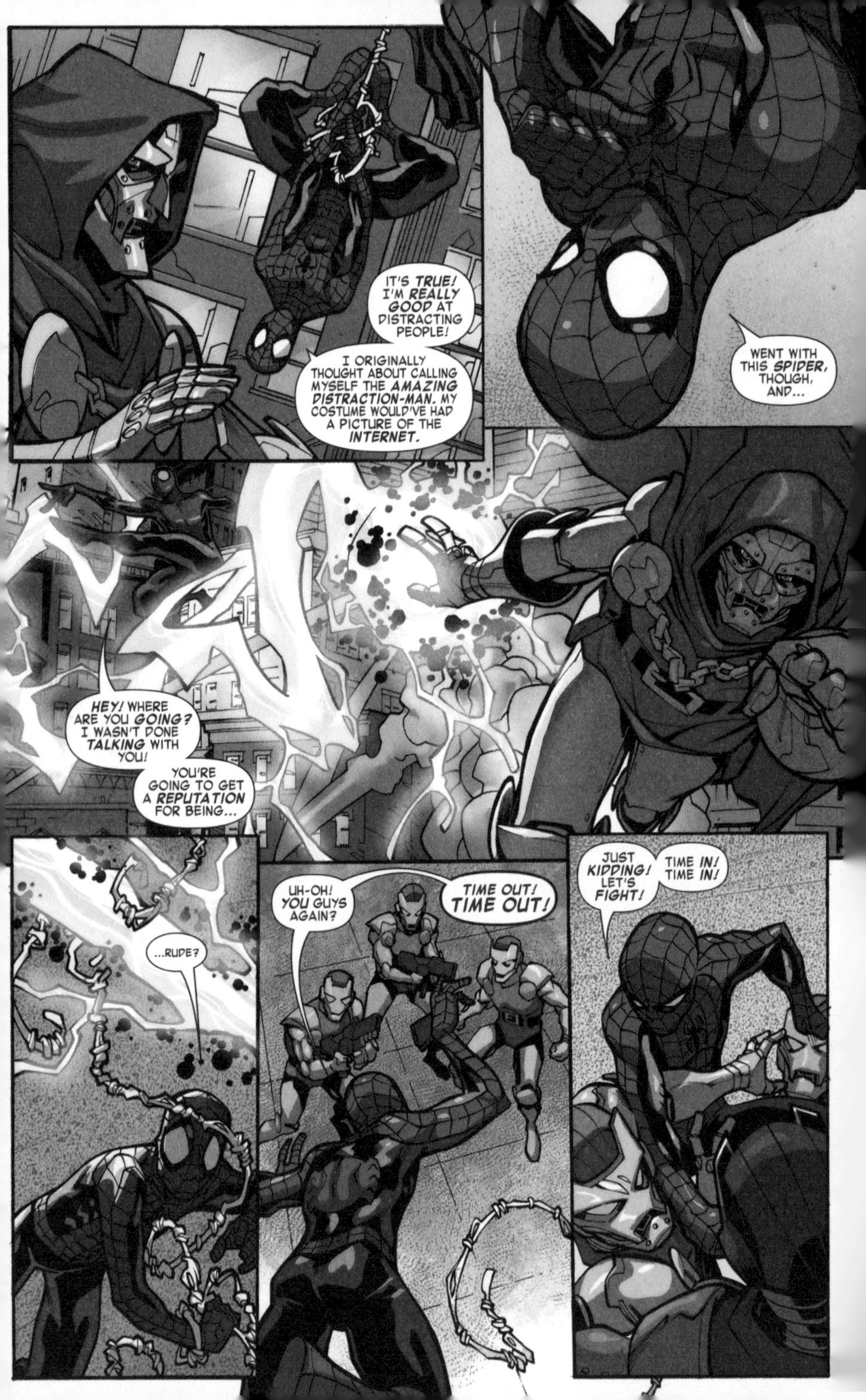
IT'S TRUE! I'M REALLY GOOD AT DISTRACTING PEOPLE!
I ORIGINALLY THOUGHT ABOUT CALLING MYSELF THE AMAZING DISTRACTION-MAN. MY COSTUME WOULD'VE HAD A PICTURE OF THE INTERNET.
WENT WITH THIS SPIDER, THOUGH, AND...
HEY! WHERE ARE YOU GOING? I WASN'T DONE TALKING WITH YOU!
YOU'RE GOING TO GET A REPUTATION FOR BEING...
...RUDE?
UH-OH! YOU GUYS AGAIN?
TIME OUT! TIME OUT!
JUST KIDDING! LET'S FIGHT!
TIME IN! TIME IN!

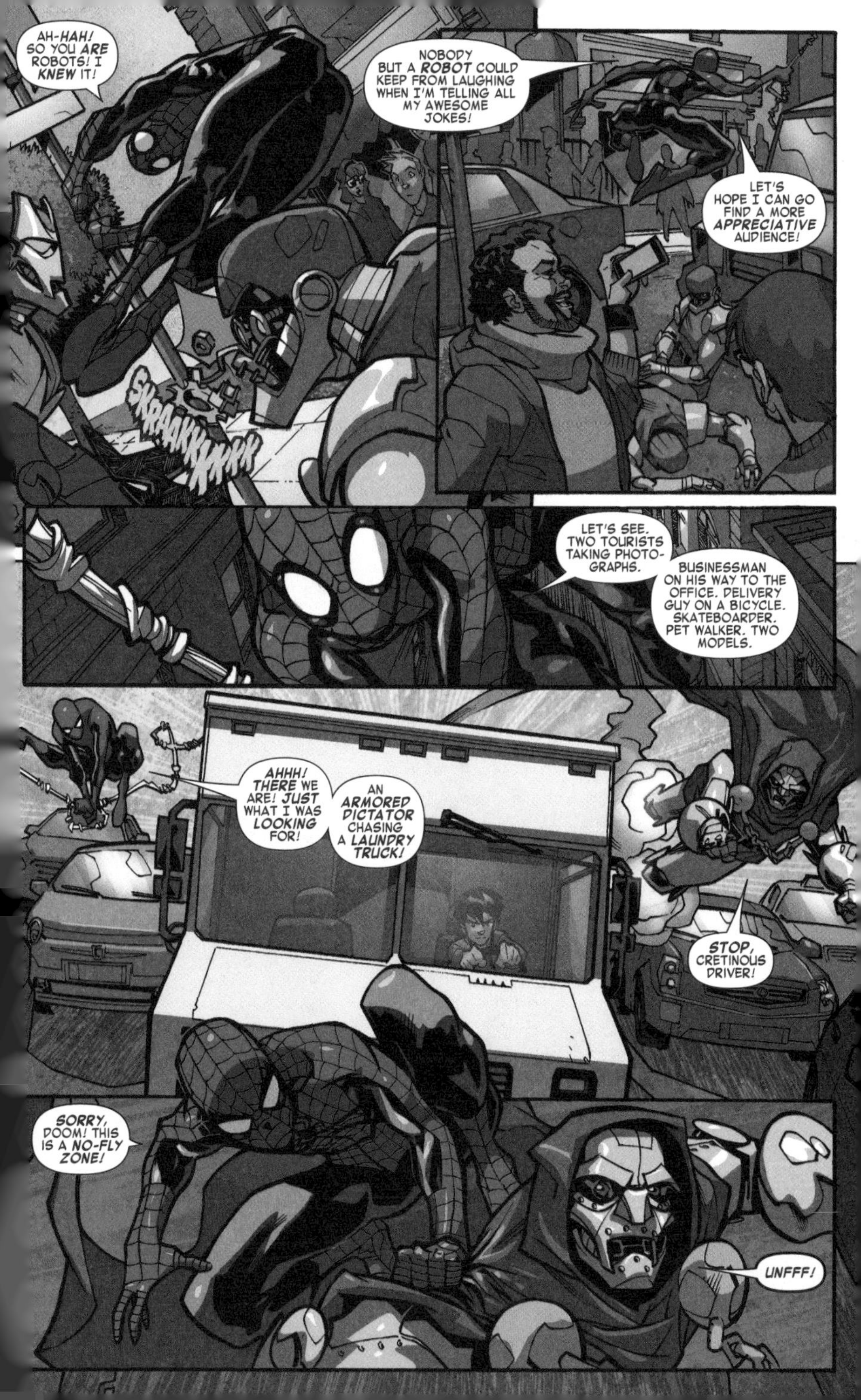
AH-HAH! SO YOU ARE ROBOTS! I KNEW IT!
SKRAAKKKKKR
NOBODY BUT A ROBOT COULD KEEP FROM LAUGHING WHEN I'M TELLING ALL MY AWESOME JOKES!
LET'S HOPE I CAN GO FIND A MORE APPRECIATIVE AUDIENCE!
LET'S SEE. TWO TOURISTS TAKING PHOTOGRAPHS.
BUSINESSMAN ON HIS WAY TO THE OFFICE. DELIVERY GUY ON A BICYCLE. SKATEBOARDER. PET WALKER. TWO MODELS.
AHHH! THERE WE ARE! JUST WHAT I WAS LOOKING FOR!
AN ARMORED DICTATOR CHASING A LAUNDRY TRUCK!
STOP, CRETINOUS DRIVER!
SORRY, DOOM! THIS IS A NO-FLY ZONE!
UNFFF!

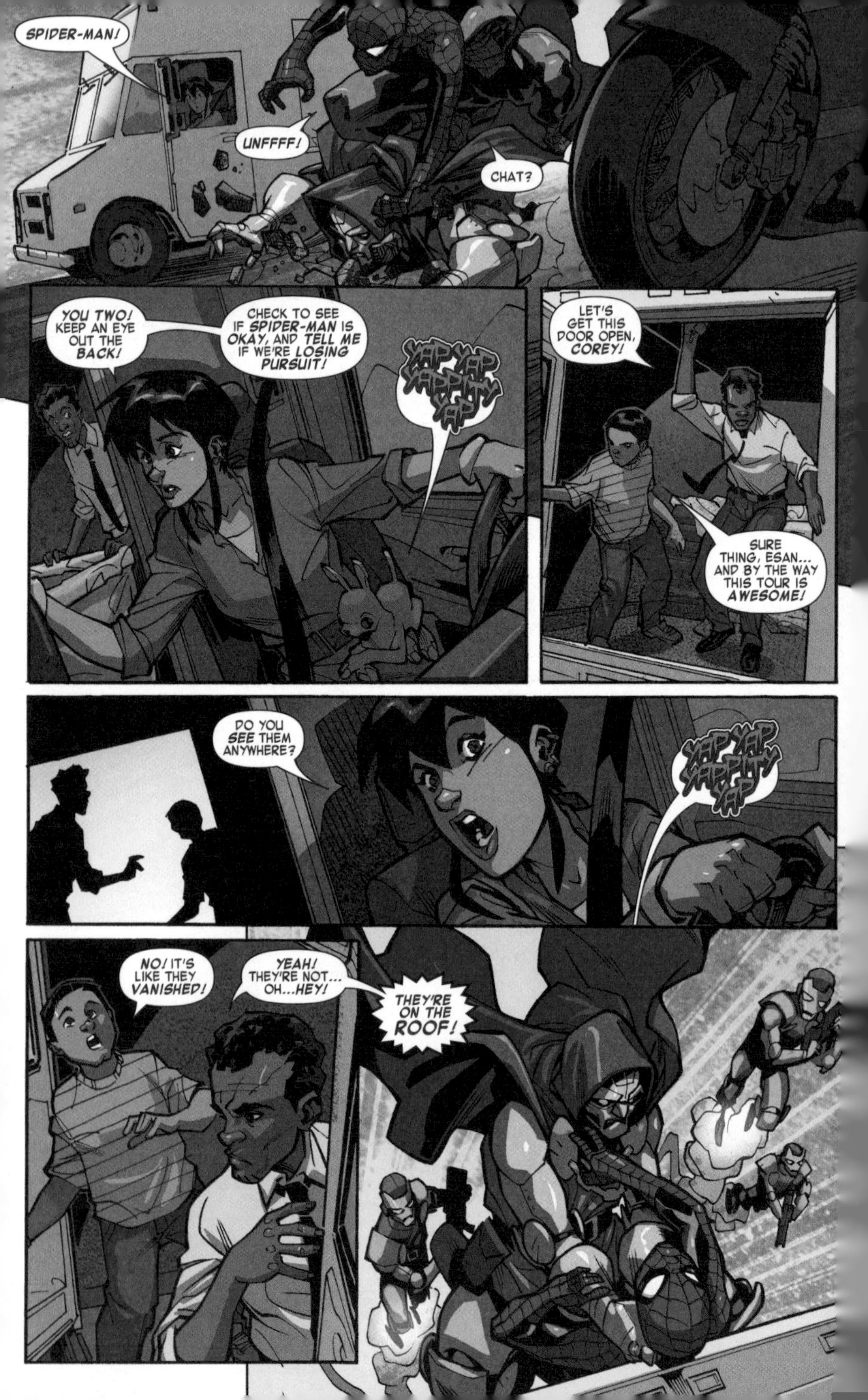
SPIDER-MAN!
UNFFFF!
CHAT?
YOU TWO! KEEP AN EYE OUT THE BACK!
CHECK TO SEE IF SPIDER-MAN IS OKAY, AND TELL ME IF WE'RE LOSING PURSUIT!
YAP YAP YAPPITY YAP
LET'S GET THIS DOOR OPEN, COREY!
SURE THING, ESAN... AND BY THE WAY THIS TOUR IS AWESOME!
DO YOU SEE THEM ANYWHERE?
YAP YAP YAPPITY YAP
NO! IT'S LIKE THEY VANISHED!
YEAH! THEY'RE NOT... OH...HEY!
THEY'RE ON THE ROOF!

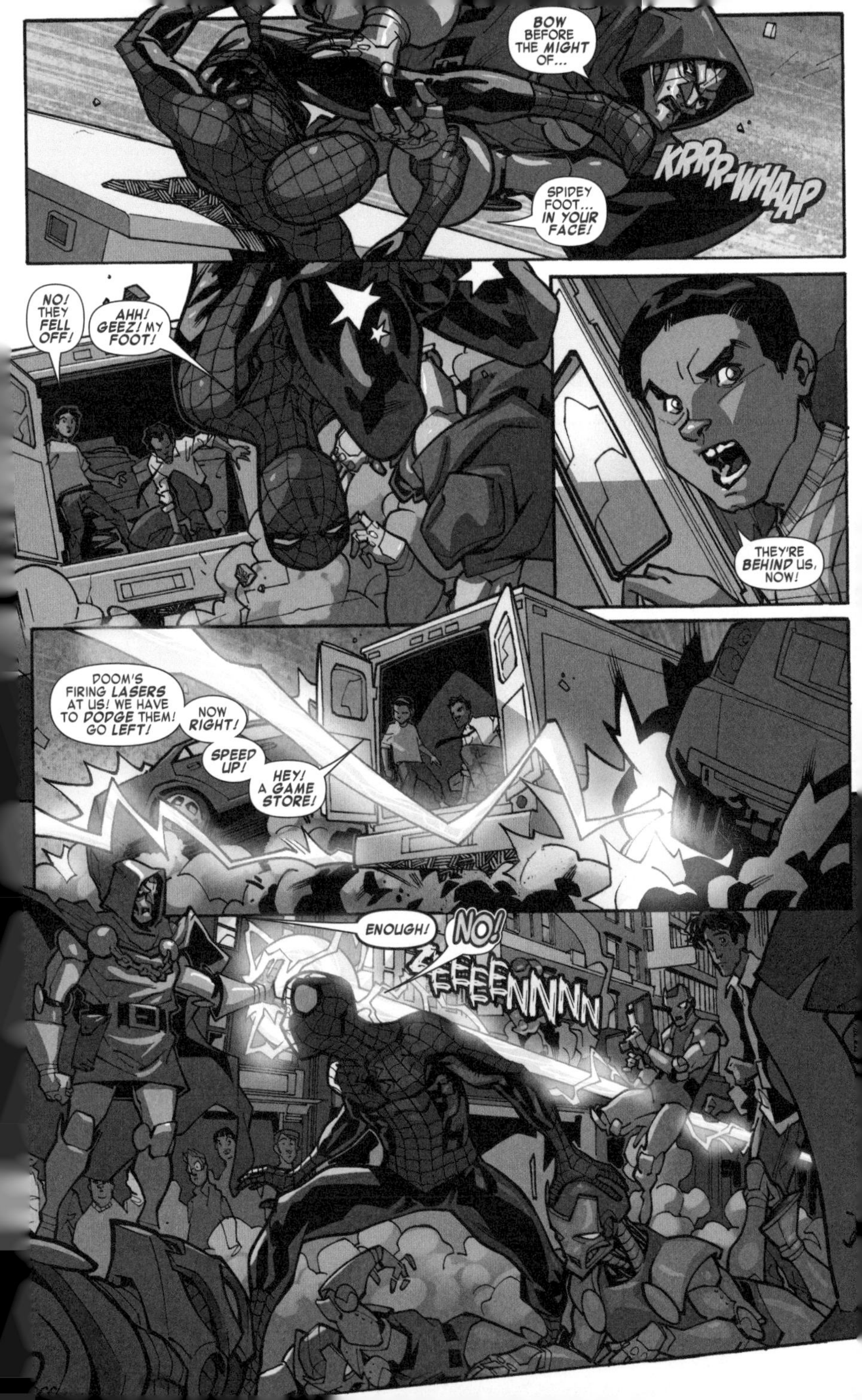
BOW BEFORE THE MIGHT OF...
KRRR-WHAAP
SPIDEY FOOT... IN YOUR FACE!
NO! THEY FELL OFF!
AHH! GEEZ! MY FOOT!
THEY'RE BEHIND US, NOW!
DOOM'S FIRING LASERS AT US! WE HAVE TO DODGE THEM! GO LEFT!
NOW RIGHT!
SPEED UP!
HEY! A GAME STORE!
ENOUGH!
NO!
EEEENNNNN

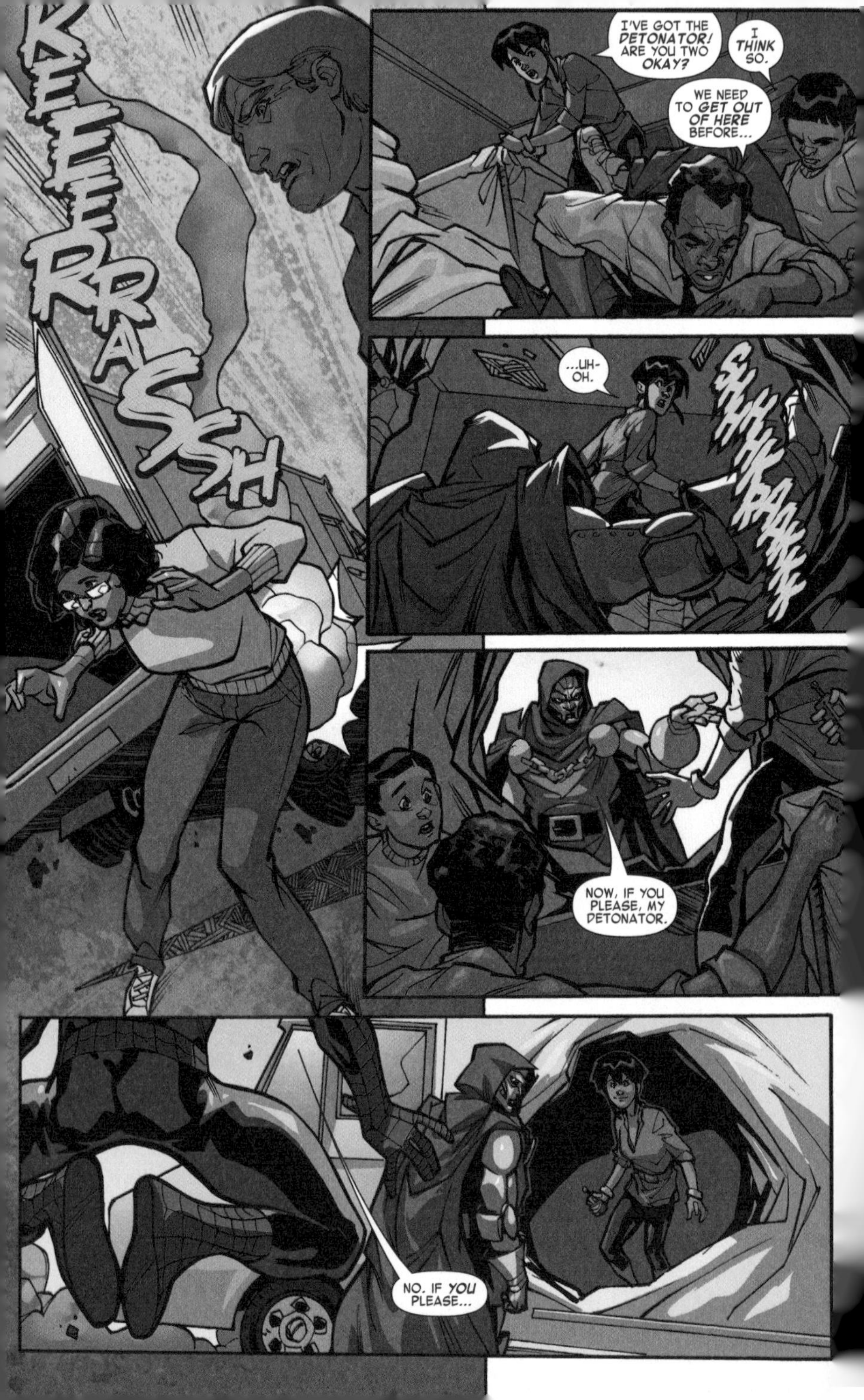
KEEERRRASSH
I'VE GOT THE DETONATOR! ARE YOU TWO OKAY?
I THINK SO.
WE NEED TO GET OUT OF HERE BEFORE...
...UH-OH.
SHHHKRAKK
NOW, IF YOU PLEASE, MY DETONATOR.
NO. IF YOU PLEASE...

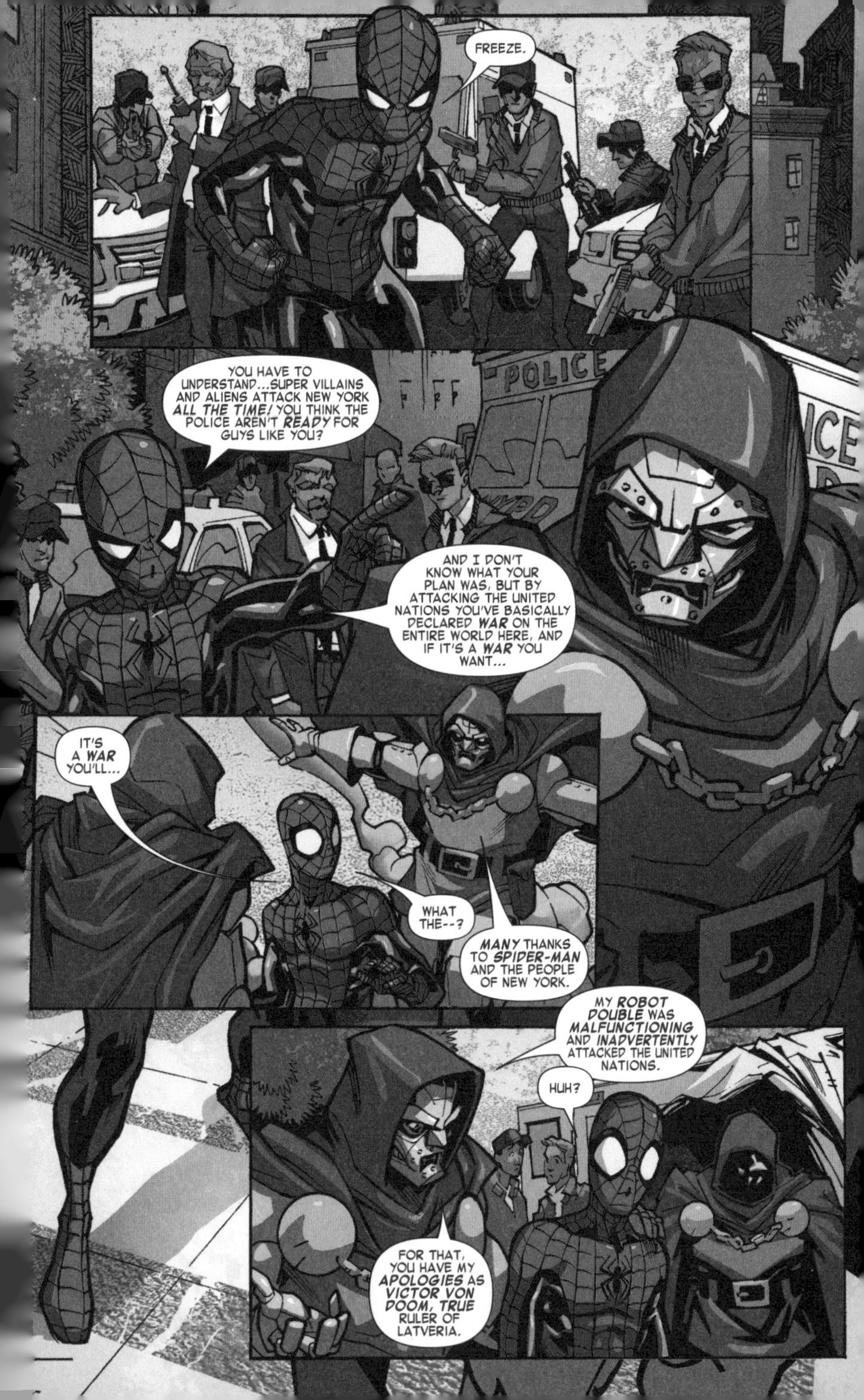
FREEZE.
YOU HAVE TO UNDERSTAND...SUPER VILLAINS AND ALIENS ATTACK NEW YORK ALL THE TIME! YOU THINK THE POLICE AREN'T READY FOR GUYS LIKE YOU?
AND I DON'T KNOW WHAT YOUR PLAN WAS, BUT BY ATTACKING THE UNITED NATIONS YOU'VE BASICALLY DECLARED WAR ON THE ENTIRE WORLD HERE, AND IF IT'S A WAR YOU WANT...
POLICE
IT'S A WAR YOU'LL...
WHAT THE--?
MANY THANKS TO SPIDER-MAN AND THE PEOPLE OF NEW YORK.
MY ROBOT DOUBLE WAS MALFUNCTIONING AND INADVERTENTLY ATTACKED THE UNITED NATIONS.
HUH?
FOR THAT, YOU HAVE MY APOLOGIES AS VICTOR VON DOOM, TRUE RULER OF LATVERIA.

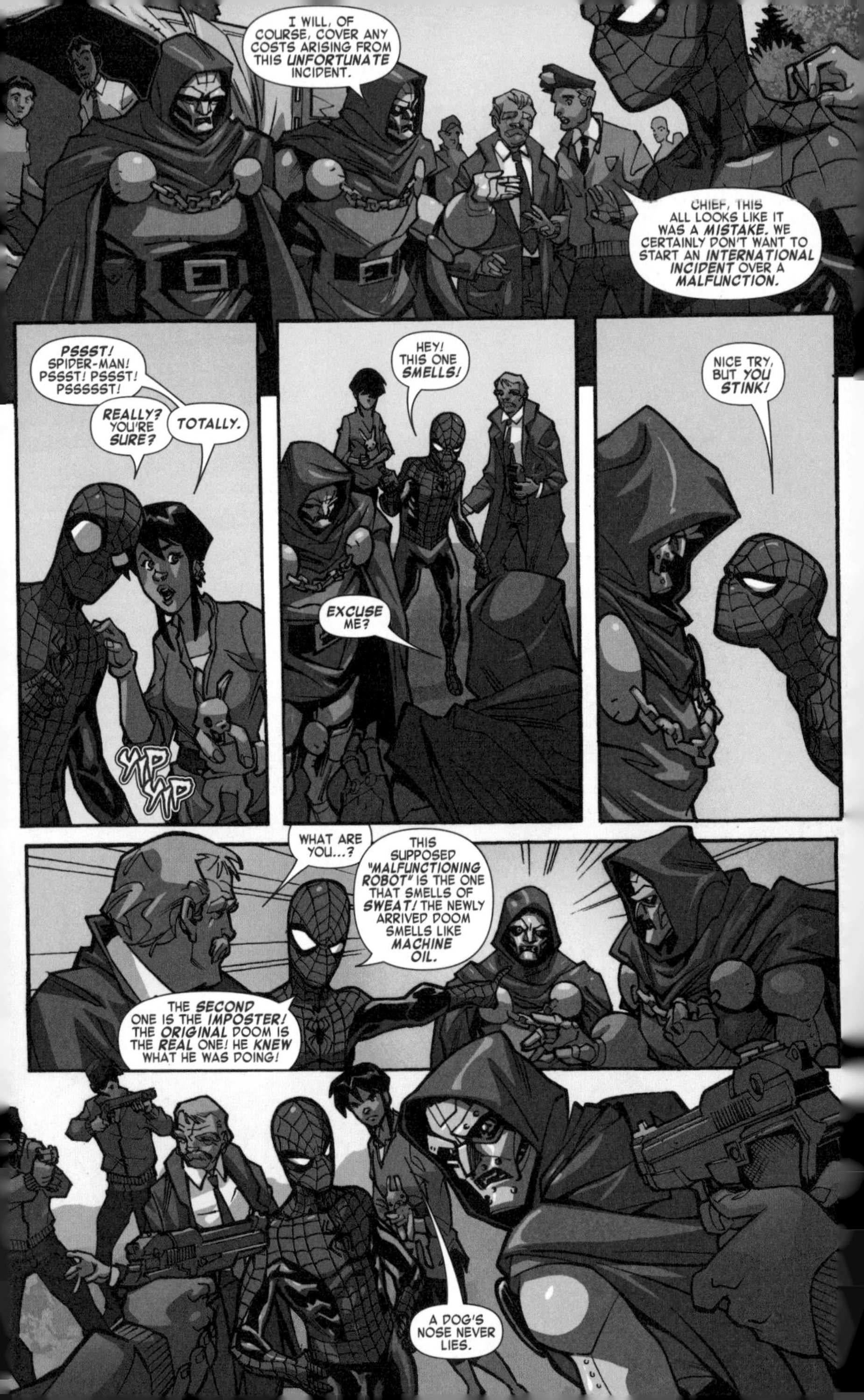
I WILL, OF COURSE, COVER ANY COSTS ARISING FROM THIS UNFORTUNATE INCIDENT.
CHIEF, THIS ALL LOOKS LIKE IT WAS A MISTAKE. WE CERTAINLY DON'T WANT TO START AN INTERNATIONAL INCIDENT OVER A MALFUNCTION.
PSSST! SPIDER-MAN! PSSST! PSSST! PSSSSST!
REALLY? YOU'RE SURE?
TOTALLY.
YIP YIP
HEY! THIS ONE SMELLS!
EXCUSE ME?
NICE TRY, BUT YOU STINK!
WHAT ARE YOU...?
THIS SUPPOSED "MALFUNCTIONING ROBOT" IS THE ONE THAT SMELLS OF SWEAT! THE NEWLY ARRIVED DOOM SMELLS LIKE MACHINE OIL.
THE SECOND ONE IS THE IMPOSTER! THE ORIGINAL DOOM IS THE REAL ONE! HE KNEW WHAT HE WAS DOING!
A DOG'S NOSE NEVER LIES.

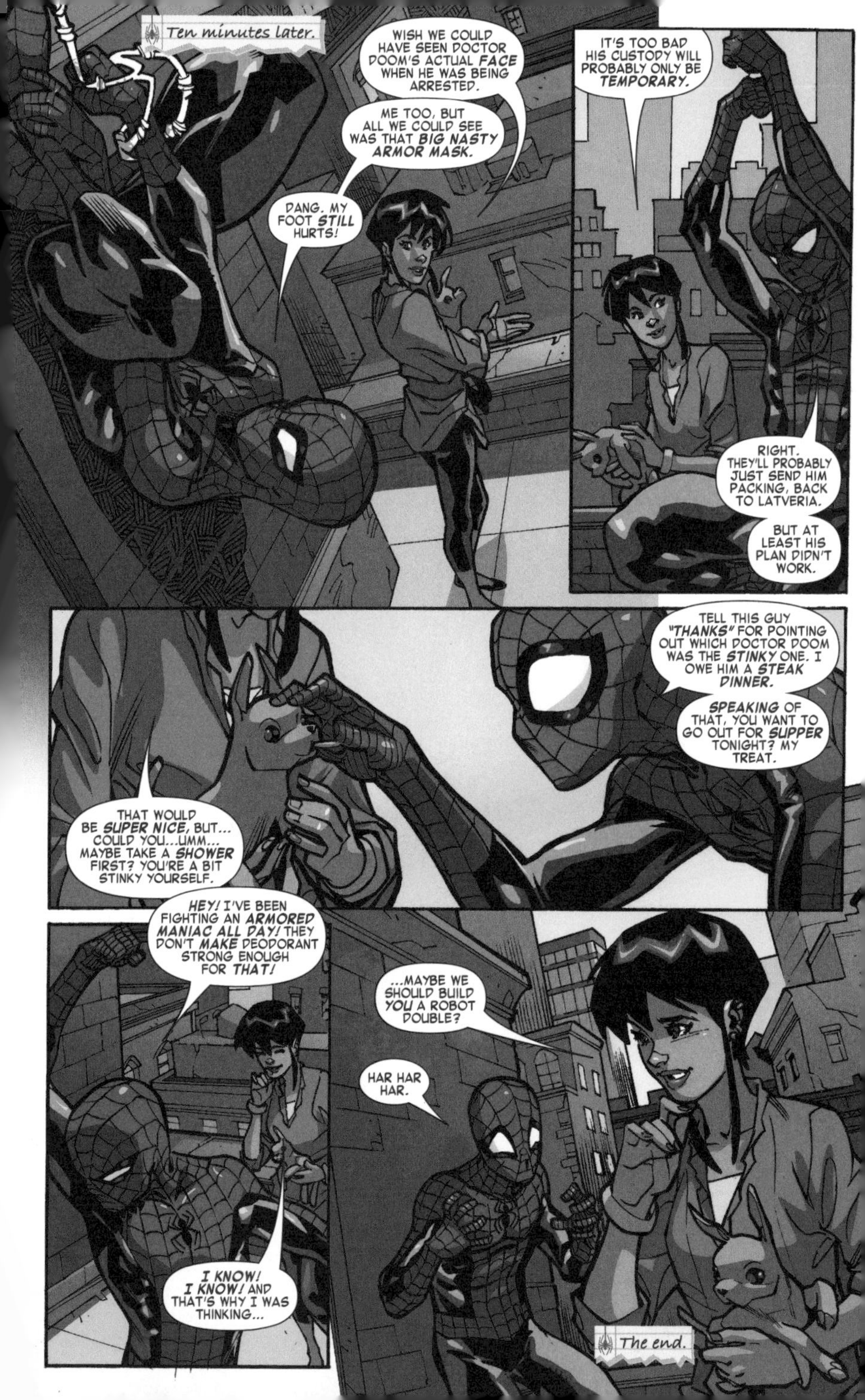
Ten minutes later.
WISH WE COULD HAVE SEEN DOCTOR DOOM'S ACTUAL FACE WHEN HE WAS BEING ARRESTED.
ME TOO, BUT ALL WE COULD SEE WAS THAT BIG NASTY ARMOR MASK.
DANG. MY FOOT STILL HURTS!
IT'S TOO BAD HIS CUSTODY WILL PROBABLY ONLY BE TEMPORARY.
RIGHT. THEY'LL PROBABLY JUST SEND HIM PACKING, BACK TO LATVERIA.
BUT AT LEAST HIS PLAN DIDN'T WORK.
TELL THIS GUY "THANKS" FOR POINTING OUT WHICH DOCTOR DOOM WAS THE STINKY ONE. I OWE HIM A STEAK DINNER.
SPEAKING OF THAT, YOU WANT TO GO OUT FOR SUPPER TONIGHT? MY TREAT.
THAT WOULD BE SUPER NICE, BUT... COULD YOU...UMM... MAYBE TAKE A SHOWER FIRST? YOU'RE A BIT STINKY YOURSELF.
HEY! I'VE BEEN FIGHTING AN ARMORED MANIAC ALL DAY! THEY DON'T MAKE DEODORANT STRONG ENOUGH FOR THAT!
I KNOW! I KNOW! AND THAT'S WHY I WAS THINKING...
...MAYBE WE SHOULD BUILD YOU A ROBOT DOUBLE?
HAR HAR HAR.
The end.

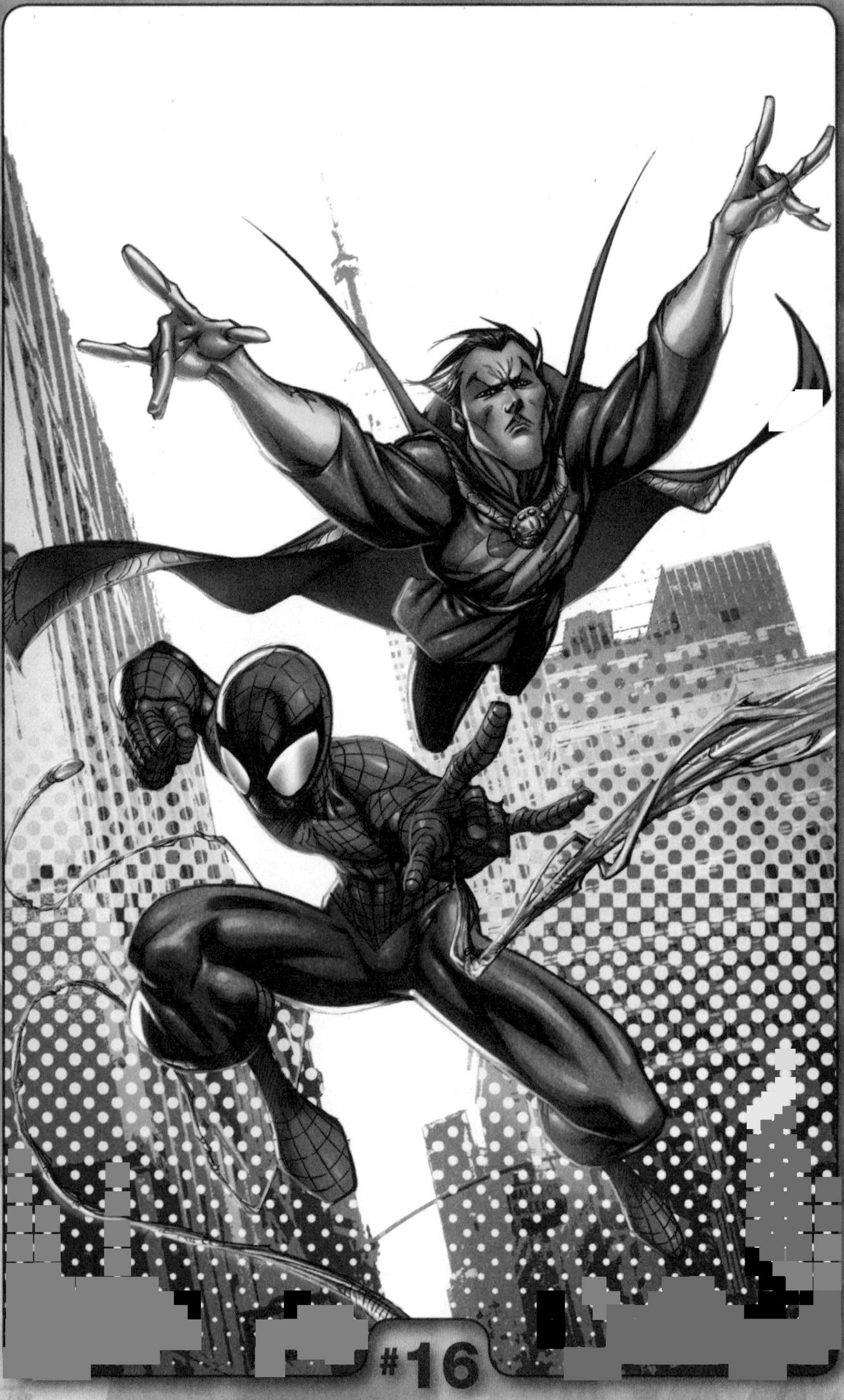
#16

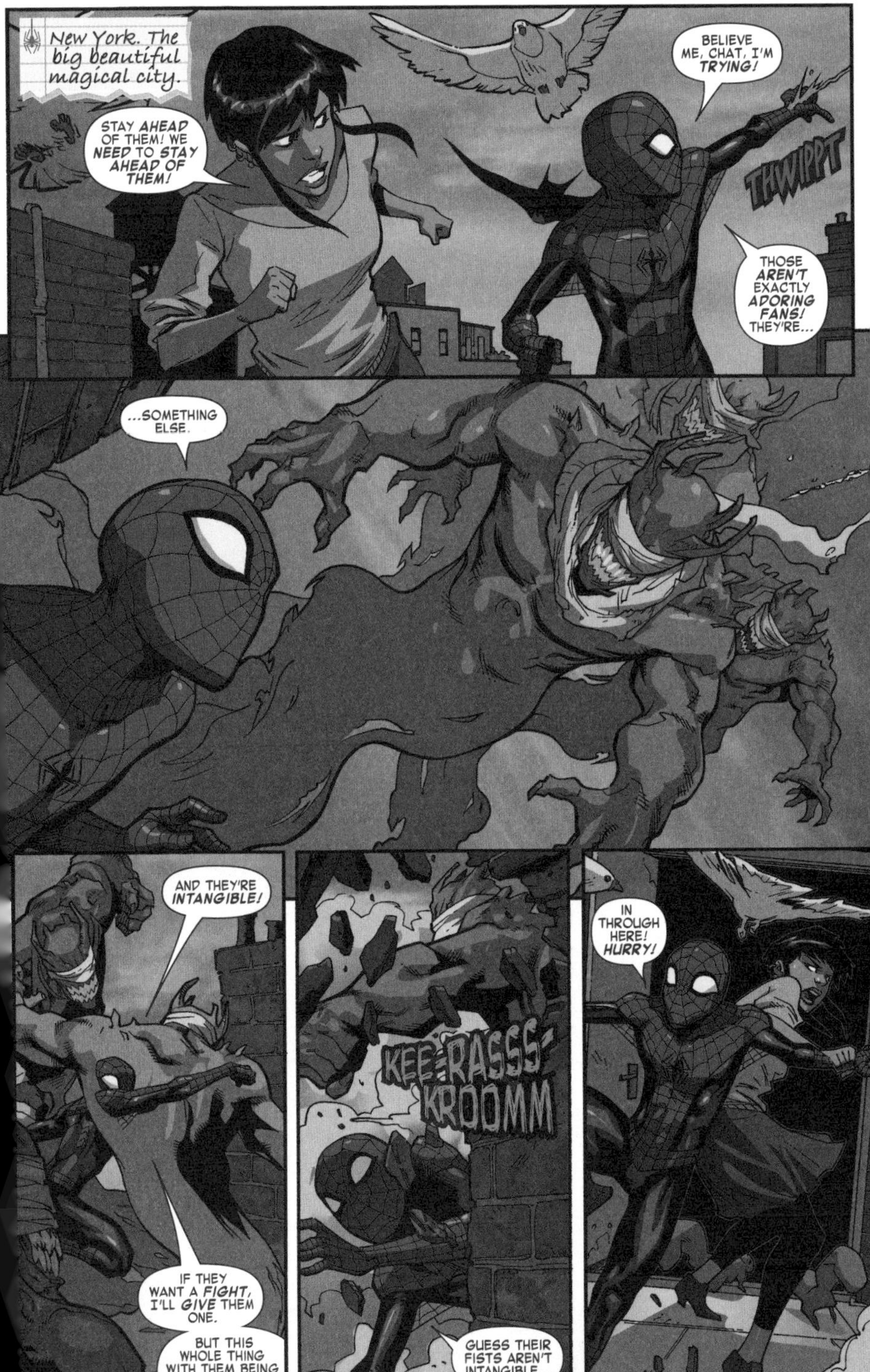
New York. The big beautiful magical city.
STAY AHEAD OF THEM! WE NEED TO STAY AHEAD OF THEM!
BELIEVE ME, CHAT, I'M TRYING!
THWIPPT
THOSE AREN'T EXACTLY ADORING FANS! THEY'RE...
...SOMETHING ELSE.
AND THEY'RE INTANGIBLE!
IF THEY WANT A FIGHT, I'LL GIVE THEM ONE.
BUT THIS WHOLE THING WITH THEM BEING INTANGIBLE...
KEE-RASSS KROOMM
GUESS THEIR FISTS AREN'T INTANGIBLE...
IN THROUGH HERE! HURRY!

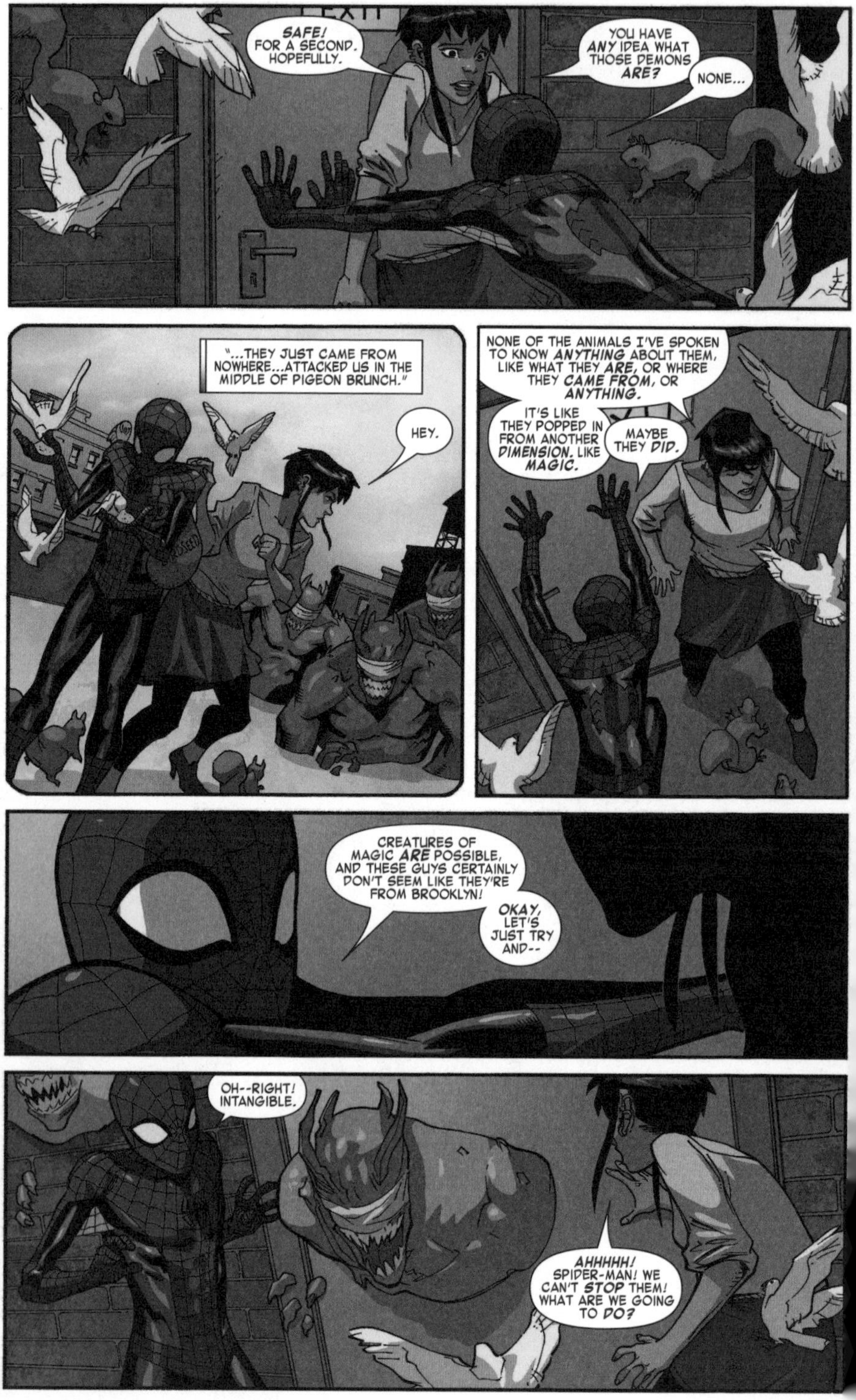
SAFE! FOR A SECOND. HOPEFULLY.
YOU HAVE ANY IDEA WHAT THOSE DEMONS ARE?
NONE...
"...THEY JUST CAME FROM NOWHERE...ATTACKED US IN THE MIDDLE OF PIGEON BRUNCH."
HEY.
NONE OF THE ANIMALS I'VE SPOKEN TO KNOW ANYTHING ABOUT THEM, LIKE WHAT THEY ARE, OR WHERE THEY CAME FROM, OR ANYTHING.
IT'S LIKE THEY POPPED IN FROM ANOTHER DIMENSION. LIKE MAGIC.
MAYBE THEY DID.
CREATURES OF MAGIC ARE POSSIBLE, AND THESE GUYS CERTAINLY DON'T SEEM LIKE THEY'RE FROM BROOKLYN!
OKAY, LET'S JUST TRY AND--
OH--RIGHT! INTANGIBLE.
AHHHHH! SPIDER-MAN! WE CAN'T STOP THEM! WHAT ARE WE GOING TO DO?

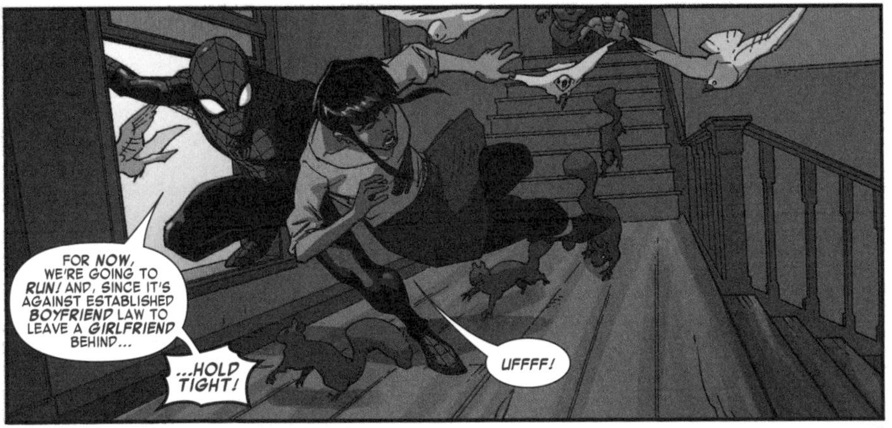
FOR NOW, WE'RE GOING TO RUN! AND, SINCE IT'S AGAINST ESTABLISHED BOYFRIEND LAW TO LEAVE A GIRLFRIEND BEHIND...
...HOLD TIGHT!
UFFFF!

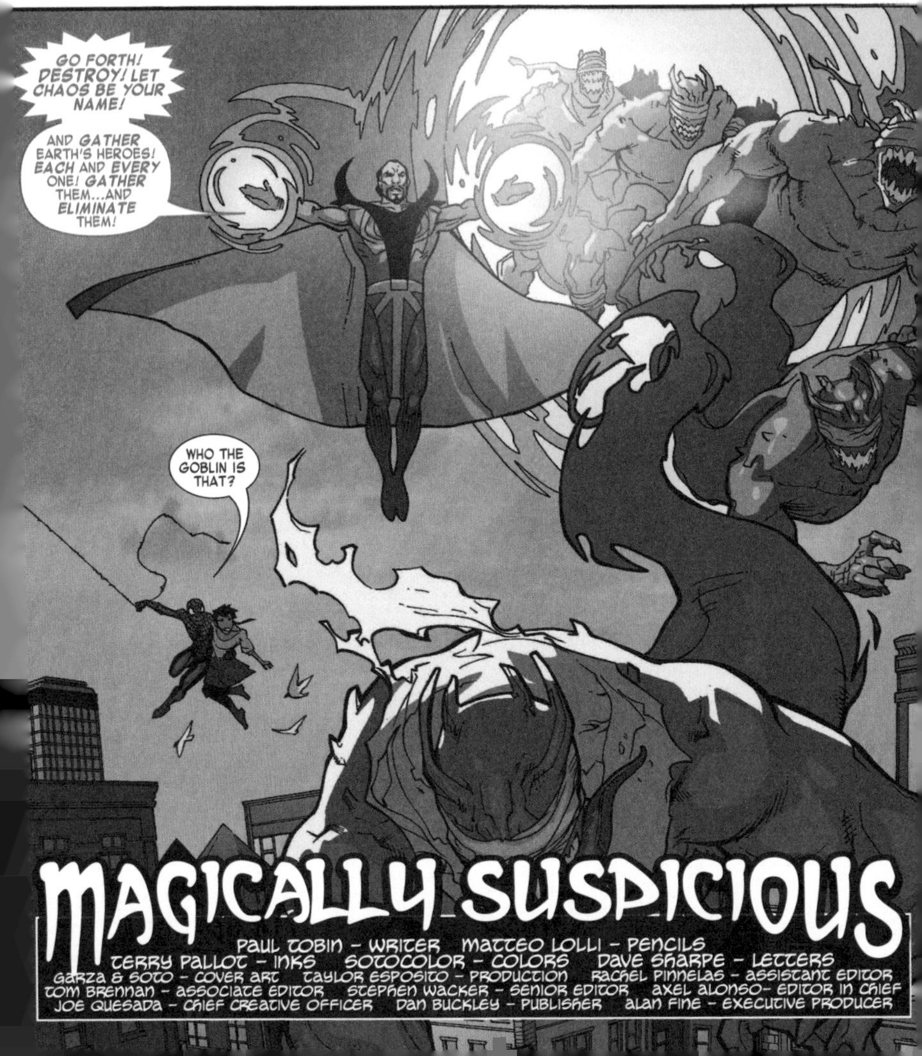
GO FORTH! DESTROY! LET CHAOS BE YOUR NAME!
AND GATHER EARTH'S HEROES! EACH AND EVERY ONE! GATHER THEM...AND ELIMINATE THEM!
WHO THE GOBLIN IS THAT?
MAGICALLY SUSPICIOUS
PAUL TOBIN - WRITER MATTEO LOLLI - PENCILS
TERRY PALLOT - INKS SOTOCOLOR - COLORS DAVE SHARPE - LETTERS
GARZA & SOTO - COVER ART TAYLOR ESPOSITO - PRODUCTION RACHEL PINNELAS - ASSISTANT EDITOR
TOM BRENNAN - ASSOCIATE EDITOR STEPHEN WACKER - SENIOR EDITOR AXEL ALONSO- EDITOR IN CHIEF
JOE QUESADA - CHIEF CREATIVE OFFICER DAN BUCKLEY - PUBLISHER ALAN FINE - EXECUTIVE PRODUCER

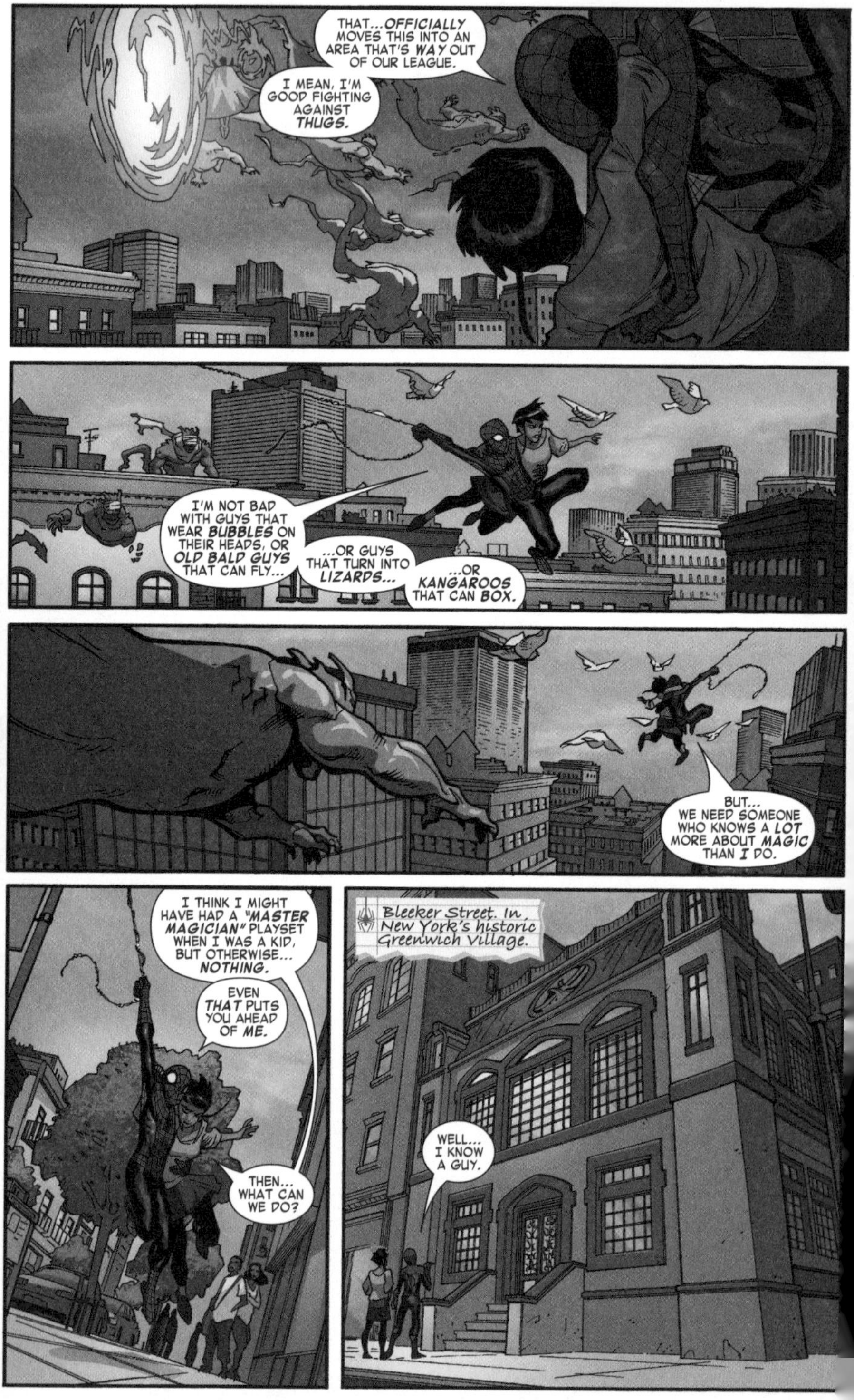

THAT...OFFICIALLY MOVES THIS INTO AN AREA THAT'S WAY OUT OF OUR LEAGUE.
I MEAN, I'M GOOD FIGHTING AGAINST THUGS.
I'M NOT BAD WITH GUYS THAT WEAR BUBBLES ON THEIR HEADS, OR OLD BALD GUYS THAT CAN FLY...
...OR GUYS THAT TURN INTO LIZARDS...
...OR KANGAROOS THAT CAN BOX.
BUT... WE NEED SOMEONE WHO KNOWS A LOT MORE ABOUT MAGIC THAN I DO.
I THINK I MIGHT HAVE HAD A "MASTER MAGICIAN" PLAYSET WHEN I WAS A KID, BUT OTHERWISE... NOTHING.
EVEN THAT PUTS YOU AHEAD OF ME.
THEN... WHAT CAN WE DO?
Bleeker Street. In New York's historic Greenwich Village.
WELL... I KNOW A GUY.

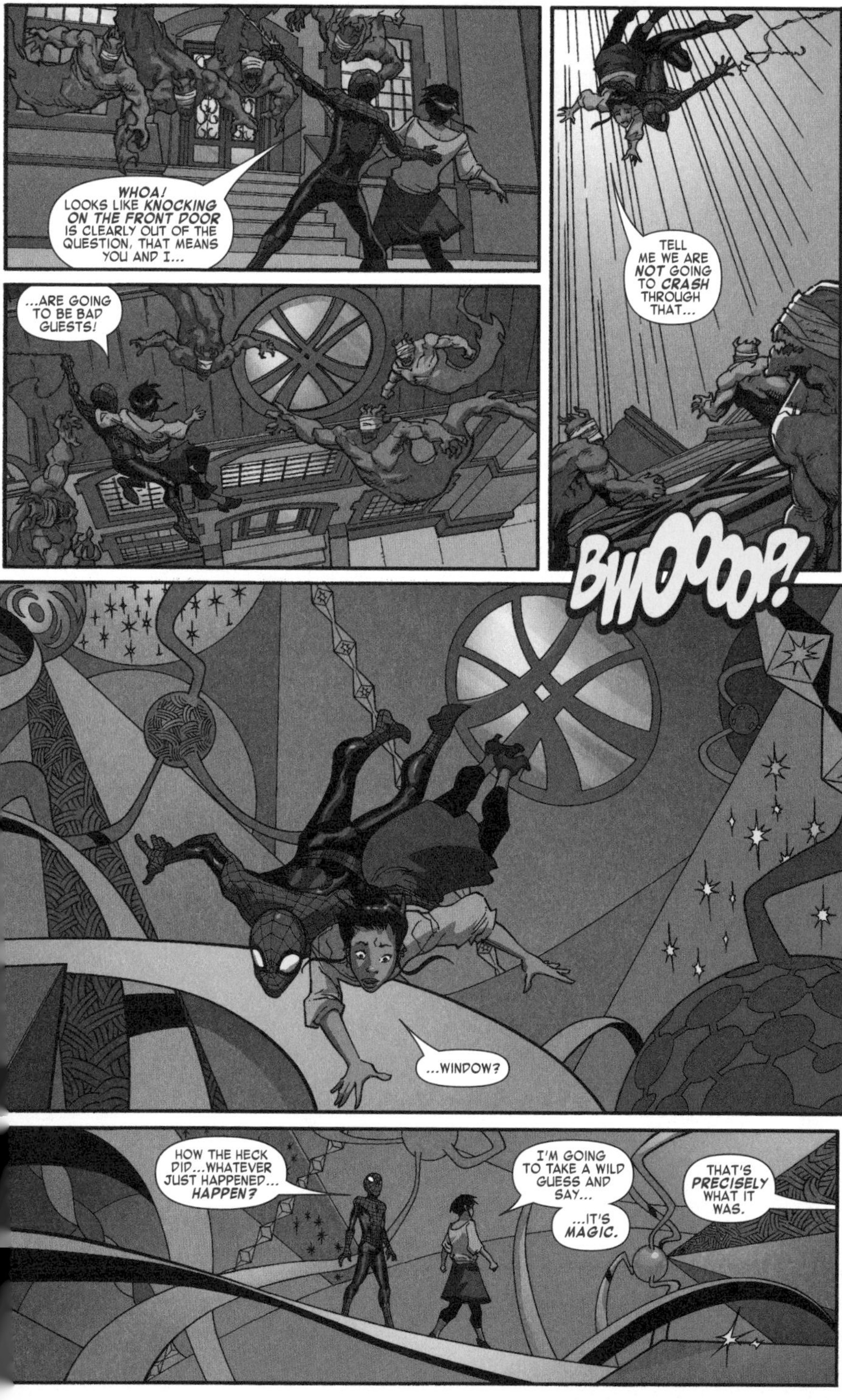
WHOA! LOOKS LIKE KNOCKING ON THE FRONT DOOR IS CLEARLY OUT OF THE QUESTION, THAT MEANS YOU AND I...
...ARE GOING TO BE BAD GUESTS!
TELL ME WE ARE NOT GOING TO CRASH THROUGH THAT...
BWOOOOP!
...WINDOW?
HOW THE HECK DID...WHATEVER JUST HAPPENED... HAPPEN?
I'M GOING TO TAKE A WILD GUESS AND SAY...
...IT'S MAGIC.
THAT'S PRECISELY WHAT IT WAS.

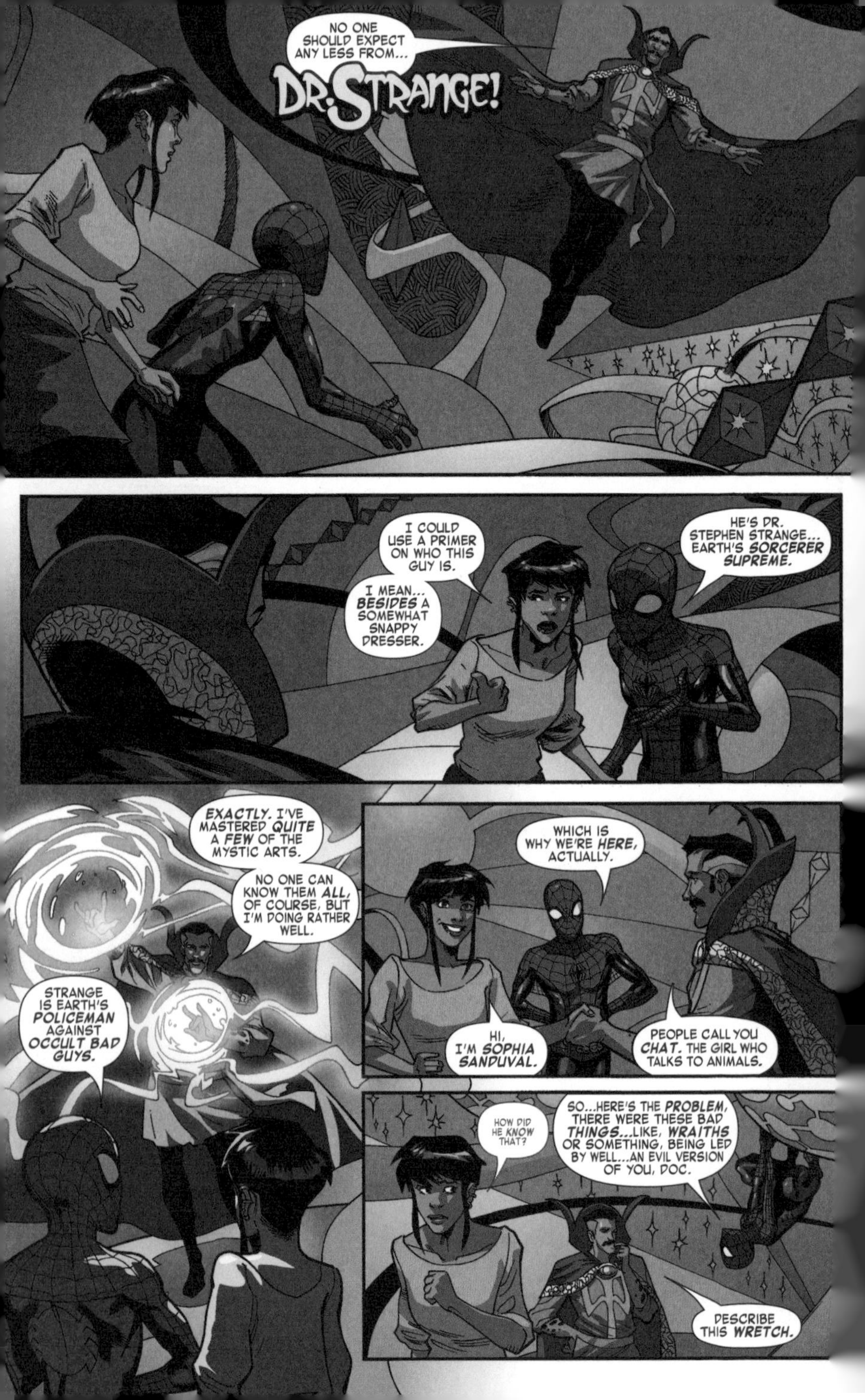
NO ONE SHOULD EXPECT ANY LESS FROM...
DR. STRANGE!
I COULD USE A PRIMER ON WHO THIS GUY IS.
I MEAN... BESIDES A SOMEWHAT SNAPPY DRESSER.
HE'S DR. STEPHEN STRANGE... EARTH'S SORCERER SUPREME.
STRANGE IS EARTH'S POLICEMAN AGAINST OCCULT BAD GUYS.
EXACTLY. I'VE MASTERED QUITE A FEW OF THE MYSTIC ARTS.
NO ONE CAN KNOW THEM ALL, OF COURSE, BUT I'M DOING RATHER WELL.
WHICH IS WHY WE'RE HERE, ACTUALLY.
HI, I'M SOPHIA SANDUVAL.
PEOPLE CALL YOU CHAT. THE GIRL WHO TALKS TO ANIMALS.
HOW DID HE KNOW THAT?
SO...HERE'S THE PROBLEM, THERE WERE THESE BAD THINGS...LIKE, WRAITHS OR SOMETHING, BEING LED BY WELL...AN EVIL VERSION OF YOU, DOC.
DESCRIBE THIS WRETCH.

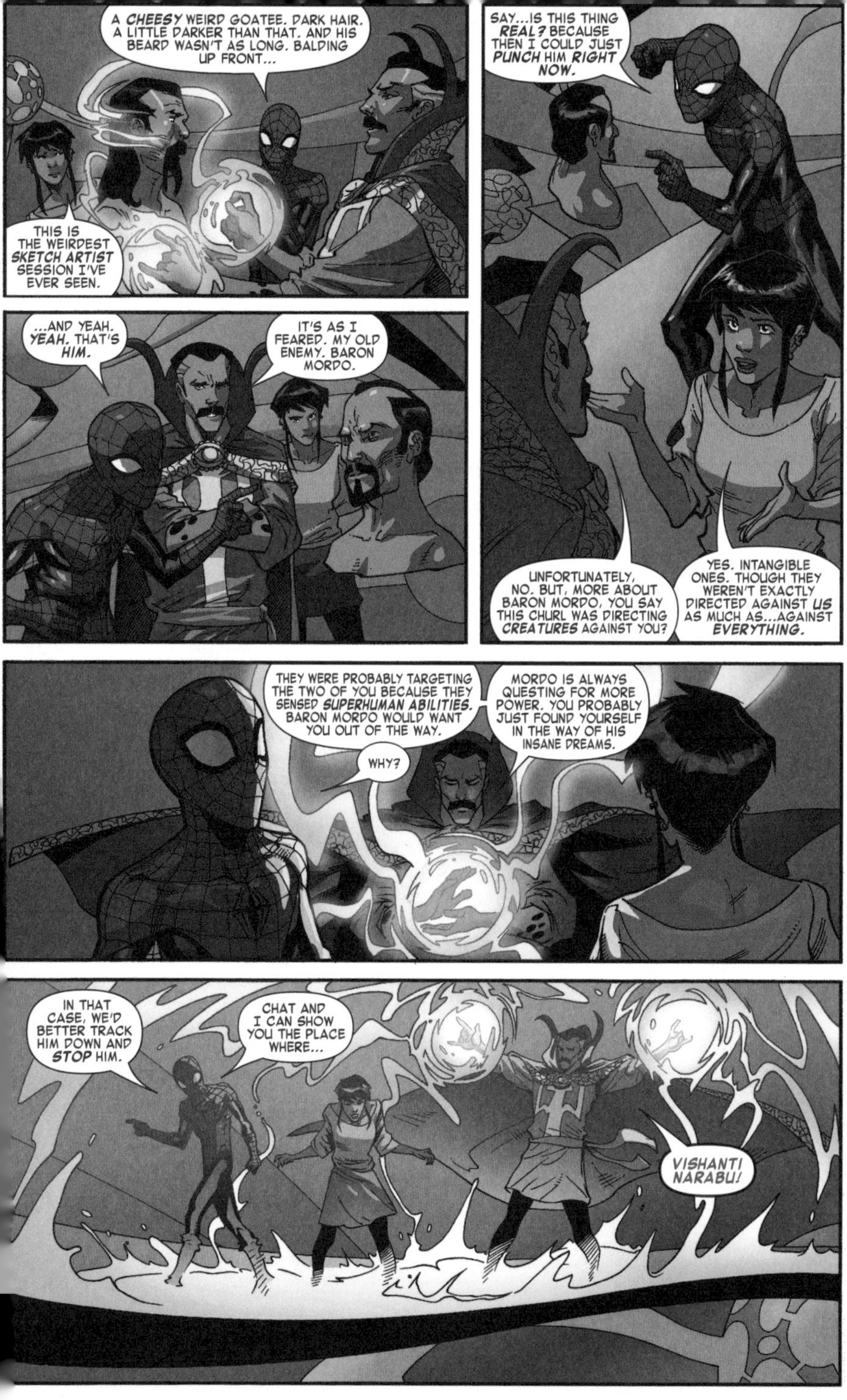
A CHEESY WEIRD GOATEE. DARK HAIR. A LITTLE DARKER THAN THAT. AND HIS BEARD WASN'T AS LONG. BALDING UP FRONT...
THIS IS THE WEIRDEST SKETCH ARTIST SESSION I'VE EVER SEEN.
...AND YEAH. YEAH. THAT'S HIM.
IT'S AS I FEARED. MY OLD ENEMY. BARON MORDO.
SAY...IS THIS THING REAL? BECAUSE THEN I COULD JUST PUNCH HIM RIGHT NOW.
UNFORTUNATELY, NO. BUT, MORE ABOUT BARON MORDO, YOU SAY THIS CHURL WAS DIRECTING CREATURES AGAINST YOU?
YES. INTANGIBLE ONES. THOUGH THEY WEREN'T EXACTLY DIRECTED AGAINST US AS MUCH AS...AGAINST EVERYTHING.
THEY WERE PROBABLY TARGETING THE TWO OF YOU BECAUSE THEY SENSED SUPERHUMAN ABILITIES. BARON MORDO WOULD WANT YOU OUT OF THE WAY.
WHY?
MORDO IS ALWAYS QUESTING FOR MORE POWER. YOU PROBABLY JUST FOUND YOURSELF IN THE WAY OF HIS INSANE DREAMS.
IN THAT CASE, WE'D BETTER TRACK HIM DOWN AND STOP HIM.
CHAT AND I CAN SHOW YOU THE PLACE WHERE...
VISHANTI NARABU!

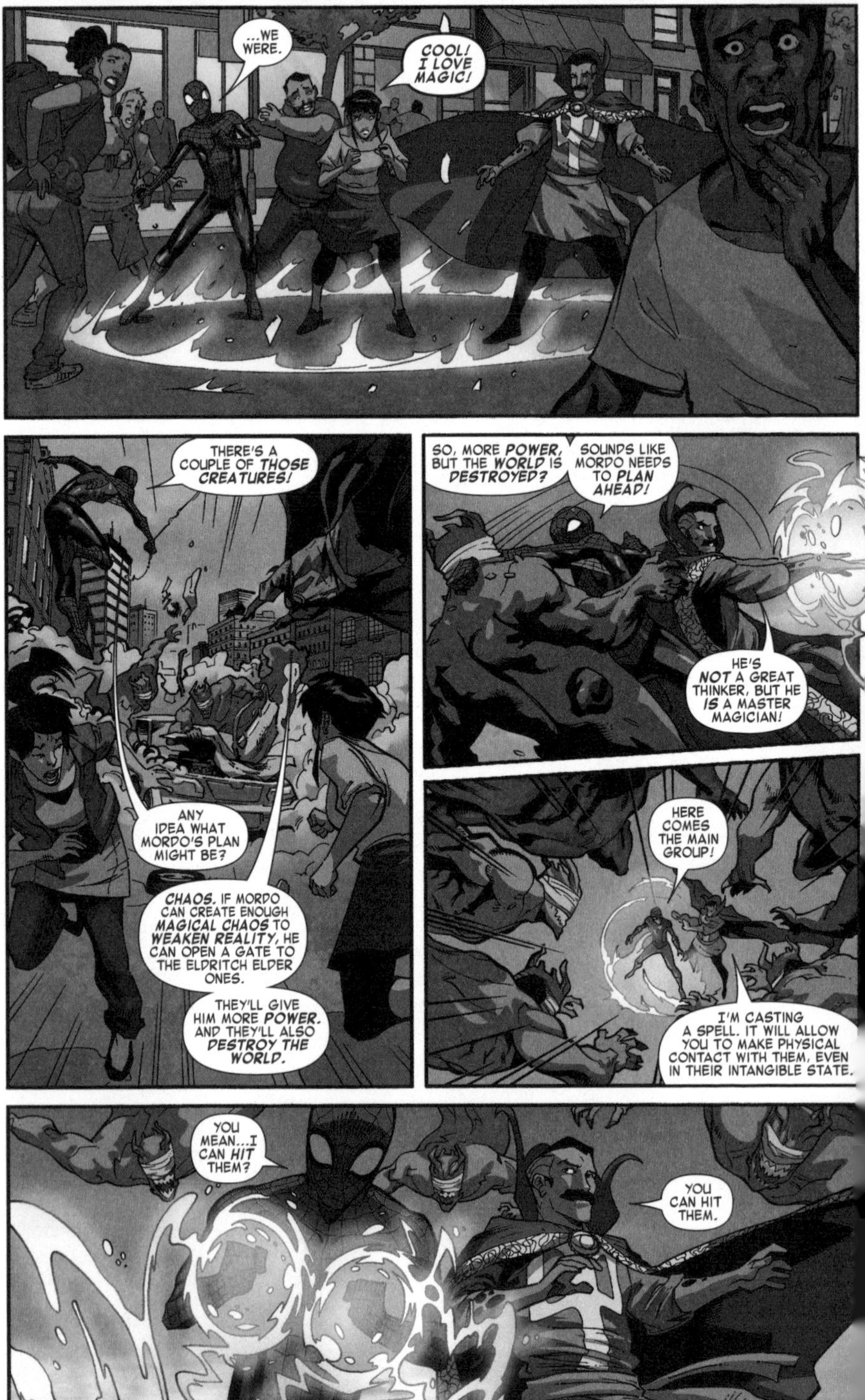
...WE WERE.
COOL! I LOVE MAGIC!
THERE'S A COUPLE OF THOSE CREATURES!
ANY IDEA WHAT MORDO'S PLAN MIGHT BE?
CHAOS. IF MORDO CAN CREATE ENOUGH MAGICAL CHAOS TO WEAKEN REALITY, HE CAN OPEN A GATE TO THE ELDRITCH ELDER ONES.
THEY'LL GIVE HIM MORE POWER. AND THEY'LL ALSO DESTROY THE WORLD.
SO, MORE POWER, BUT THE WORLD IS DESTROYED?
SOUNDS LIKE MORDO NEEDS TO PLAN AHEAD!
HE'S NOT A GREAT THINKER, BUT HE IS A MASTER MAGICIAN!
HERE COMES THE MAIN GROUP!
I'M CASTING A SPELL. IT WILL ALLOW YOU TO MAKE PHYSICAL CONTACT WITH THEM, EVEN IN THEIR INTANGIBLE STATE.
YOU MEAN...I CAN HIT THEM?
YOU CAN HIT THEM.

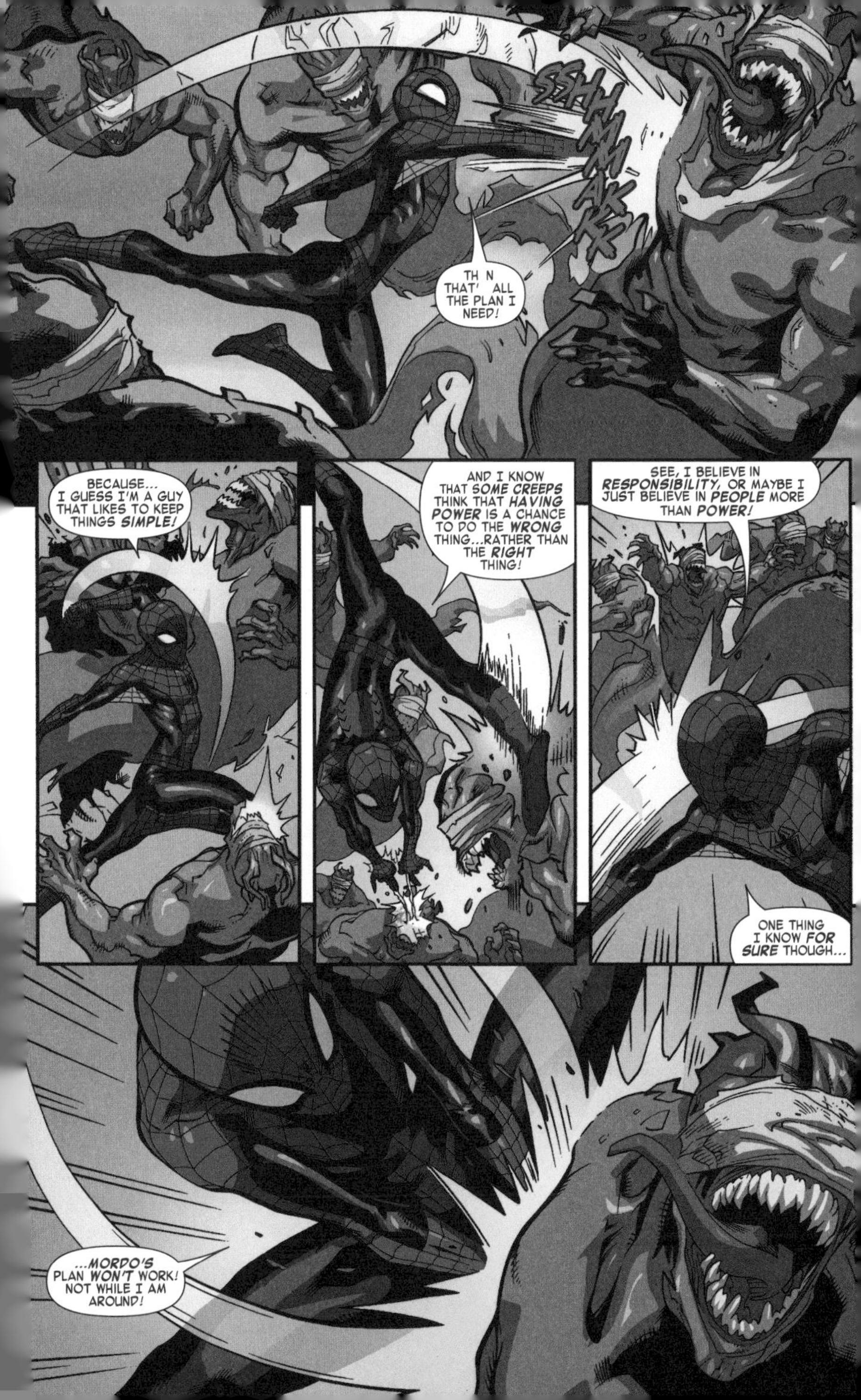
SSHHMMAKKK
TH N THAT' ALL THE PLAN I NEED!
BECAUSE... I GUESS I'M A GUY THAT LIKES TO KEEP THINGS **SIMPLE!**
AND I KNOW THAT **SOME CREEPS** THINK THAT **HAVING POWER** IS A CHANCE TO DO THE **WRONG** THING...RATHER THAN THE **RIGHT** THING!
SEE, I BELIEVE IN **RESPONSIBILITY**, OR MAYBE I JUST BELIEVE IN **PEOPLE** MORE THAN **POWER!**
ONE THING I KNOW **FOR SURE** THOUGH...
...**MORDO'S** PLAN **WON'T** WORK! NOT WHILE I AM AROUND!

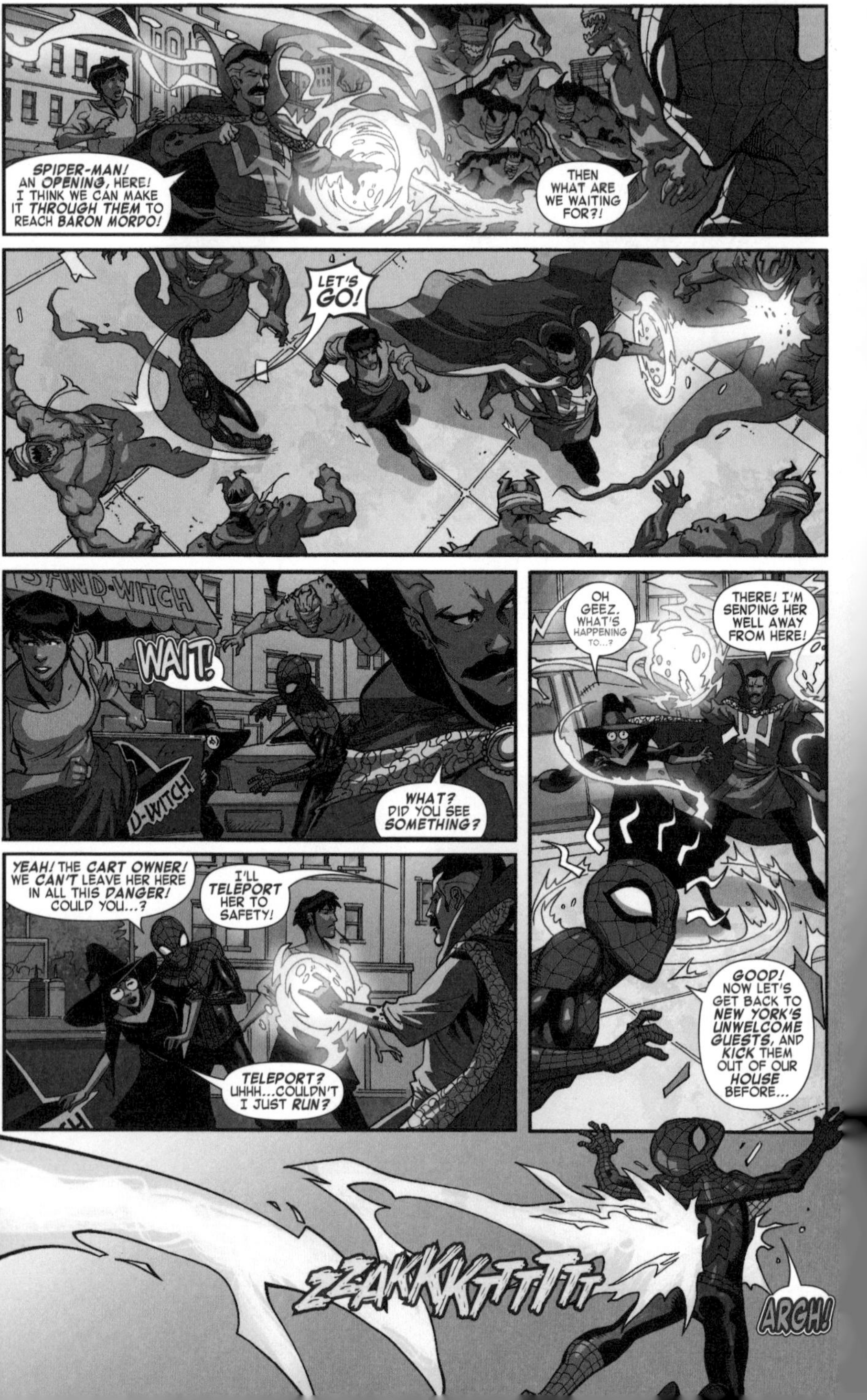
SPIDER-MAN! AN OPENING, HERE! I THINK WE CAN MAKE IT THROUGH THEM TO REACH BARON MORDO!
THEN WHAT ARE WE WAITING FOR?!
LET'S GO!
SAND-WITCH
WAIT!
WHAT? DID YOU SEE SOMETHING?
D-WITCH
YEAH! THE CART OWNER! WE CAN'T LEAVE HER HERE IN ALL THIS DANGER! COULD YOU...?
I'LL TELEPORT HER TO SAFETY!
TELEPORT? UHHH...COULDN'T I JUST RUN?
OH GEEZ. WHAT'S HAPPENING TO...?
THERE! I'M SENDING HER WELL AWAY FROM HERE!
GOOD! NOW LET'S GET BACK TO NEW YORK'S UNWELCOME GUESTS, AND KICK THEM OUT OF OUR HOUSE BEFORE...
ZZAKKKKTTTTTT
ARGH!

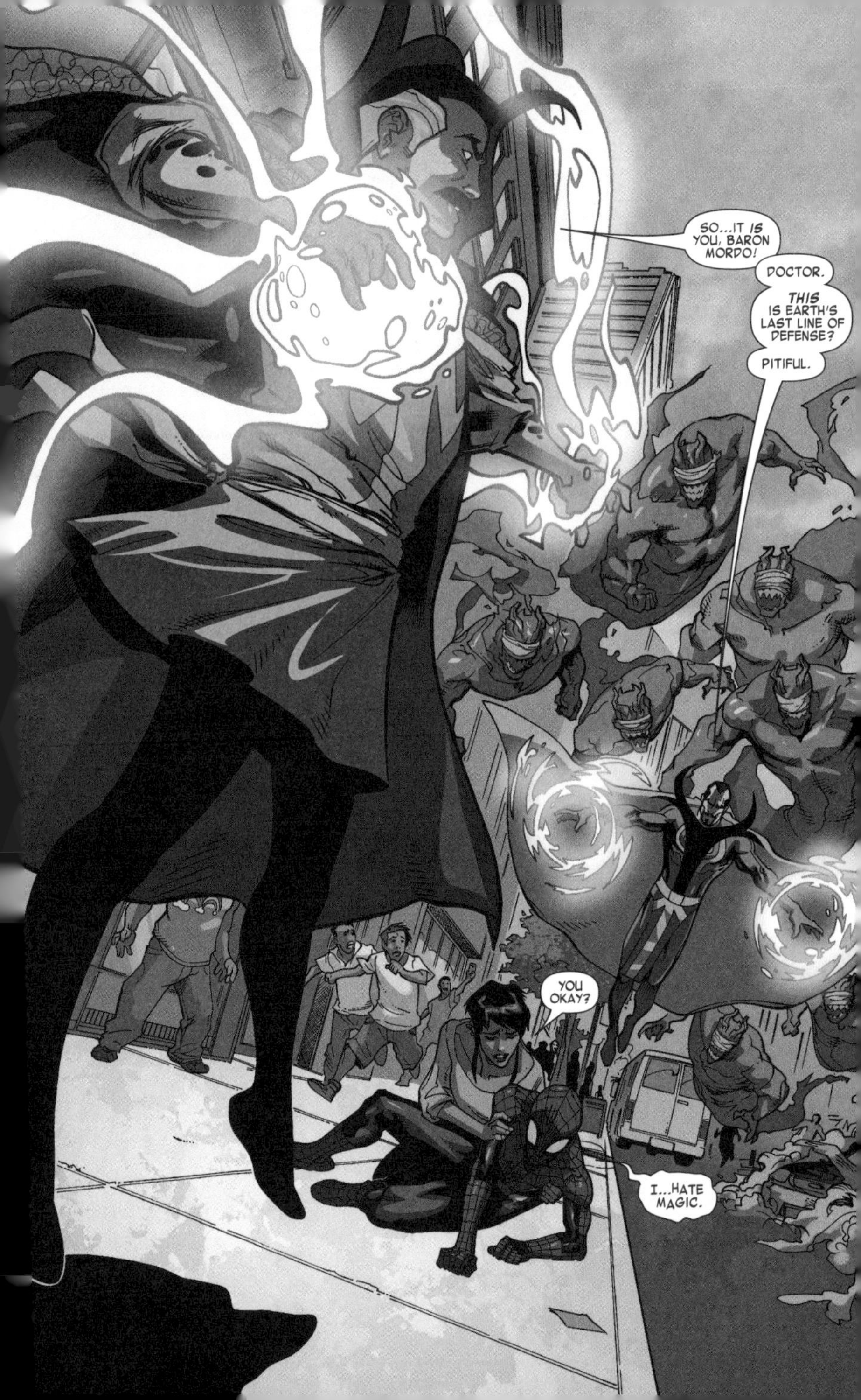
SO...IT *IS* YOU, BARON MORDO!
DOCTOR.
THIS IS EARTH'S LAST LINE OF DEFENSE?
PITIFUL.
YOU OKAY?
I...HATE MAGIC.

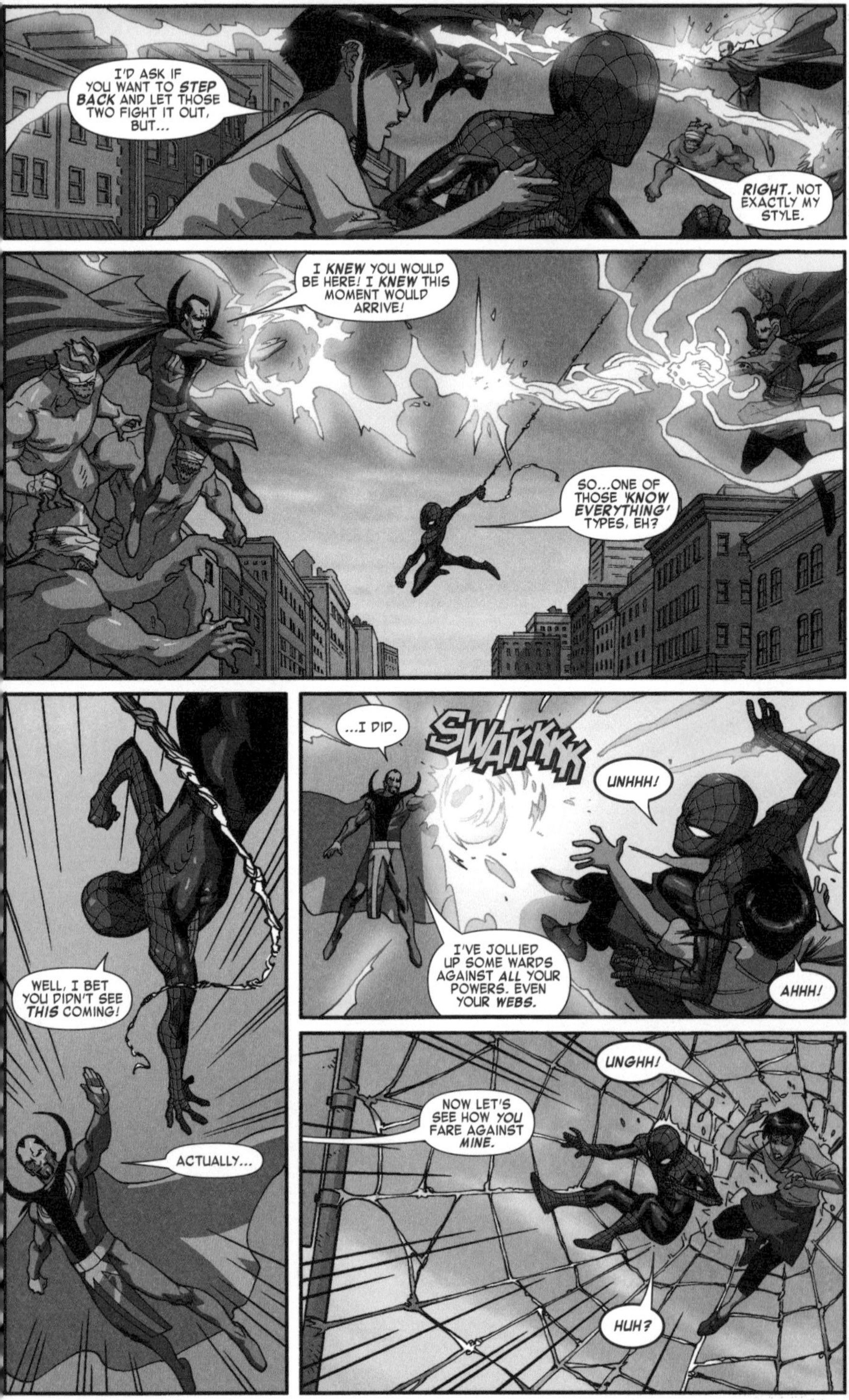
I'D ASK IF YOU WANT TO STEP BACK AND LET THOSE TWO FIGHT IT OUT, BUT...
RIGHT. NOT EXACTLY MY STYLE.
I KNEW YOU WOULD BE HERE! I KNEW THIS MOMENT WOULD ARRIVE!
SO...ONE OF THOSE 'KNOW EVERYTHING' TYPES, EH?
WELL, I BET YOU DIDN'T SEE THIS COMING!
ACTUALLY...
...I DID.
SWAKKKK
UNHHH!
I'VE JOLLIED UP SOME WARDS AGAINST ALL YOUR POWERS. EVEN YOUR WEBS.
AHHH!
UNGHH!
NOW LET'S SEE HOW YOU FARE AGAINST MINE.
HUH?

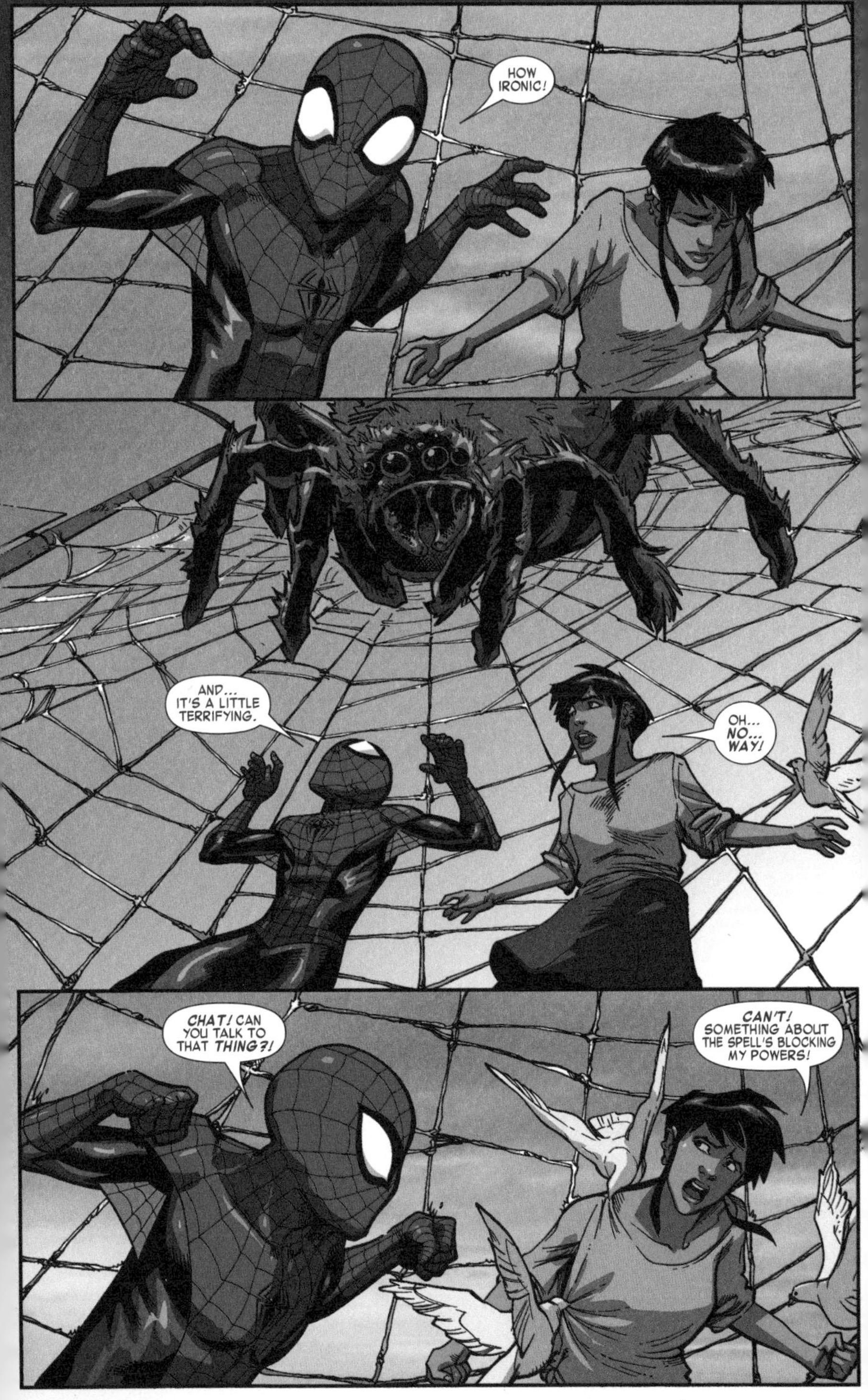
HOW IRONIC!
AND... IT'S A LITTLE TERRIFYING.
OH... NO... WAY!
CHAT! CAN YOU TALK TO THAT THING?!
CAN'T! SOMETHING ABOUT THE SPELL'S BLOCKING MY POWERS!

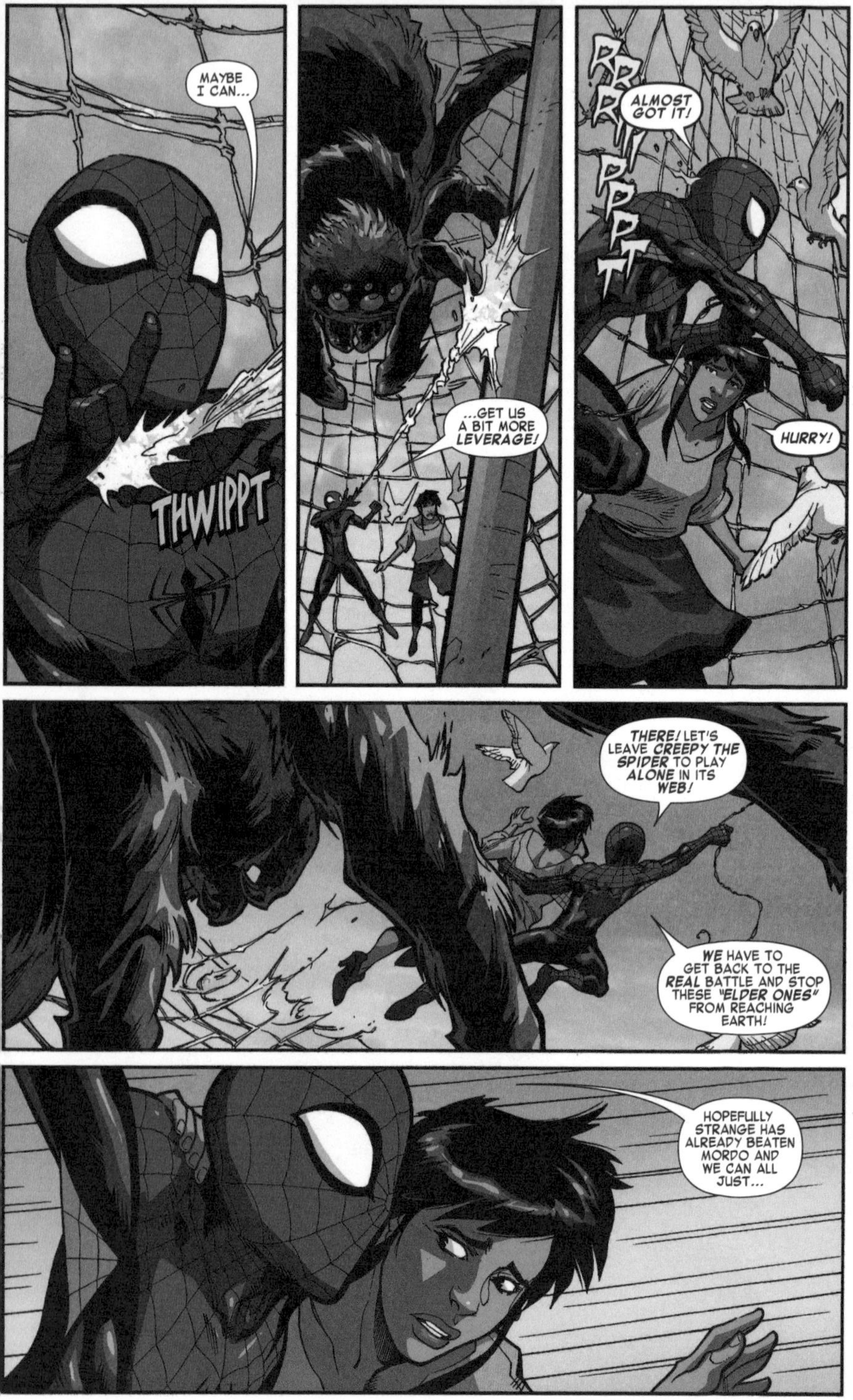
MAYBE I CAN...
THWIPPT
...GET US A BIT MORE LEVERAGE!
RRRIIPPPT
ALMOST GOT IT!
HURRY!
THERE! LET'S LEAVE CREEPY THE SPIDER TO PLAY ALONE IN ITS WEB!
WE HAVE TO GET BACK TO THE REAL BATTLE AND STOP THESE "ELDER ONES" FROM REACHING EARTH!
HOPEFULLY STRANGE HAS ALREADY BEATEN MORDO AND WE CAN ALL JUST...

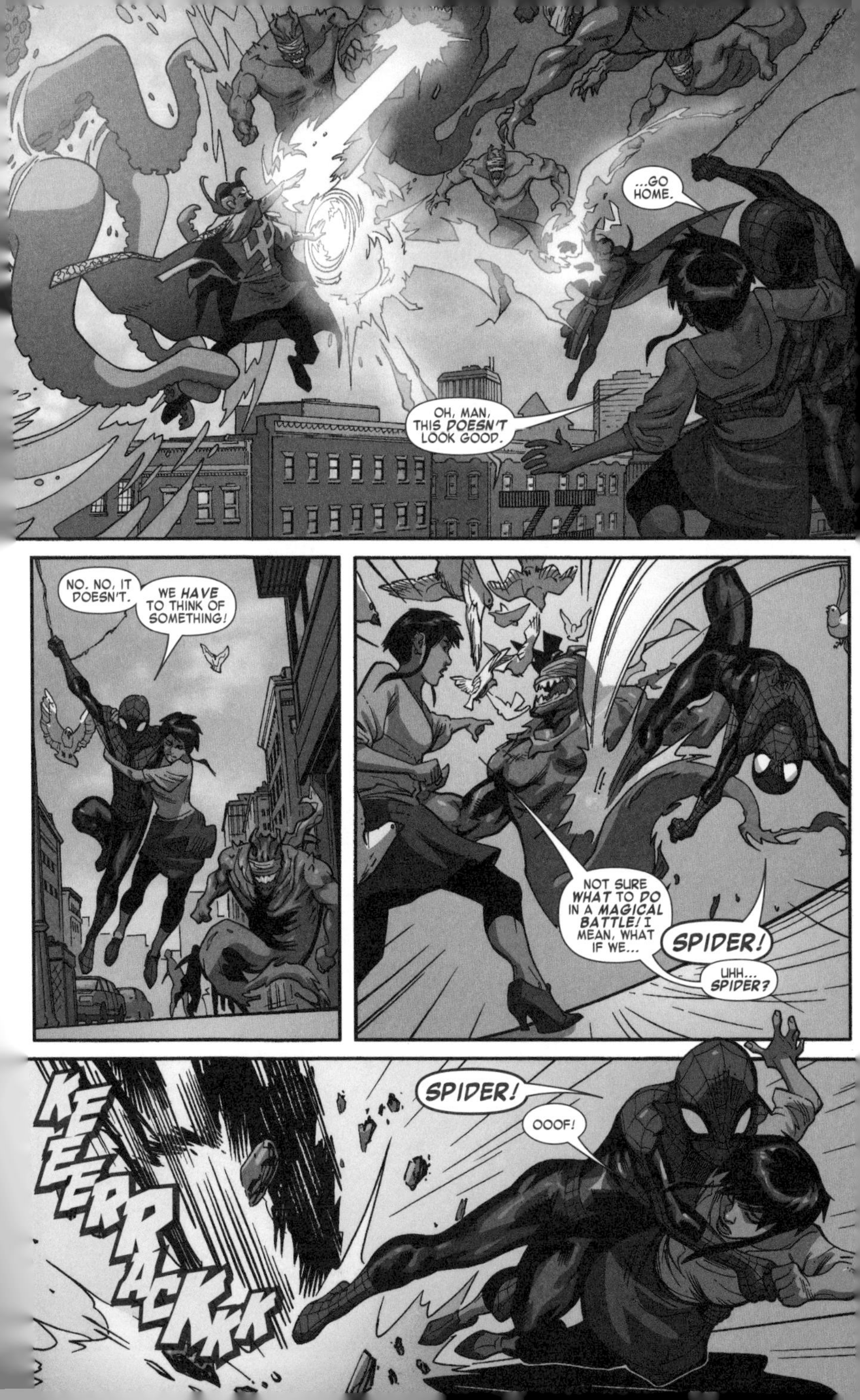
...GO HOME.
OH, MAN, THIS DOESN'T LOOK GOOD.
NO. NO, IT DOESN'T.
WE HAVE TO THINK OF SOMETHING!
NOT SURE WHAT TO DO IN A MAGICAL BATTLE! I MEAN, WHAT IF WE...
SPIDER!
UHH... SPIDER?
KEEERRACKKK
SPIDER!
OOOF!

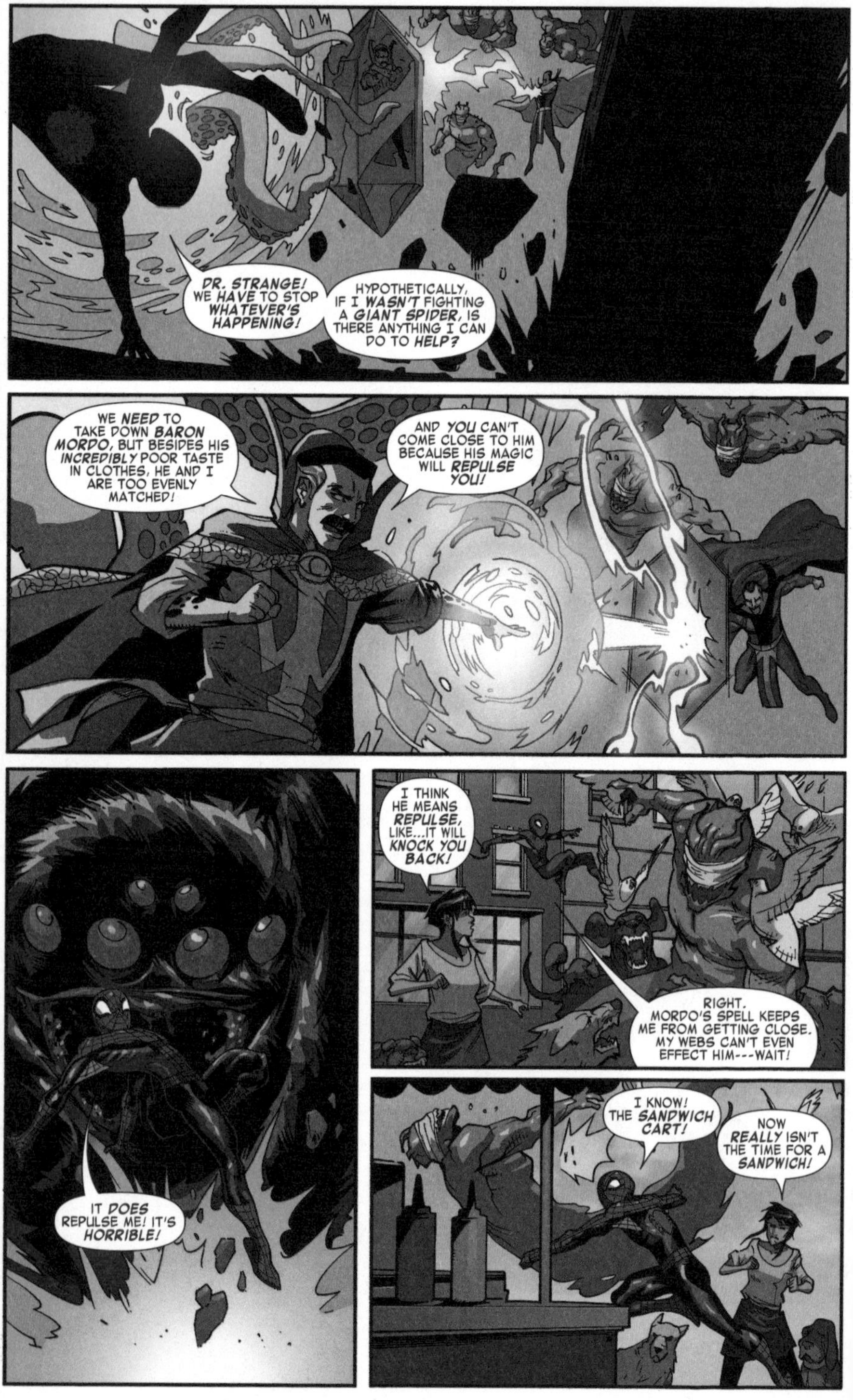

DR. STRANGE! WE HAVE TO STOP WHATEVER'S HAPPENING!
HYPOTHETICALLY, IF I WASN'T FIGHTING A GIANT SPIDER, IS THERE ANYTHING I CAN DO TO HELP?
WE NEED TO TAKE DOWN BARON MORDO, BUT BESIDES HIS INCREDIBLY POOR TASTE IN CLOTHES, HE AND I ARE TOO EVENLY MATCHED!
AND YOU CAN'T COME CLOSE TO HIM BECAUSE HIS MAGIC WILL REPULSE YOU!
IT DOES REPULSE ME! IT'S HORRIBLE!
I THINK HE MEANS REPULSE, LIKE...IT WILL KNOCK YOU BACK!
RIGHT. MORDO'S SPELL KEEPS ME FROM GETTING CLOSE. MY WEBS CAN'T EVEN EFFECT HIM---WAIT!
I KNOW! THE SANDWICH CART!
NOW REALLY ISN'T THE TIME FOR A SANDWICH!

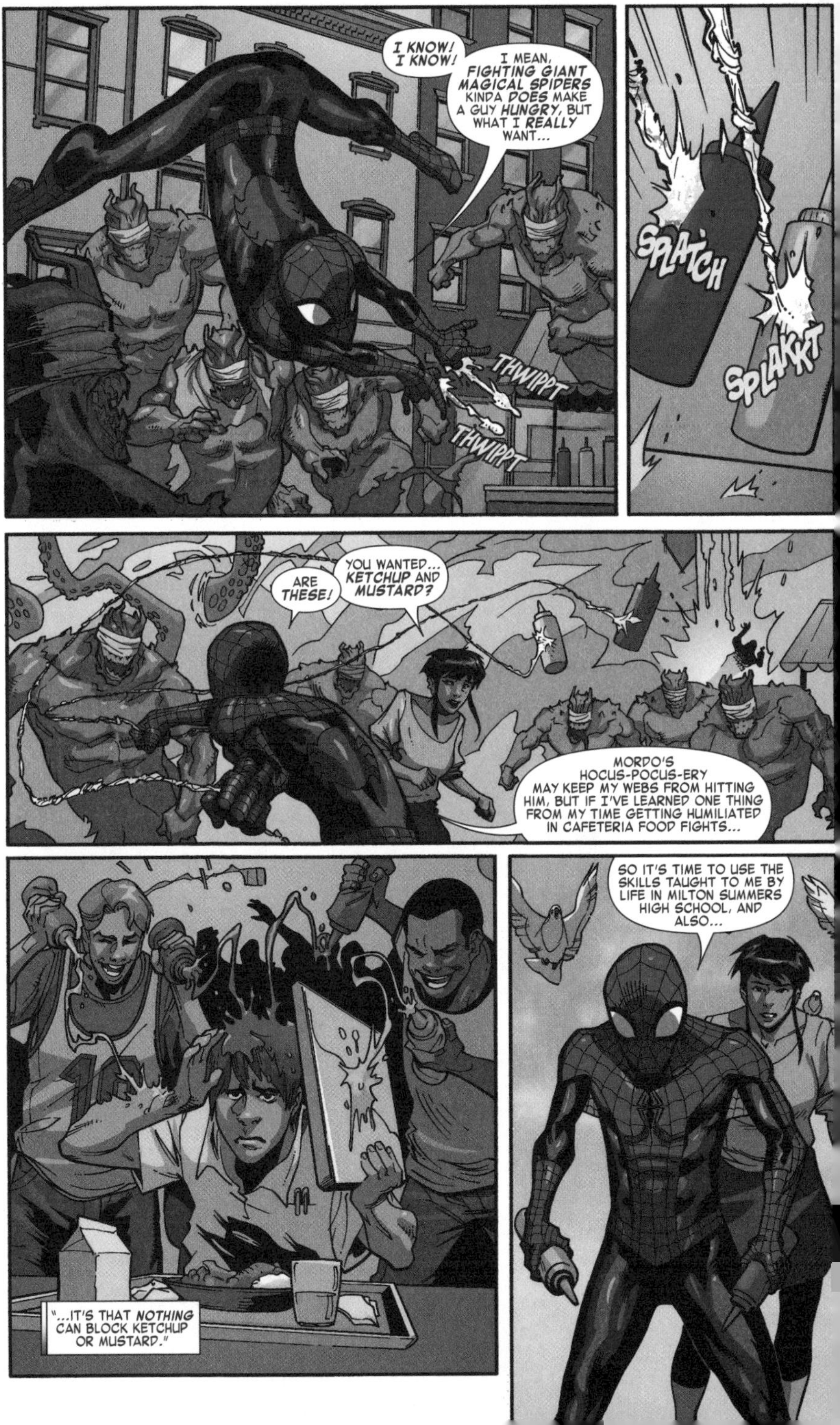
I KNOW! I KNOW!
I MEAN, FIGHTING GIANT MAGICAL SPIDERS KINDA DOES MAKE A GUY HUNGRY, BUT WHAT I REALLY WANT...
THWIPPT
THWIPPT
SPLATCH
SPLAKKT
YOU WANTED... KETCHUP AND MUSTARD?
ARE THESE!
MORDO'S HOCUS-POCUS-ERY MAY KEEP MY WEBS FROM HITTING HIM, BUT IF I'VE LEARNED ONE THING FROM MY TIME GETTING HUMILIATED IN CAFETERIA FOOD FIGHTS...
"...IT'S THAT NOTHING CAN BLOCK KETCHUP OR MUSTARD."
SO IT'S TIME TO USE THE SKILLS TAUGHT TO ME BY LIFE IN MILTON SUMMERS HIGH SCHOOL, AND ALSO...

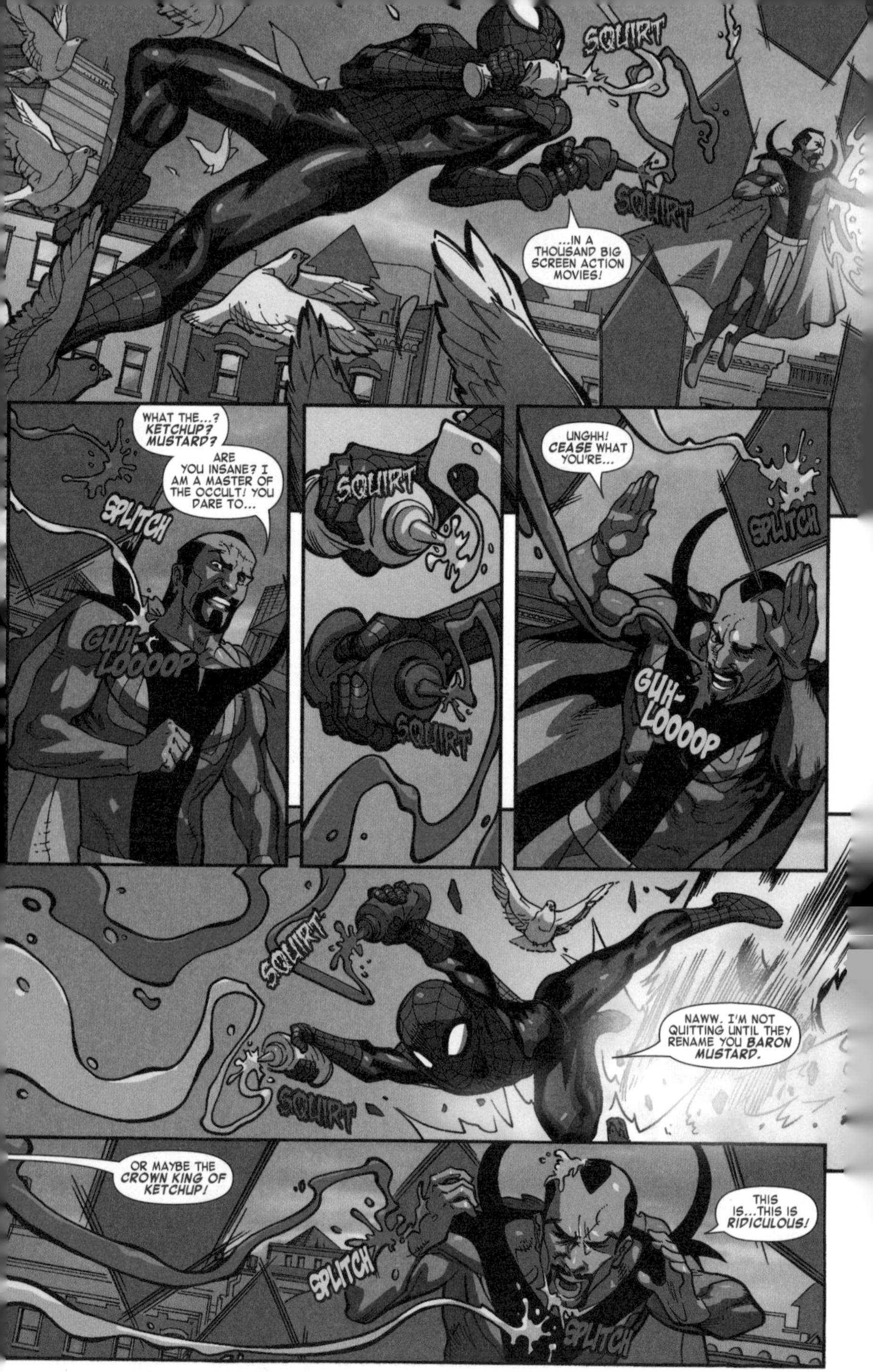
SQUIRT
SQUIRT
...IN A THOUSAND BIG SCREEN ACTION MOVIES!
WHAT THE...? KETCHUP? MUSTARD?
ARE YOU INSANE? I AM A MASTER OF THE OCCULT! YOU DARE TO...
SPLITCH
GUH-LOOOOP
SQUIRT
SQUIRT
UNGHH! CEASE WHAT YOU'RE...
SPLITCH
GUH-LOOOOP
SQUIRT
SQUIRT
NAWW. I'M NOT QUITTING UNTIL THEY RENAME YOU BARON MUSTARD.
OR MAYBE THE CROWN KING OF KETCHUP!
THIS IS...THIS IS RIDICULOUS!
SPLITCH
SPLITCH

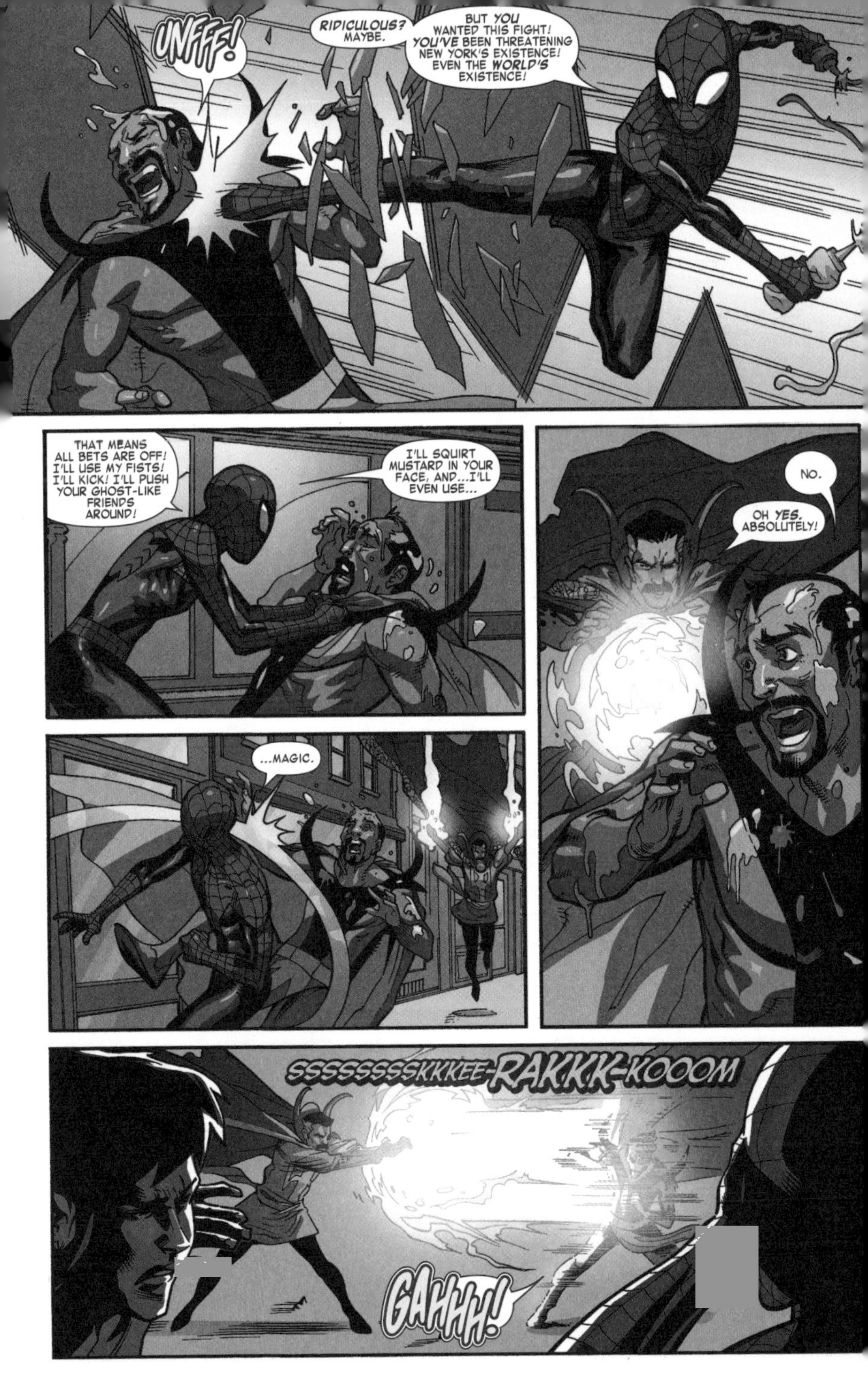
UNFFF!
RIDICULOUS? MAYBE.
BUT YOU WANTED THIS FIGHT! YOU'VE BEEN THREATENING NEW YORK'S EXISTENCE! EVEN THE WORLD'S EXISTENCE!
THAT MEANS ALL BETS ARE OFF! I'LL USE MY FISTS! I'LL KICK! I'LL PUSH YOUR GHOST-LIKE FRIENDS AROUND!
I'LL SQUIRT MUSTARD IN YOUR FACE, AND...I'LL EVEN USE...
...MAGIC.
NO.
OH YES. ABSOLUTELY!
SSSSSSSSKKKEE-RAKKK-KOOOM
GAHHH!

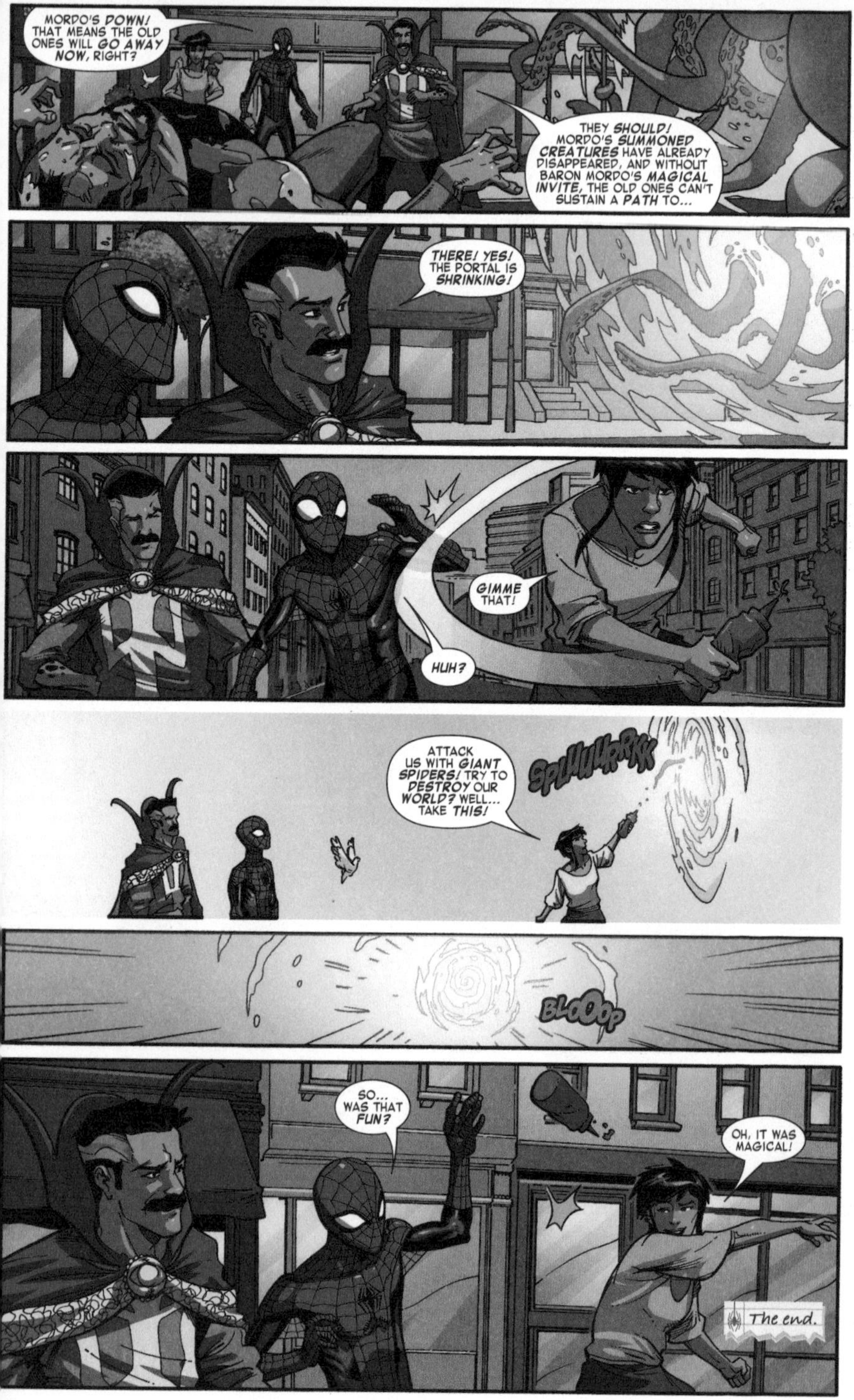
MORDO'S DOWN! THAT MEANS THE OLD ONES WILL GO AWAY NOW, RIGHT?
THEY SHOULD! MORDO'S SUMMONED CREATURES HAVE ALREADY DISAPPEARED, AND WITHOUT BARON MORDO'S MAGICAL INVITE, THE OLD ONES CAN'T SUSTAIN A PATH TO...
THERE! YES! THE PORTAL IS SHRINKING!
GIMME THAT!
HUH?
ATTACK US WITH GIANT SPIDERS! TRY TO DESTROY OUR WORLD? WELL... TAKE THIS!
SPLUUURRKK
BLOOOP
SO... WAS THAT FUN?
OH, IT WAS MAGICAL!
The end.

BONUS PINUPS

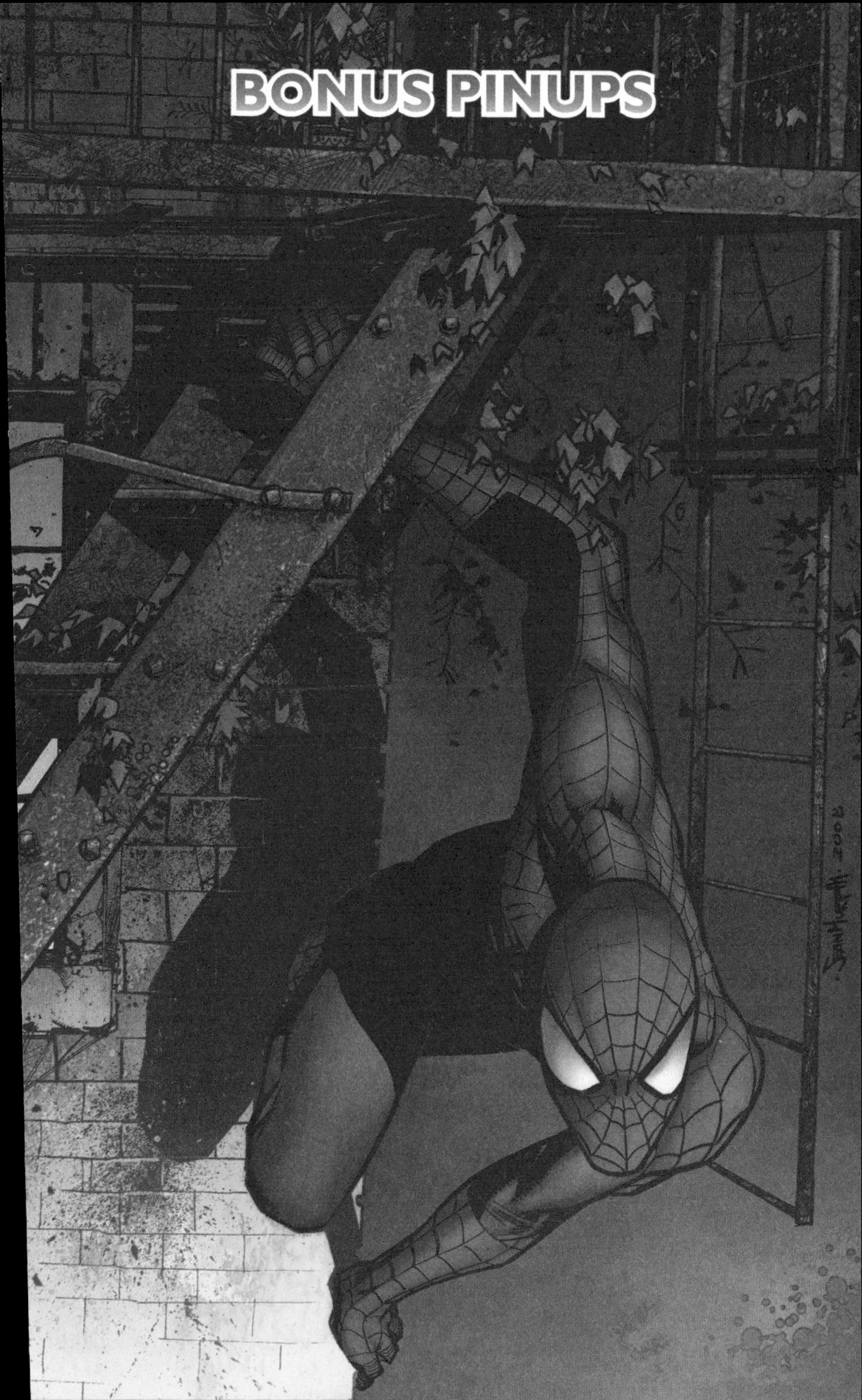

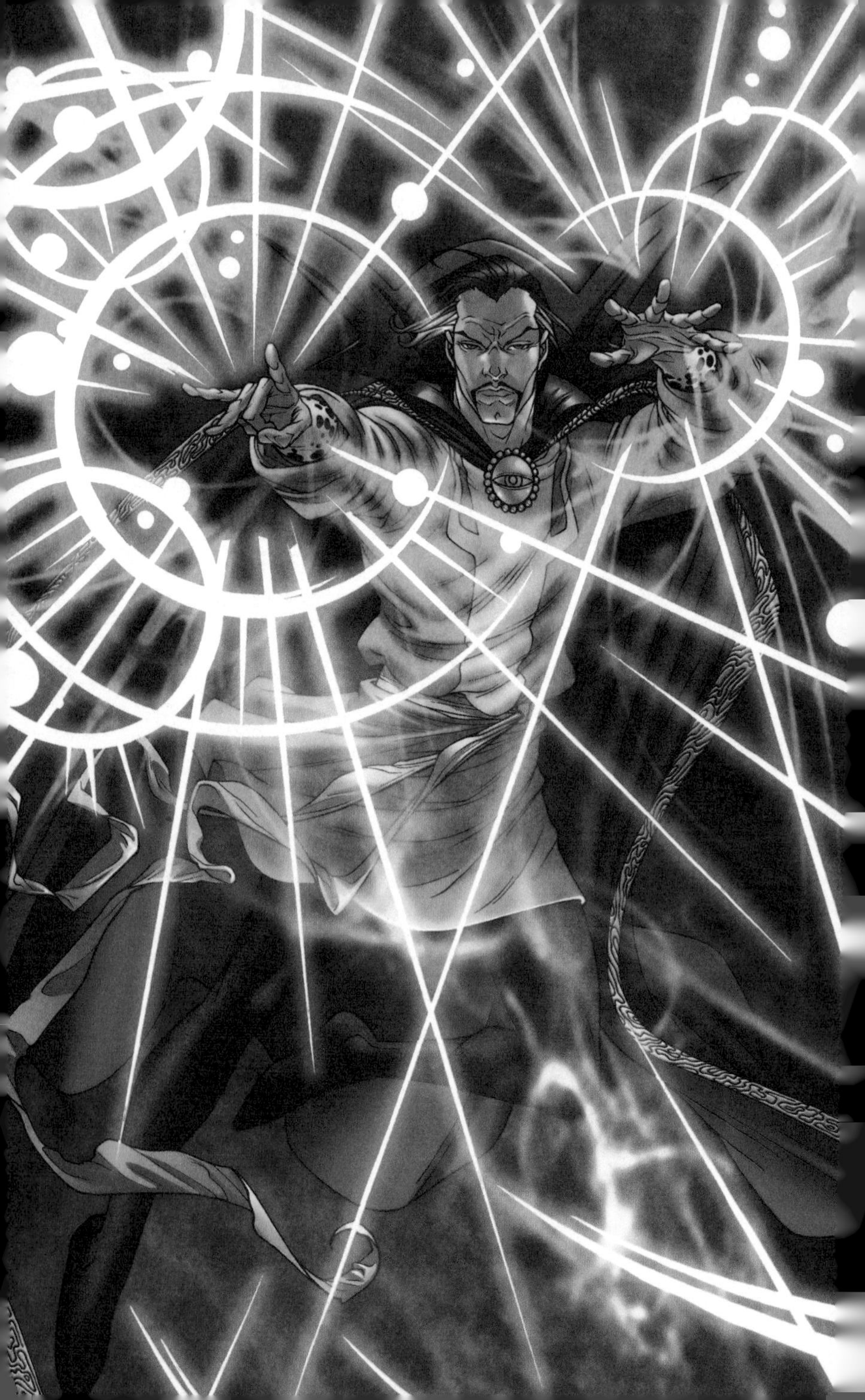

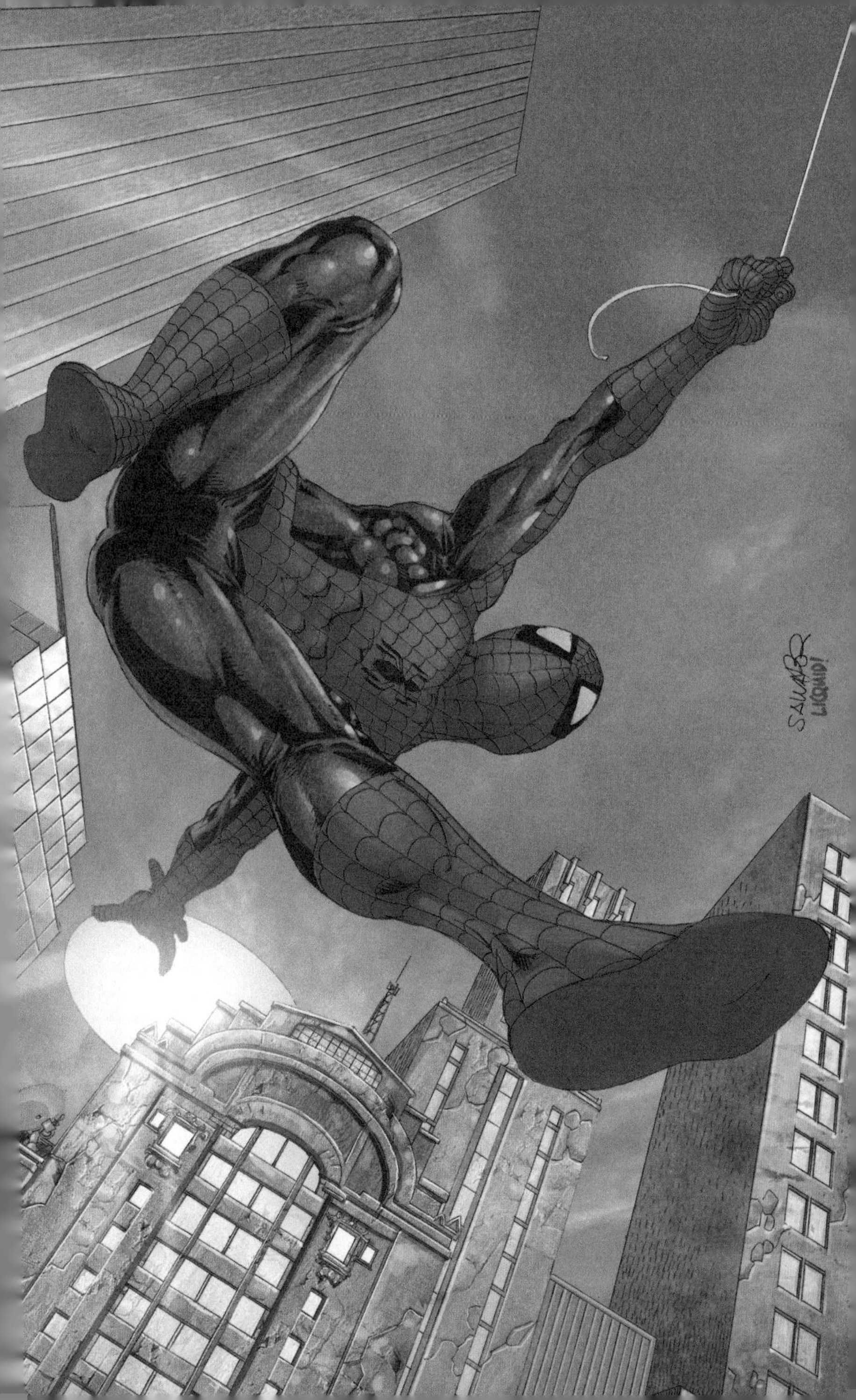
LIQUID!

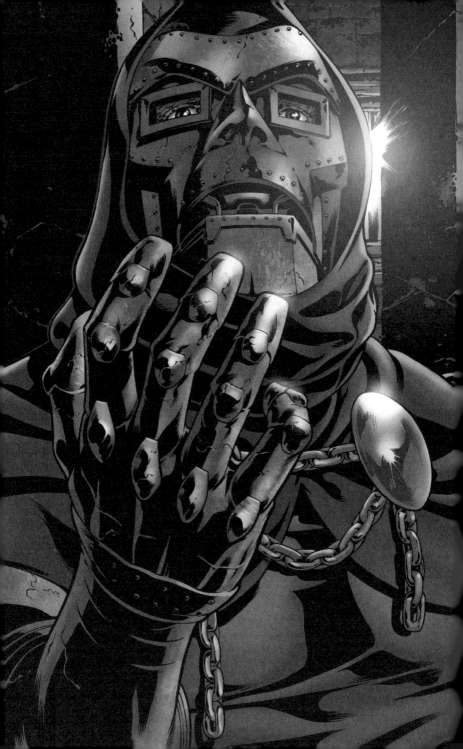

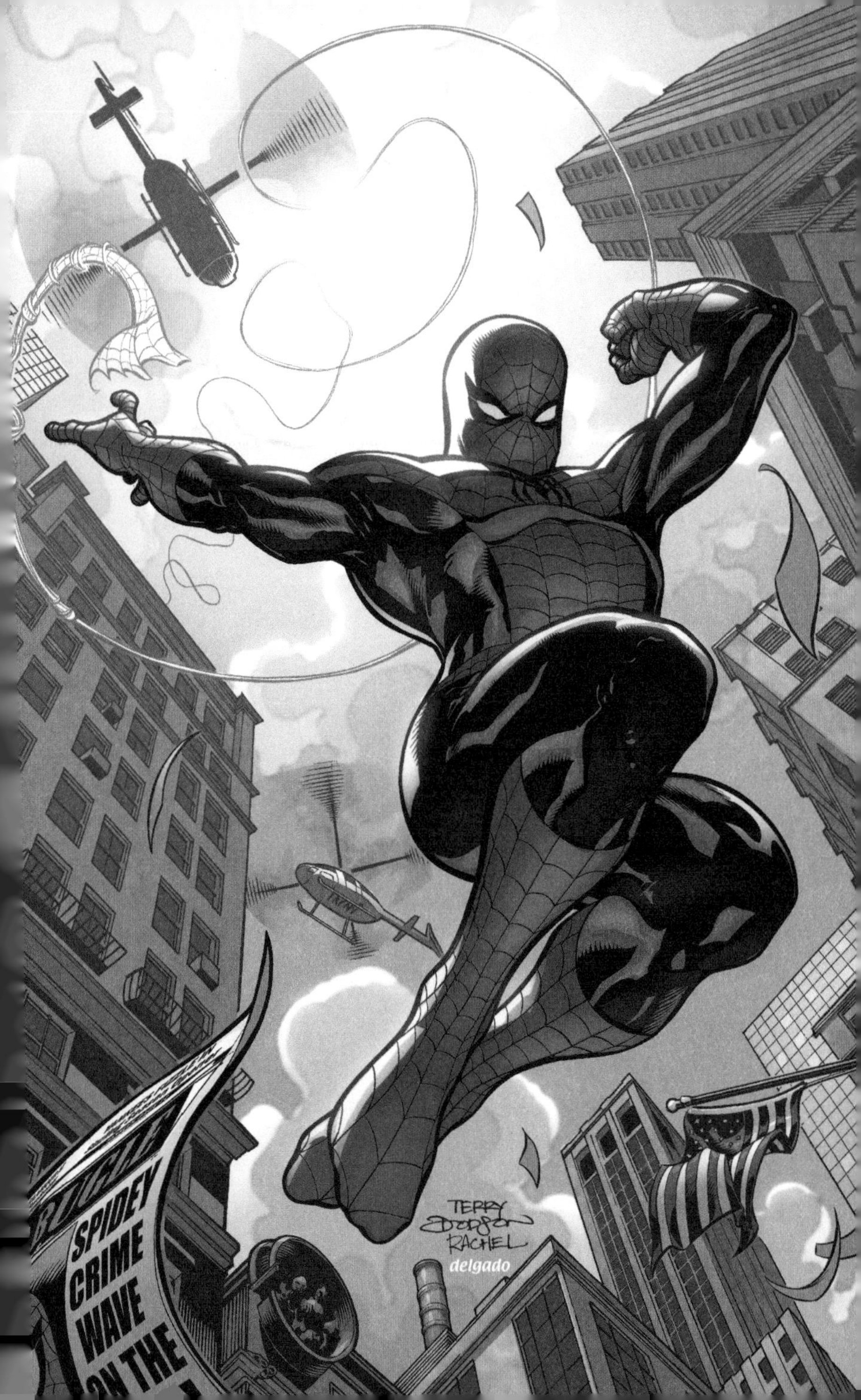
SPIDEY
CRIME
WAVE
TERRY DODSON RACHEL
delgado

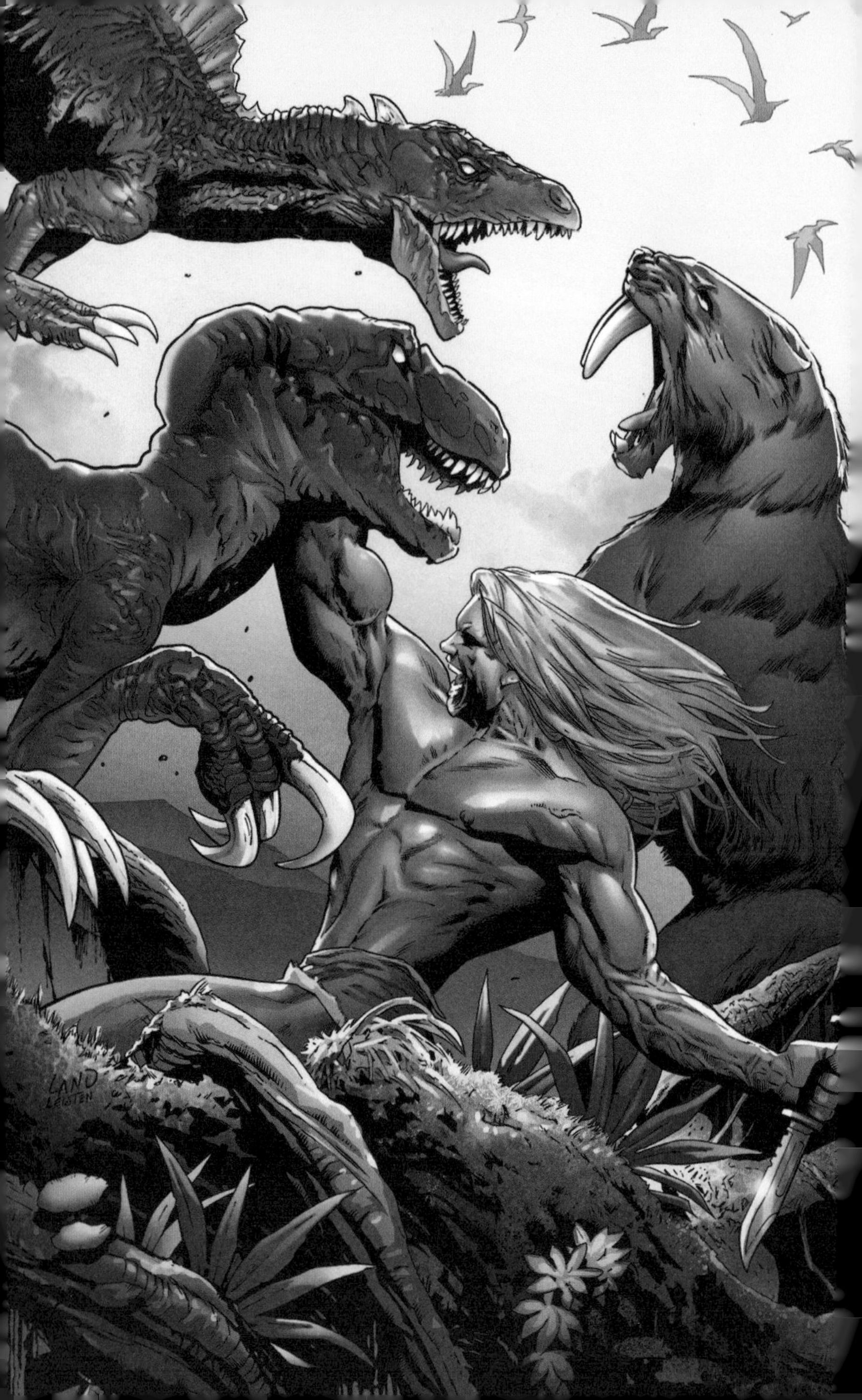